Contents

Introduction   xi

Part I   **Between economics and ecology: sustainability in political**   1
          perspective

     1   The uncertain quest for sustainability: public discourse   3
          and the politics of environmentalism
          Douglas Torgerson

     2   Sustainable development as a power/knowledge system: 21
          the problem of 'governmentality'
          Timothy W. Luke

     3   Towards a sustainable future: the organizing role of   33
          ecologism in the north–south relationship
          Hector R. Leis and Eduardo J. Viola

Part II   **Environmental policy-making: beyond industrial ideology and**   51
          technocratic strategy

     4   The unnatural policies of natural resource agencies: 53
          fishery policy on the Sacramento River
          Michael Black

     5   Environmental technology and the green car: towards a   66
          sustainable transportation policy
          Lamont C. Hempel

     6   The North American Free Trade Agreement and the   87
          environment: economic growth versus democratic politics
          Derek Churchill and Richard Worthington

     7   Environmental policy in Chile: the politics of the   104
          comprehensive law
          Eduardo Silva

Contributors

Michael Black is a visiting professor of political science at Harvey Mudd College in Claremont, California. He is a San Francisco-based environmental policy analyst who writes about issues confronting the arid western regions of the USA, the social-ecological impact of science and technology and economic development. He is currently writing *California's Last Salmon: the Unnatural Policies of Natural Resource Agencies*, a book exploring policy responses to endangered Pacific salmon.

Derek Churchill is currently conducting an environmental education and outdoor leadership training programme for the non-profit organization, Outward Bound. A graduate of Pomona College, his recent research interests have centred on environmental sustainability and the North American Free Trade Agreement.

Frank Fischer is professor of political science at Rutgers University. His most recent books include *Technocracy and the Politics of Expertise* and *Evaluating Public Policy*. Frequently a guest scholar at the Free University and the Science Centre of Berlin, he is currently engaged in a comparative study of environmental policy in Germany and the USA. Among other journals, he serves on the editorial board of *Industrial and Environmental Crisis Quarterly*.

Maarten A. Hajer teaches at the Ludwig-Maximilians University of Munich in Germany, where he specializes in environmental politics and technology policy. The author of *City Politics: Hegemonic Projects and Discourse* and *The Politics of Environmental Discourse: Ecological Modernization and the Policy Process*, he also serves as a book review editor for *Industrial and Environmental Crisis Quarterly*. He is currently engaged in research on the automobile and its environmental problems.

Lamont C. Hempel is an associate professor of Public Policy in the Center for Politics and Economics at the Claremont Graduate School, Claremont, California. He is the author of *Environmental Governance: The Global Challenge*.

Hector R. Leis is a professor of environmental politics and policy in the Department of Social Science at the Universidade Federal de Santa Catarina, Brazil. He has served as the coordinator of the Forum of Brazilian Non-governmental organizations at the UN Conference on Environment and Development.

Timothy W. Luke is professor of political science at Virginia Polytechnic Institute and State University in Blacksburg, Virginia. The author of *Screens of Power* and *Ideology and Soviet Industrialization*, he has written extensively on social theory, comparative politics and international political economy.

Jo McCloskey is a senior lecturer in corporate responsibility and marketing within the Centre for Risk and Crisis Management at the Business School of Liverpool John Moores University. She has previously lectured at Leicester Business School and in colleges in Ireland and Africa.

Robert Paehlke is a professor of political science and environmental studies and resource studies at Trent University, Ontario, Canada. Included among his publications are *Environmentalism and the Future of Progressive Politics* and *Managing Leviathan: Environmental Politics and the Administrative State*, coedited with Douglas Torgerson. He has also served as an editor of the journal *Alternatives: Perspectives on Society, Technology and Environment*.

Paul Shrivastava is the Howard Scott Professor of Management at Bucknell University in Pennsylvania. An expert on industrial and environmental accidents and crisis management, he is the author of *Bhopal: Anatomy of a Crisis* and *Greening Business: Towards Sustainable Corporations*. He serves as the editor-in-chief of *Industrial and Environmental Crisis Quarterly*.

Eduardo Silva teaches political science at the University of Missouri in St Louis and is a member of the University's Center for International Studies. In addition to his work on Chilean politics, he writes about environmental issues in Latin America generally. Currently he is at work on a book entitled *The Politics of Conservation and Sustainable Development: Natural Forest Policy in Latin America*.

Denis Smith is professor of management at the University of Durham. His publications include *Business and the Environment: Implications for the New Environmentalism* and *Waste Location: Social Aspects of Waste Management, Hazards and Disposal*, coedited with M. Clark and A. Blowers. His main research interests are in the areas of environmental risk assessment, corporate responsibility and crisis management.

Douglas Torgerson teaches political studies and administrative studies at Trent University in Ontario, Canada, and currently serves as editor of the journal *Policy Sciences*. Included among his many publications are *Industrialization* *and Assessment: Social Impact Assessment as Social Phenomena* and *Managing Leviathan: Environmental Politics and the Administrative State*, coedited with Robert Paehlke. He has also taught environmental studies at York University and the University of Toronto.

Eduardo J. Viola is a professor in the Department of Political Science and International Relations at Universidade de Brasilia, Brazil, where he specializes in environmental politics and policy. He is co-author of the Brazilian Report on Environment and Development for the UN Conference on Environmental Development.

Rodney White is professor of geography and director of the Institute for Environmental Studies at the University of Toronto in Canada. He is author of *North, South, and the Environmental Crisis* and of *Urban Environmental Management*.

Richard Worthington directs the Program in Public Policy Analysis at Pomona College in Claremont, California. He has written extensively about science, technology and environmental policy. Currently he is working on *The Human Dimensions of Global Production*, a book exploring the shift from an international society of sovereign nation-states to that of a global political economy.

Introduction

The conquest of the earth is not a pretty thing when you look into it too much.
(Joseph Conrad: *The Heart of Darkness)*

During the two past decades, green politics and environmental policy have emerged as major issues on the political agendas of all industrialized nations. As a consequence of countless environmental threats, at times real disasters – for example, the Chernobyl nuclear catastrophe that frightened the entire world, the Bhopal toxic chemical leak that killed 26,000 people and injured thousands more, or the Love Canal toxic waste site that led to the complete disruption of a community and its social fabric – the environment has captured the public mind. Moreover, as the 1992 Earth Summit in Rio made clear, environmental crisis is positioned to become the most pressing international challenge of the twenty-first century. In recent years a widespread sense of urgency for concerted action has been expressed as the search for a sustainable future.

The growth of such concern has spawned a very active – even at times aggressive – environmental movement. In a relatively short period of time, the environmental 'green revolution' has established itself as one of the most progressive worldwide political forces. For this reason, many activists and observers in western countries deem this 'fierce green fire' a genuine success story. Environmentalists can now point to extensive media coverage, green parties, steady approval ratings in opinion polls, increased financial resources and a global network comprising thousands of groups. Even more significant, the movement can claim important successes in the legislative and regulatory arenas, not to mention a growing number of proponents in the boardrooms of major multinational corporations.

But there are problems that caution against optimism. One is that such environmental successes scarcely match the accelerating pace of environmental degradation. Each decade has only brought new and more serious ecological problems to the top of the environmental agenda. Whereas the environmental movement of the 1960s concentrated on pesticides, air and water pollution, the 1970s ushered in the overconsumption of energy, overpopulation and the dangers of nuclear radiation. In the 1980s the movement added toxic waste hazards, the ozone hole and the destruction of the tropical rain forests to its list of major concerns. Then the 1990s added some of the most serious environmental problems yet, in particular global warming, biodiversity and a revisitation of the population explosion. Some argue that we might have as little as 40 years to come to grips with such problems – that is, about a generation. If we have not succeeded by then, according to this argument, environmental degradation and economic decline are likely to feed upon one another, leading to a downward spiral of social and political disintegration. Given this possibility, numerous writers predict that the wars of the twenty-first century will be fought over the question of who controls and uses the globe's increasingly scarce and costly supply of natural resources.

A second problem concerns the globalization of the environmental crisis. Whereas nation-states are the constructions of an earlier historical era, today's social and ecological forces defy traditional international categorization. For example, transnational companies are engaged in a worldwide coproduction of goods. Basic to this global political economy are new technologies of telecommunication and computers that link up a geographically dispersed web of scientists, technicians, producers and users into a coherent whole. In the process, investment has become a global activity in which trillions or more dollars change hands daily. Such mobility of capital and labour has transformed the terrain occupied by once-autonomous nation-states.

This profound economic shift was accompanied by the realization in the 1980s that many environmental problems had also transcended national boundaries. No longer could environmental policy remain concerned with a dirty river here or a toxic waste dump there. Issues such as the ozone hole, global warming, the disappearance of rain forests, unchecked pollution expansion and nuclear catastrophe all underscored the global dimensions of the ecological crisis. Such problems make it clear that none of us can escape the international consequences of the environmental crisis. In the context of the third world, the word 'crisis' is almost an understatement.

The transnational character of many of our most critical environmental problems seriously complicates the search for effective policy solutions. For one thing, international governmental organizations, such as the United Nations, not to mention international non-governmental organizations (NGOs), remain politically quite weak compared to national regimes. They lack both the resources and regulatory authority to take decisive action in transnational issues. By and large, they are often relegated to an advisory role with little more than the force of moral suasion.

For another thing, as the chapter on NAFTA by Worthington and Churchill illustrates, environmental protection now cuts across complicated issues of international political economy, particularly those concerned with development. For instance, a problem like global warming directly confronts the tensions between overconsumption and population explosion (see White, Appendix on global warming). As Leis and Viola make clear in their chapter on north–south relationships, such an issue pits the wealthy northern industrial countries against the poverty-ridden southern 'developing' and 'underdeveloped' countries. The international effort to reduce the increase of greenhouse gases often comes down to the high consumption northern countries lecturing their poor southern counterparts to curtail industrialization in the name of a sustainable future. In the view of the southern countries, as characterized by Silva in his chapter on Chile, the hypocritical northern perspective only extends the sordid history of colonial and postcolonial domination. Desperately struggling to increase their standard of living for burgeoning populations, the poor countries argue that it is now their turn to develop. (Witness China's recent decision to elevate the production of the automobile to a top priority in its push for industrialization, a major blow to the struggle to abate the greenhouse effect.) If the wealthy nations are so concerned with sustainable economic development, argue the developing countries, the northern countries should curtail their own wasteful consumption. (Given the fact that the average citizen in a country like the USA consumes up to 40 times more energy per day than an average member of a third-world nation, the argument is not easy to dismiss.) Such economic disparities have set off sharp international tensions with no immediate or apparent resolutions. In the meantime, more greenhouse gases are spewed into the atmosphere at ever-increasing rates and the earth continues to get warmer.

A third problem concerns the proliferation of environmental theories and philosophies. During the past decade an outpouring of environmental theorizing has created serious divisions among environmentalists themselves. Although in many ways the products of the movement's own successes, such divisions make it difficult to organize concerted environmental action. Once saving the earth was established on the agenda, environmental politics turned to the even more difficult questions concerned with prioritizing specific policy goals and strategies. In the process, an increasingly divided environmental camp has found itself beset with internal disputes. In this context, groups such as Greenpeace, tree-huggers, green marketers, anti-toxic activists and Smokey the Bear often coexist uneasily with one another; issues such as ozone holes, spotted owls, free-trade agreements and electric vehicles frequently pose complicated policy paradoxes.

In ideological terms, these combatants extend across the political spectrum. In addition to mainstream reformers, they include 'deep ecologists', 'ecofeminists', 'eco-Marxists', the 'environmental justice' movement, 'ecowarriors', 'corporate environmentalists' and, last but not least, the 'anti-environmentalists'. In many ways, this latter group is the most worrisome, given its close proximity to money and power. As the environmental embodiment of right-wing movements, the anti-environmentalists argue that the ecological crisis is a Trojan Horse invented by discredited socialists still seeking ways to attack capitalism.

Basic to this ideological clash, as Shrivastava explains, are issues about the capacity of western institutions to redress or reverse environmental crisis. On one end of the environmental spectrum are the 'dark greens'. They view the environmental problem as lodged in the very assumptions and practices of advanced industrial society and its consumption-driven way of life. For many of these environmentalists, nothing short of radical transformation is required to save us from the looming disaster ahead. They call for the return to small-scale technologies, decentralized bioregions and participatory democracy. Some of the more apocalyptic among them altogether refuse to co-operate with the existing institutional system.

At the other end of the environmental continuum are the corporate environmentalists. For corporate environmentalists the radical prescription is entirely misguided, as it rejects the very institutions and beliefs held to be sacred in advanced industrial societies. Acknowledging the need to take environmental degradation seriously, corporate environmentalists look for solutions within the parameters of established western institutions, free-market capitalism and liberal democracy in particular. As McCloskey and Smith point out, those who advocate the 'greening of business' advance a reformist rather than radical environmental strategy. Concretely stated, strategy can be approached through socially responsible managerial practices, an argument critically examined by Shrivastava. The task is to build environmental criteria into the existing technoindustrial trajectory. Indeed, corporate environmentalists argue that economic growth is the very precondition for solving environmental problems; it generates the resources essential for shaping workable solutions.

This brings us to the fourth and final issue, namely the concept of 'sustainable development'. Sustainable development, as opposed to sustainability more generally, has rapidly emerged as the environmental slogan of national and international organizations, the United Nations in particular. Envisioned as a strategy to save the earth for future generations, sustainable development is the organizing concept of a joint north/south global project suited to the environmental challenges of the twenty-first century. The unusually widespread popularity of the concept may be attributed to the hidden contradictions and ambiguities of the term. Due to its nebulous assumptions, different proponents have been able to read competing meanings into the concept of sustainability. For some, especially those in the developing world, it means dramatic curtailments of economic growth in industrialized countries accompanied by large redistributions of income to the developing countries. For others, particularly the leaders of the industrialized countries, it means only reconciling economic growth with the ancillary goals of environmental protection. The fact that different groups can read competing meanings into sustainability has made it possible for the concept to generate widespread support.

That sustainable development should paper over crucial environmental disagreements is no accident. Indeed, the Brundtland report explicitly introduced the term as a conceptual bridge to bring together environmentalists and industrialists. Such a conceptual move, however, is not without political implications. As Douglas Torgerson shows in the first chapter of the book, sustainable development is an effort to rescue and protect economic growth from its environmental critics. Formulated in this way, the approach is a concrete expression of corporate environmentalism. By reframing environmental discourse to accommodate industrialism, it seeks to subsume environmentalists in a discussion grounded in the interests of business and industry. Conceptualized in this way, sustainable development is much more than a normative goal; it also constitutes the basis of a planning methodology for the management of an industrially sustainable future.

Sustainable development is thus firmly rooted at the logics of modernity and industrialism. Even though the concept officially acknowledges the cultural diversity and complexity of the global sphere, sustainable development narrowly frames the environmental crisis as a scientific problem, amenable to risk assessment and technological solutions. It is a framework that has given birth to technocratic cadres of sustainable development experts who, as Timothy Luke argues, would seek to disassemble, recombine and subject the natural environment to suit the needs of sustainable economic strategies. Most important here is the idea that experts can calculate and plan the 'carrying capacities' of local and regional ecosystems.

There are two problems here. The first is that the approach presumes that our knowledge is sophisticated enough to reveal the limits of nature, permitting us to exploit resources safely up to that limit. Everything to date about environmental science raises serious questions about the validity of this assumption. Second, as Fischer argues, a technocratic approach underplays the essential role of social and economic choices in the creation and resolution of environmental problems. Rather than treating the basic social and economic prerequisites of our daily lives as *causes* of environmental degradation, the problem is reconceptualized as an *effect* of such behaviour. By taking everyday behaviour as given, scientists can thus concentrate on finding technical solutions capable of mitigating problematic environmental side-effects. Such 'technological fixes', as Black's chapter illustrates, makes it possible for decision-makers to ignore the economic and social implications that must be basic to the search for a sustainable strategy. In so far as scientific and technological solutions are treated as 'neutral and objective', and hence outside the human context, human beings are disengaged from the consequences of their actions, as well as the obligation to take responsibility for them.

Consider, for instance, the way in which the US automobile industry and the federal government in Washington approach the automobile and its environmental problems. Although the automobile is responsible for a host of environmental problems, the one that has compelled regulatory action is air pollution. As Hempel points out in his chapter on the green car, the primary response to air pollution has been the development of the catalytic converter and, more recently, the electric car. Both of these technological fixes are designed to allow Americans to continue using the automobile and the transportation patterns which it has hitherto shaped. This means that air quality can be improved, but only in ways that neglect other serious environmental problems caused by the car, in particular traffic congestion. (Indeed, some evidence suggests that the electric car may lead to even more cars on the road, not less, than the internal combustion engine vehicle.) Thus, people's preferences to transport themselves from one place to another in a given vehicular mode are taken as given by this technical perspective. Missing here is the essential fact that mobility is itself a 'socially constructed' concept, rather than simply a given preference. Once we acknowledge the social foundations of mobility we can begin to rethink the meaning of the concept itself – or, as one writer has put it, we can think about how to move from 'automobility' to 'multimobility'. Transcending narrow technical solutions, such an approach requires us to think more systematically about how we in fact want to live together and what role technical solutions would play in selecting alternative scenarios. Whereas the technological fix is at best a short-term piecemeal solution, only a more comprehensive exploration of the basic social patterns underlying our environmental problems can help us to structure long-term sustainable solutions.

The basic social and economic assumptions underlying the environmental crisis constitute the core concerns of a green politics. Despite numerous attempts to appropriate or manipulate the term 'green' – especially those on the part of self-serving businesses seeking new ways to market products – an authentic green politics remains committed to the conviction that environmental problems are firmly rooted in our way of life. No environmental problem can be solved in isolation of our economic enterprises, public institutions or personal lives. Moreover, green politics is basically participatory politics. Emphasizing diversity and inclusiveness, the green movement seeks to build political and economic institutions that facilitate the development of an environmental democracy. The point is driven home by Paehlke in his chapter on environmental values and democratic policy-making.

It is to these kind of green commitments that *Greening Environmental Policy* is devoted. Rather than focusing on environmental policy solutions *per se* – solutions that at present are beyond the reach of even the savviest of experts – this volume focuses on the need for political and institutional structures that facilitate building a democratic consensus about sustainability, as well as the institutional decision-making processes required to translate such consensus into effective policy solutions. Toward this end, *Greening* seeks to open up the discussion of sustainability to include a wider set of economic and social values and goals. In particular, it strives to do this by creating new social and political spaces in which national and global social experimentation, together with new forms of social learning, may occur. Such deliberation and experimentation must include our understanding of nature and our relationship to it, our beliefs about the idea of progress, our capability of measuring and predicting the carrying capacities of our ecological systems and the ability of the institutions basic to industrialism – whether capitalist or socialist – to guide us towards a sustainable future. Only by freely and openly debating such questions can we begin to move beyond the pre-emptively narrow, short-term industrial and technological strategies that dominate contemporary environmental policy-making. Such deliberation means abandoning political decision processes which inherently privilege the views of élite industrialists and their political spokespersons who regularly relegate the environmental crisis to a secondary priority. In place of environmental decisions generally made in the interests of corporate élites, if not by them directly – decisions which typically emphasize private sector solutions at the expense of the public interest – we need solutions that include a broader range of individuals and groups. Beyond biased decision processes, as Hajer argues, we need to develop reflexive institutional arrangements capable of resolving conflicting policy preferences regarding problems and solutions. Such institutional forums would assist in 'demonopolizing' knowledge and decision-making at the broadly normative levels of agenda-setting, as well as the more concrete levels of policy implementation. Specifically, such institutional change would make it possible to open up to public scrutiny and deliberation the kinds of deceptive biases hidden in an industrially conditioned version of sustainable development.

The book pursues these political and institutional concerns in three parts. Part I of the book, 'Between economics and ecology: sustainability in political perspective', is concerned with an exploration of the contradictions and ambiguities underlying the concept of sustainable development. Focusing on both the national and global aspects of the question, Torgerson, Luke, Leis and Viola explore the implications of these ambiguities for the organization of concerted political action. Part II, 'Environmental policy-making: beyond industrial ideology and technocratic strategy', critically examines the clash between industrial priorities and the struggle for environmental protection. The role of economic ideology in framing policy deliberation and the use of the technocratic strategies to formulate and implement environmental policy thread together the contributions by Black, Hempel, Churchill and Worthington, and Silva. Finally, Part III, 'Towards a sustainable future: environmental values, institutions and participatory practices', focuses on the need for environmental renewal. Paehlke, Hajer, Fischer, Shrivastava, McCloskey and Smith underscore the need to rethink our environmental values and to pay special attention to the hidden politics that often lurk behind institutional practices. Most importantly, they stress the need to create the kinds of public spaces needed to nurture participatory democracy and social experimentation in environmental policy-making. Only a democratic society, it is argued, can provide the foundations of a sustainable future.

Frank Fischer
Michael Black

PART I

Between economics and ecology: sustainability in political perspective

Part I begins with Douglas Torgerson's examination of the basic origins and development of environmentalism. Specifically, he probes the transformation of environmental discourse from a focus on the 'limits of economic growth' to an emphasis on sustainability. In the process, Torgerson illustrates the way in which the concept of sustainability rescues economic growth from the earlier discourse on limits and sets out an approach to environmental protection that is comfortably adjusted to the requirements of the existing corporate-industrial order. Broad public debate about the meaning of sustainability gives way to a discourse organized by technical experts and central managers. For Torgerson, the only viable alternative to this instrumentalization of environmental policy is a strategy positioned between the incrementalism of traditional management and the radical green call for fundamental societal changes. Torgerson calls for a new 'incremental radicalism'.

Timothy Luke addresses the same problem from a different perspective. Focusing on the contradictions of sustainable development, he seeks to show the ways in which the term shifts basic power/knowledge relationships that undergird western institutions. Fundamental to the concept is the emergence of cadres of sustainable development experts who profess knowledge about basic environmental goals and practices. Technocratically, these experts shift around concepts and practices independently of social and political context. Luke draws on Foucault's theory of 'governmentality' to show how the environment is embedded in a host of power/knowledge relations that are not amenable to standard reformist strategies of the type advanced by leading sustainable development theorists.

Hector Leis and Eduardo Viola take up these issues in the international context of north–south relationships. After outlining the environmental disorders of the global biosphere, they examine the major international reports concerned with environment and development, especially as they pertain to the relationship of so-called first to third-world countries. From a third-world perspective the concepts of sustainable development advanced by these reports are seen to be inherently problematic. The future of a greener, sustainable relationship between north and south, they argue, depends on the development of a new international order based on the theory and practices of what they choose to call 'ecologism', a perspective that combines a deep grasp of ecological processes with an ethical expansion of human consciousness.

1

The uncertain quest for sustainability: public discourse and the politics of environmentalism

DOUGLAS TORGERSON

Trent University, Canada

Upon entering the public scene, environmentalism disturbed the established discourse of advanced industrial society. While technically focused discourse could usually overwhelm concerns about the morality of dominating nature, doubt about the human *ability* to dominate nature was more worrisome. The future was dramatically thrown into question, and the doubt proved especially troubling when expressed through the scientistic idiom of technical discourse.

Widely promulgated photographs of the earth from lunar spacecraft combined with computer models (e.g. Meadows *et al.*, 1972) to emphasize the finitude of the planet. The image of a finite earth questioned a central premiss of public discourse – the managerialist assumption that, as part of the conquest of nature, there were no practical limits to the advance of industrialization. With this premiss in doubt, the confident pursuit of progress came to be at least partially eclipsed by a new, uncertain quest for sustainability.

The central thrust of environmentalism in public discourse has been to raise doubts about the potential of the natural resource base to sustain established patterns of human activities. The main question has centred on how these activities might have to be modified, curtailed or transformed to achieve sustainability. In particular, the evident need to change the path of industrial development has given rise to recommendations for incremental reform and, more dramatically, for radically green alternatives for development, varyingly grim or utopian. Similarly, answers to the question of how sustainability might be achieved have varied from a process of basic social and historical change, requiring the mobilization of social movements, to a better process of policy planning and management.

Environmentalism in the late 1960s and early 1970s initially injected the notion of 'limits' into public discourse. Although a concern with sustainability was obviously the implicit counterpart to a concern with limits, environmentalism did not inject the focus of 'sustainability' into public discourse until the

1980s when the idea of 'sustainable development' became salient (e.g. World Commission, 1987). Examining the transformation of environmentalism from a discourse of limits to a discourse of sustainability, this chapter both draws attention to an ambivalence of environmentalism within a broader ideological field and suggests a strategic orientation for environmentalism in the shifting context of public discourse.[1]

The discourse of limits

Environmentalism has emerged in the closing decades of the twentieth century amid apocalyptic visions, some frightening, some hopeful. Images of chaos and death, the extinction of human life, the destruction of the web of life on earth – these have comingled with utopian images of a restored humanity living peacefully, happily and harmoniously as part of a revitalized nature. Among all these images, different varieties of environmentalism have advanced various diagnoses of environmental difficulties, together with different prescriptions. What is common is the perception that human activities, interacting with broader natural contexts, have repercussions which seriously jeopardize the well-being of humanity, if not nature itself.

Environmentalist views have thus thrown into question the hopeful vision of progress which had previously transfixed advanced industrial society. Despite a half-century marked by two world wars and the great depression, technological developments allowed the image of an orderly industrial civilization more than to survive. By mid century, this image could be revived through an ideology of industrialization, resistant to doubts about industrial progress and insulated from criticism by a technocratic idiom.[2] The key image, clearly advanced as early as nineteenth-century positivism, arose from the modern conception of progress and was based on enormous confidence in the capacity of human knowledge to exert control – to grasp and shape the world in a manner useful to human beings. Questioning this confidence and raising the spectre of limits, environmentalism not only challenged an idea to which modern culture had become accustomed but also provoked an incredulous, even hostile, reaction.

Environmentalist diagnoses covered the spectrum from the identification of perplexing – yet potentially manageable – environmental problems to the nightmarish vision of an environmental catastrophe, in which humanity would be thrown out of the 'balance of nature' unless the character and direction of industrial civilization were fundamentally altered. These diagnoses, even the more modest ones, were at odds with an ideological context pervaded by confidence in industrial progress. Now, it seemed, the future might not work after all. At least, the future no longer simply presented a set of challenges for which human drive and ingenuity could be assumed as adequate. The spectre of limits meant that collapse and catastrophe loomed as possible, perhaps even as likely – by some accounts, indeed, as virtually inevitable.

Denial of limits: the ideological context

The modern belief in the possibility of mastering all things through calculation has developed as the key feature of the ideology of industrialization. Well before the onset of industrialism, a precise knowledge of natural regularities was seen as key to the human control of nature. In the early phases of industrialization, technological innovation remained a product of largely piecemeal endeavours. The prospect of dominating nature – of shaping it, without limit, in accord with human interests – was rendered increasingly plausible as technological innovation became subject to systematic research and development. As part of the march of progress, indeed, the domination of nature became the historical mission of humanity.

This mission was necessarily an intellectual one, requiring 'the progress of the human mind' through rational discipline and scientific investigation. Yet the intellectual dimension of progress was part of a broader change in the order of governance. Eliminating confusion and error in favour of clarity and knowledge, progress advanced to an orderly, efficient industrial civilization guided by an impersonal reason. Progress in the collective mastery of nature would thus also be part of humanity's advance to a type of governance which – though freed from the dogmatic oppression of the feudal and monarchial forms – retained its singularity of purpose. From the time of the Enlightenment, indeed, belief in progress was based not only on the advance of knowledge but also on confidence in centralized power: 'The experience of what the royal authority could achieve encouraged men to imagine that one enlightened will, with a centralized administration at its command, might accomplish endless improvements in civilization' (Bury, 1955, p. 76).

The ideology of industrialization may thus be traced to an image of unity – an image of unified knowledge, purpose and power: the administrative mind (Torgerson, 1990, pp. 120–1; cf. Bordo, 1992). Impartial reason, in this image, exercises a supreme, unquestionable authority in pursuit of the universal well-being of humanity. Detached from mundane conflict and error, the administrative mind projects a benign aura of assured mastery. Under the unified direction of this mind, an otherwise confusing and uncertain world becomes calculable and controllable. While given a distinctive form with the emergence of administrative thought in the early twentieth century, this image has been a key characteristic of the modern age, significantly influenced by early modern philosophy and anticipated by the image of cosmic order in medieval political theology.

The irony of the ideology of industrialization resides in its obviously mythic character: for it is a rationalized myth, a myth which poses as being beyond myth and superior to it.[3] The touchstone of the myth is the belief that scientific knowledge offers a power capable of subduing and controlling the forces of nature for a collective human purpose. The myth provides orientation to the journey of 'modern man', signposts comfortably identifying and labelling the features of the terrain while offering coherent directions. Yet this orientation cannot itself be contained by the scope of the scientific knowledge which the myth portrays as its rational foundation.

Despite its rationalized imagery, the ideology of industrialization is at odds with the scientistic epistemology it celebrates. This is clear not only from its sweeping conceptualization of history but also from its unbounded confidence in the capacity of human design to control nature for human benefit. Modern scientific and technological achievements, however impressive they might be, do not by themselves offer sufficient basis for the conviction that the problems they confront – and perhaps create – can actually be solved. And they certainly do not allow for a faith in technology which ridicules doubt as if it were a violation of scientific method. Such faith is secured only by implicit appeal to the image of an administrative mind overcoming conflict and trouble, diversity and plurality, to guide and govern a unified humanity with a singularity of purpose.

Precise limits to the power of technology cannot, of course, be definitely established on scientific grounds, for this would rule out the possibility that unanticipated innovations could provide solutions to problems which seem to be insoluble. Whatever present difficulties and past mistakes might be portrayed, there is no scientific knowledge which must necessarily shake confidence in the capacity of technology. What is striking and significant about the ideology of industrialization, though, is precisely the unshakable character of its confidence. Although resting on the perceived progress of scientific technology, this confidence cannot itself be celebrated as part of scientific knowledge.

The ambivalence of environmentalism

The perception of environmental crisis has animated the emergence of environmentalism as a counterideology (Paehlke, 1989), but environmentalism has itself exhibited significant ambivalence. This ambivalence is evident in the divergence between strategic orientations calling either for incremental reform or radical transformation. Especially in its more radical variants, environmentalism tends to unsettle both the image of the administrative mind and the ideology of industrialization. However, even as environmentalism throws conventional notions into question, it remains marked by them. Paradoxically, perhaps, environmentalism retains significant roots in industrialism, particularly in the conservation movement of the progressive era.

As a phenomenon of the late twentieth century, environmentalism took a distinctive form in the late 1960s and early 1970s. This early period was followed by a time of both decline and consolidation, until the subsequent revival of environmentalism in the late 1980s and early 1990s. The advent and revival of environmentalism, conveniently marked by the first Earth Day in 1970 and its twentieth anniversary in 1990, of course exhibit significant differences, particularly in a shift in emphasis from 'limits' to 'sustainability'. What the two periods of environmentalism none the less share is a legacy linking them to the progressive conservation movement of the early twentieth century.

Emerging in an ideological context still influenced by images of the progressive era, environmentalism signals continuity with, as well as departure from, industrialism. For progressivism was part of this broader ideological context and became institutionalized as a central element in the advance of the administrative state and the industrialized economy.

The early conservation movement also emerged with the same pattern of ideological and institutional development that gave rise to the rationalized economic and administrative edifice of advanced industrial society. Indeed, Frederick Taylor, the founder of 'scientific management', saw fit to advance his seminal proposals in the language of the conservation movement: future human well-being depended upon the efficient use of human labour as well as the efficient use of natural resources. This link between scientific management and conservation was by no means spurious, however, for both formed part of the wider progressive movement, which pictured human progress in terms of the advance of science, technology and industry. The conservation movement did exhibit an ambivalence between industrialist and naturalist tendencies – represented, respectively, by the figures of Gifford Pinchot and John Muir – but the principal impact on public policy and administration followed a 'gospel of efficiency' in managing natural resources for industrial development.[4]

Even though radical tendencies in environmentalism and related cultural developments in the 1960s and 1970s threw the progressive faith into question, contemporary environmentalism partly continues and partly resists this conservationist legacy. The resource conservation framework is paradoxically reinforced even as it is threatened. Given the perception of crisis, the tradition of resource conservation seems to provide at least some intellectual and institutional ground upon which to muster a response.

The ambivalence of environmentalism is today evident in differences over goals. The environmentalist goal is viewed in divergent ways, which roughly divide between two opposing positions: 1) the idea that a thorough transformation of advanced industrial society is needed; and 2) the opposing position which, while accepting the need for difficult adjustments and reforms, none the less holds that the basic socioeconomic form may remain intact – may, indeed, be adopted by newly industrializing countries. In terms of practical strategy, the more radical environmentalist position tends away from association with established institutions of policy and management, placing reliance on oppositional activities of a diverse social movement. The contrary position tends towards a managerialist orientation that, in depending upon the reform of established institutions, seeks an association with them. What is striking about this divergence is that, despite the extraordinary uncertainty of the enterprise, each camp often seems convinced that – however great the uncertainty – it is right and the other is wrong, even in the camp of the enemy (cf. Lewis, 1992, pp. 2–6, 247–51).

From limits to sustainability

The perception of environmental crisis animating the dramatic rise of environmentalism in the late 1960s and early 1970s was announced in various ways and with different emphases. By far the most dramatic announcement, however, was *The Limits to Growth* (Meadows *et al.*, 1972), which attracted attention both because it employed a computer-orientated method and because its sponsor, the Club of Rome, consisted of members of the international élites of science, business and government. While the source and style of *The Limits to Growth* provoked concern and attracted enormous publicity, its message was ultimately too blunt and dismal, too at odds with the ideological context, for it to be acceptable.

The centrepiece of *The Limits to Growth* was a computer model of the 'world system' portraying the prospect of 'overshoot and collapse' if trends of exponential growth were not significantly curtailed (*ibid.* Ch. 3, p. 166). The study sought an alternative which, while providing for 'the basic material requirements' of the population, would be 'sustainable' (*ibid.* p. 158). This possibility – termed 'the state of global equilibrium' – was found in the idea of 'the stationary state', particularly as adapted by Herman E. Daly (e.g. 1973) from John Stuart Mill's mid-nineteenth-century work, *Principles of Political Economy*.

In responding to the image of an end of growth (which had haunted classical political economy since Adam Smith), Mill raised the question of the purpose of growth: 'Towards what ultimate point is society tending by its industrial progress?' (1965, Vol. 3, p. 752). Unlike Smith, Mill was not averse to the prospect of a stationary state, but indeed saw in it an improvement of the human condition. Once productive capacity became advanced, the chief question became one of how to enhance distribution rather than production. Disaffected with 'struggling to get on' as an 'ideal of life' (*ibid.* p. 754), Mill decisively revised the myth of progress by, in effect, identifying the stationary state as the goal of growth. Concerned about the possibility of 'the world with nothing left to the spontaneous activity of nature', Mill held out the hope that human beings 'will be content to be stationary long before necessity compels them to it' (*ibid.* p. 756). To this end, Mill sketched an image of progress without the continuous growth of capital or population (*ibid.* pp. 756–7):

> It is scarcely necessary to remark that a stationary condition of capital and population implies no stationary state of human improvement. There would be as much scope as ever for all kinds of mental culture, and moral and social progress; as much room for improving the Art of Living, and much more likelihood of its being improved, when minds ceased to be engrossed by the art of getting on. Even the industrial arts might be earnestly and successfully cultivated, with this sole difference, that instead of serving no purpose but the increase of wealth, industrial improvements would produce their legitimate effect, that of abridging labour. Hitherto it is questionable if all the mechanical inventions yet made have lightened the day's toil of any human being. They have enabled a greater population to live the same life of drudgery and imprisonment, and an increased number of manufacturers and others to make fortunes. They have increased the comforts of the middle classes. But they have not yet begun to effect those great changes in human destiny, which it is in their nature and in their futurity to accomplish.

Mill's vision of progress without the growth of capital or population provided *The Limits to Growth* with an enticing image with which to affirm the stability of an equilibrium state as a desirable goal. Yet, while authors of the report quoted the first few lines of this passage (Meadows *et al.*, 1972, p. 175; cf. Meadows, Meadows and Randers, 1992, pp. 211–212), it is doubtful that they, or the Club of Rome sponsors, regarded with anything like Mill's serious-ness the prospect of a world without growth, in which technology and its continual refinement could – through fairer distribution – eliminate toil and provide for an improved art of living. Crucial parts of the passage, indeed, were not quoted. The 'picture of the equilibrium state', the authors admitted, was 'idealized': 'The only purpose in describing it at all is to emphasize that global equilibrium need not mean an end to progress or human development' (Meadows *et al.*, 1972, p. 179).

By invoking images of vitality and dynamism within the context of an equilibrium state, *The Limits to Growth* sought to avoid the connotation of stagnation often surrounding the notion of stability. None the less, the attrac-tive prospect of a progressive future without growth was clearly subordinated to the distinctly more modest aim of avoiding a threatened global catastrophe. This theme, while central to the published report, was even more clearly domi-nant in the film version of *The Limits to Growth*. What is offered there is not a dream of utopia but the hope of a secure order.[5]

The film opens with chaotic images of pollution and destruction, a voice-over depicting the potential catastrophic collapse of the world system and accompanying music from Wagner. Suddenly, the turbulence recedes; the scene becomes calm, quiet, opening on to a clean, bright room: the computer comes into view as the solution, the saviour. A scientistic, technocratic imag-ery, pervades the film as a counter to the threat of disaster, thereby offering a promise of salvation through technical expertise. Experts are interviewed, and they seem to agree. Despite the advent of environmental crisis, there is thus a reassuring consensus on the need for rational planning to bring about orderly change on a revolutionary scale.

Both in its book and film versions, *The Limits to Growth* possessed an ironic, rhetorical power: the ideology of industrialization was thrown into doubt through the very technocratic imagery which normally sustains the ideology. Supported by such imagery, the 'doom and gloom' focus on limits captured the popular imagination, but was too threatening to the ideology of industrialization. *The Limits to Growth* thus provoked a vociferous reaction from many academics, journalists, business leaders and politicians – sometimes in the form of carefully considered criticism and sometimes in the form of an angry response to the study's apparent lack of faith in technology and progress (see, e.g. Cole *et al.*, 1973; Rosenbluth, 1976; Vargish, 1980).

By directly challenging the confident expectations of industrialism, however, the environmentalist focus on limits during the late 1960s and early 1970s came eventually to pay the price of declining credibility. Environmentalists began to recognize that, for them to be taken seriously amid the prevailing industrialism of public discourse, a shift was necessary in the focus of their message. The revival of environmentalism in the late 1980s (Paehlke, 1992) placed the en-vironment on the agenda of public discourse without directly violating the reign-ing myth. A 'win-win' solution to the environmental crisis was formulated in terms of 'sustainable development', particularly as defined by the Brundt-land Commission: 'development that meets the needs of the present without compromising the ability of future generations to meet their own needs' (World Commission, 1987, p. 43). 'The concept of sustainable development,' according to the commission, 'provides a framework for the integration of environmental policies and development strategies – the term "development" being used here in *its broadest sense*' (*ibid.* p. 40, emphasis added).

The discourse of sustainability

Sustainable development certainly sounds like a good idea. How could anyone reasonably object to something that is obviously meant to resolve environmental problems and promote the enduring well-being of humanity? Yet, as soon as one begins to question the idea, it turns out to have a variety of meanings, along with varying implications for nature and humanity (cf. Redclift, 1987; O'Riordan, 1988). Ironically, the idea appears to carry the same presuppositions which, environmentalism had charged, supported unsustainable development in the first place – especially, the confident expectation that development, in any conventional meaning of the term, can actually be sustained.

This irony has not always been missed by environmentalists, but the focus on sustainable development now allows environmentalism to enter established circles of policy debate. For the reform-orientated, incrementalist wing of environmentalism (e.g. Lewis, 1992), this is a welcome prospect. The radical wing of environmentalism (e.g. Merchant, 1992) tends, in contrast, to reject sustainable development as an oxymoron, stressing ecological fragility and objecting to the technically focused, human-centred character of the discourse. While remaining outside established policy circles, these radicals are also often pressed to frame their arguments in terms of sustainability; for public discussion concerning the environment has become primarily a discourse of sustainability.

Even if a previously critical edge of environmentalism has thus become dulled, there still remains room to question the meaning of sustainable development. The term cannot be contained within the conventionally technical framework of policy debate, but emerges as a disputed symbol which harbours potential threats to that very framework. While seemingly at ease with incrementally focused discourse, the term also alludes to a broader context and provides an opening for explicit disputes about the meaning of development and the shaping of the future (cf. Merchant, 1992, Ch. 9).

What does sustainable development mean? Since the term was propelled into public discourse in 1987 by the report of the Brundtland Commission (World Comission, 1987), a plethora of definitions has emerged – by one count, at least 40 significant efforts (see Pearce, Markandya and Barbier, 1989, Annex; Brooks, 1992, p. 408). In technical management terms, the goal of sustainable development requires a precisely specified objective, an operational definition, to guide planning and determine success. However, the notion of sustainable development cannot readily be reduced to a technical framework, and necessarily draws attention to considerations which such a framework neglects.

Even if agreement could be reached on an operational definition, the task of implementation would clearly overwhelm the technical capacities of any existing or imaginable institution. Keeping track of quantifiable flows of energy and materials, for example, is a task so vast – as one commentator has ironically observed – that it would threaten to exhaust the capabilities of the entire labour force (Norgaard, 1994, Ch. 2). Even this information would be far short of what would be necessary: knowledge of both quantifiable and unquantifiable flows through the systematic integration of the measurements in a comprehensive model. In the light of the scope of knowledge needed to pursue sustainable development in a technocratic manner, a staggering human ignorance is evident (cf. Gibson, 1992). The quest for sustainability cannot but be uncertain.

With any technological innovation or industrial project, events join an array of variables that is both inexhaustible and ambiguous. Even if one takes for granted many conventional assumptions concerning the conceptualization and categorization of phenomena, there are always more variables than can be identified, much less measured with any precision, or even counted. The inexhaustibility and ambiguity, while possibly obscured through precise operationalizations and measurements in narrowly defined contexts, none the less become obvious when one tries to imagine the sum of all innovations and projects, including their relationships to one another. The idea of sustainable development as an orientating vision rather than a precise formula is thus at times suggested (e.g. Lee, 1993, p. 198): 'Sustainable development is not a policy objective so much as it is a vision of appropriate human endeavor on the planet we inhabit.'

Yet such vision is obviously open to dispute. Indeed, uncertainty, combined with differing interests and perspectives, ensures that the quest for sustainability cannot comfortably be contained by the terms of technical discourse, but is pressed into a political context where the meaning of key terms is vigorously contested. Much room is thus left for debate. Still, the prevailing focus on sustainable development reflects the kind of background consensus often needed to mobilize support for limited policy initiatives.

Sustainable development thus operates much like other objectives in public discourse: it has meanings which are 'multiple', 'conflicting' and 'vague'. The meanings are multiple and conflicting because the plurality of political actors wants 'many things' and 'different things'. The meanings are vague because the vagueness allows for a coalescence of potentially opposed actors to work together for an apparently common end; they can do this without generating the antagonisms that would be sure to arise from an effort to establish a comprehensive strategy to attain a precisely delimited objective (Majone and Wildavsky, 1984, p. 168).

In the world of environmental politics, the ambiguity of sustainable development thus often seems attractive because it fosters enhanced co-operation among one-time opponents, the proverbial strange bedfellows of political life. In contrast to the prevailing, nearly unrelieved acrimony of earlier environmental politics, environmentalists and industrialists now have at least the appearance of a common ground. The vagueness of 'sustainable development', a weakness in terms of technical discourse, gains a certain political strength because it allows political actors 'to proceed without having to agree also on exactly what to do' (*ibid.* p. 168; cf. O'Riordan, 1988; Hajer, 1992, p. 30).

Of course this political strength is more attractive to environmentalists focused on the prospect of incremental reforms than to environmentalists advocating radical social transformation. Yet apparently limited incremental reforms may have consequences which set in motion or converge with larger changes (cf. Weiss and Woodhouse, 1992). Because of fear of this possibility, the radical environmentalist rejection of compromise with industrial interests is indeed mirrored, in anti-environmentalist circles, by an equally sharp condemnation of business 'appeasement' of environmentalism: sustainable development is a term which serves 'to mask an anti-industrial agenda' (Salsman, 1993, pp. 119, 124) because the idea is 'so vague that it can be stretched to suit anyone's purpose to restrain capitalist development' (Woiceshyn and Woiceshyn, 1993, p. 145). Despite continuing attempts to reduce the notion of sustainable development to technical terms, the discourse of sustainability thus contains ambiguities and uncertainties which, in a public context of differing interests and perspectives, renders the discourse inescapably political.

Whatever sustainable development may have meant to the Brundtland Commission and to the many who have since proffered definitions, the significant rhetorical impact arose from a smooth co-ordination and reconciliation of what, in the previous discourse of limits, had appeared as opposites: sustainability and development. Environmentalism could thus advance with a motto which escaped the stigma of 'limits to growth', countering the claim that environmentalism was a doctrine of hopelessness which would deny progress and consign most of the humanity – particularly the underdeveloped nations – to impoverished stagnation. While the Brundtland Commission presented a familiar litany of environmental problems, its tone was strikingly upbeat (World Commission, 1987, p. 28):

> We also found grounds for hope: that people can cooperate to build a future that is more prosperous, more just, and more secure; that a new era of economic growth can be attained, one based on policies that sustain and expand the Earth's resource base; and that the progress that some have known over the last century can be experienced by all in the years ahead.

There is a vagueness to the term 'development' since, in a broad sense, the term can mean a process of change involving distinct alternatives to the established pattern. The Brundtland Commission in fact seems to play upon this vagueness by saying that it intends development in 'its broadest sense'. However, the text repeatedly suggests that this broadest sense is actually rather narrow, amounting to no more than a fairly conventional notion of 'progress' (*ibid.* pp. 27–8, 37, 43). What the commission's concept of sustainable development thus lacks is a vision of alternative historical possibilities, such as the dramatic redefinition of progress advanced by Mill and repeated by contemporary environmentalists, including the authors of *The Limits to Growth*.

The term 'sustainable development' suggests a comfortable reconciliation with the presuppositions of the ideology of industrialization. Indeed, the discourse on sustainable development includes ambiguities and associations which make for two crucial equations that appear in a more or less explicit manner:

1. Sustainable = sustained.
2. Development = growth.

In the discourse of sustainable development, there is an explicit appearance of phrases such as 'sustained development' and 'sustainable economic growth'. Not only are these phrases more in keeping with the ideology of industrialization than 'sustainable development', but also sustainability is thus implicitly put at ease with what had appeared to be its opposite: sustained economic growth (e.g. Turner, 1988; cf. Brooks, 1992, p. 404). With such associations, the rhetoric of sustainable development helps to render plausible such notions as the 'greening' of business and sets the stage for a significant change at least in the tone, and perhaps even in the substance, of environmental politics.

Environmental politics and 'sustainable development'

Early reports of environmental crisis tended to cast the politics of the environment in terms of a stark opposition between environmentalists and industrialists. At the time of Earth Day 1970, there were disagreements among environmentalists about whether to promote the reform of established institutions or to adopt a posture of radical opposition. Yet the spectre of falling prey to co-optation by industrial interests loomed over the debate and was widely recognized as a danger. Proponents of environmentalism generally took it for granted that the existing pattern of industrial development was deeply flawed. The very controversy, indeed, reinforced a cultural dimension which characterized environmental politics at the time – an evocative, festive, unruly, almost carnival atmosphere at odds with the severe tone of advanced industrial society and its administrative state (see Paehlke and Torgerson, 1990). In this context, fears of ecological catastrophe could readily alternate with Utopian visions of nature and humanity in harmony.

As the 1970s advanced, however, there came a period of institutionalization, in which many of the sharply oppositional features of environmentalism were at least partially smoothed over. According to Samuel P. Hays's description of this change in the American context, politics tended to be eclipsed by 'environmental management'; broad 'public debate' gave way to a discourse that was orientated to 'centralized direction by technical experts' and guided by 'the terminology and conceptual focus of management' (1989, pp. 393–4). The institutionalization of environmental concern meant an entry of environmentalism into the world of administration, but entry into this world also meant adaptation to it (*ibid.* p. 405): 'Environmental management linked private and public agencies in reinforcing and supportive relationships of common perception, purpose, and choice. Such relationships were influenced heavily by tendencies from all sides toward stability and predictability in system management.' In this world, the antagonism between environmentalist and industrialist was attenuated by the emergence of 'a middle ground' of environmental professionals who, while environmentally informed and concerned, came increasingly under the influence of a concerted corporate attempt to control the focus of the discourse. Given what they viewed as an inescapable 'conflict between economics and environmental objectives' (*ibid*. pp. 410–11), corporate advocates maintained that environmental initiatives should carry a heavy burden of proof – waiting always upon indisputable scientific conclusions and, with cost-benefit analysis instituted as 'the central language of public discourse over environmental policy', following technocratic decision procedures (*ibid*. pp. 412–13). In the administrative world of the environmental professional, controversy came to be seen as a problem leading to irrationality and policy stalemate (*ibid*. pp. 410–11). A contentious environmental politics should give way to reason, to discussions largely limited to calm, deliberate administrative settings (*ibid*. pp. 414–15).

Despite this call to administrative reason, a sharp political polarization remained between environmentalist and industrialist camps. In response to an increasingly organized environmental movement that for a time enjoyed wide popular support, business interests mobilized both to resist environmental regulation and to reclaim public opinion. By 1980, for example, a business-sponsored National Coalition for Growth was in place in the USA to challenge the environmentalist views advanced in connection with the tenth anniversary of Earth Day (*ibid*. p. 413). Protagonists in both the environmentalist and industrialist camps could readily assume that the interests of the two sides were diametrically opposed. If environmentalists tended to view business – perhaps, indeed, the entire system of corporate capitalism – as the problem, as being necessarily anti-environmentalist, business proponents in turn tended to accept an anti-environmentalist role, implicitly if not explicitly, viewing environmentalism as a direct threat to business legitimacy.

Caught between opposing environmentalist and industrialist forces, environmental professionalism influenced both, reducing the conflict to some extent. By the twentieth anniversary of Earth Day, indeed, both environmentalist and industrialist figures could voice enthusiasm for business as at least a partial solution to environmental problems. This enthusiasm pictured business – in contrast to the state – as an innovative, flexible, adaptive institution, able to respond quickly to the signals of the market. Business responsiveness included the creation of lines of 'green' products to meet consumer concerns. More significantly, this responsiveness involved new technologies and productive processes designed in a context which combined environmentalist influence with intense international competition. The new technologies often proved to be both profitable and environmentally friendly, enhancing efficiency while reducing the through-put of resources and the generation of pollutants (cf. World Commission, 1987, pp. 211–13). Despite continuing conflicts, discussion was now possible among environmentalists, environmental professionals and business leaders – with or without government officials. 'Sustainable development' provided a focus for discussion (cf. Davis, 1991; Bruton and Howlett, 1992): it was a term which, unlike 'limits to growth', seemed consistent with the ideology of industrialization. As a book on the 'greening' of business indeed indicates, 'sustainable development accentuates the positive' (Davis, 1991, p. 26).

The advent of 'sustainable development' as a focus of environmentalist discussion heralds the ascent of an incrementalist strategy that involves deliberate accommodation with established institutions orientated to the promotion of industrialism. Yet the radical strain of environmentalism remains suspicious both of the notion of 'sustainable development' and of any move towards compromise. Plant (1991, p. 3), offering a radical viewpoint in explicit opposition to incrementalism, thus sees hope in an economic catastrophe: 'the very best thing for the planet might be a massive world-wide economic depression. Amid the terrible hardships this would create for countless people, at least the machinery would stop for a while, and the Earth could take a breather.' Needless to say, the range of potential consequences arising from such economic dislocation does not seem to have been carefully considered. Placing no real hope in the potential of incremental reform, however, radical environmentalism tends to vacillate between romantic and catastrophic scenarios of social change.

Radical environmentalism is of course composed of diverse, often conflicting, elements – such as social ecology, deep ecology and ecofeminism – but these elements tend to coalesce in clear opposition to established institutions.[6] With a rejection of established institutions and 'sustainable development', radical environmentalists advance sustainability as a goal to be attained through a strategy generally relying on the counterinstitutions and decentralized initiatives of a diverse social movement (cf. Carroll, 1992).

Radical environmentalists characteristically reject compromise while emphasizing imperatives of thoroughly transforming established institutions and ways of viewing the human/nature relationship. Sustainable development, in this view, is a contradiction in terms that simply serves to obscure intellectual and moral failures. With this uncompromising posture, radical environmentalism serves to set in relief the domain of the administrative mind and the risk that environmentalist initiatives might well be absorbed and rendered ineffective by it. An enduring feature of environmental politics from its early period to today is thus the ambivalence and tension between strategies of incremental reform and radical opposition, and this tension has placed its mark on the discourse of sustainability.

Conclusion

Contemporary environmental policy and management, while shaped through their institutionalization in the administrative world, at least partly remain achievements of an environmentalism critical of this world and its prevailing industrialist ideology. The radical critique is right to emphasize that established institutions have an enormous capacity to absorb and reshape divergent initiatives. The promotion of sustainable development, in this regard, seems virtually programmed to reinforce the existing order and pattern of development. However, it is a mistake to think that such an initiative is somehow intrinsically destined to have this effect; for the outcome depends on the dynamics of a broader context, of which radical environmentalism is itself a part.

The propensity for the dominant form to co-opt and absorb oppositional elements is clear enough. This does not argue for the insignificance of incremental changes in that form, however, but for the importance of a radical opposition to counter co-optive tendencies and to maintain a tension, without which the administrative form would be prone to close in further upon itself. Emerging tendencies towards new forms of environmental policy and management are not inherently destined to be still-born, but have ambivalent potentials which depend on a context that often defies administrative control (cf. Torgerson, 1990, pp. 140–5). The many meanings and connotations of 'sustainable development', in this regard, signal no neat concept, but a range of ideas whose very indeterminacy and contestability help to suggest previously unheard-of possibilities.

The industrialist faith in progress offered a mode of closure to the world of public discourse: a form of 'uncertainty absorption' (March and Simon, 1958, pp. 164–5) which inhibited the serious consideration of alternatives to the conventional path of development. By advancing a discourse of sustainability, environmentalism now provokes uncertainties with implications for the very shape of public life. Although the dominant accent of the discourse on sustainability appears to fit comfortably with a technical administrative focus, with a cautiously incremental approach and with the steady advance of industrialization, this discourse of sustainability also has the potential to disrupt the prevailing contours of public discourse. Central to the concern with sustainability, after all, there remain doubts about the very possibility of maintaining the conventional path of progress.

In this context, the environmentalist ambivalence between incrementalism and radicalism does not appear as necessarily requiring a definitive resolution through some either/or decision. The always-shifting ground of public discourse suggests another approach. The prospect emerges of an environmentalist strategy, decentred in its orientation, breaking decisively with the epistemological presuppositions of the administrative mind. The ambivalence and tension of a diverse social movement might thus be retained, the apparent alternatives combined within the general orientation of an 'incremental radicalism' (cf. Torgerson, 1994). This approach continues to accept the responsibility of critical judgement but – acknowledging the uncertainty of the quest for sustainability – gives up the presumptuous notion of somehow comprehensively controlling the future.

Efforts to forge a sustainable future unavoidably confront profound uncertainties which, although endemic to human endeavours, were before obscured by the unquestioned faith in future progress – by the sense of an overall, virtually predetermined direction to human affairs. Attempts to assimilate the discourse of sustainability to prior expectations, to rehabilitate conventional notions of progress under the heading of sustainability, are undercut from the outset because the discourse itself has arisen from doubts about the possibility of fulfilling those very expectations.

Such doubts also provoke questions of desirability, for uncertainty about the direction of development suggests an element of choice. Not only do environmental issues become increasingly salient but also a space begins to open in public discourse for reflection on the purpose and direction of development in the modern world (Hajer, 1995a; 1995b). No longer ruled out of consideration by a supposed imperative of progress (cf. Leiss, 1990), such concerns become a potential focus for serious public deliberation through new forms of democratic politics.

Despite the character of prevailing tendencies in environmental policy and management, there are indeed countertendencies promoting a revised agenda of inquiry and practice. What these developments anticipate is an approach that rejects the dominance of the administrative mind in favour of practices in which the stance of detached calculation and control is replaced by a distinctly human world of uncertain judgements and interactions (Paehlke and Torgerson, 1990, pp. 292ff; Torgerson and Paehlke, 1990).

This approach to environmental policy and management abandons the apolitical façade characteristic of administration under industrialist expectations: the accent of the approach is instead placed on a democratic agenda of developing 'participatory expertise' (Fischer, 1990; 1993) and 'discursive designs' (Dryzek, 1987; 1990). Without accepting as fixed the present form of administration in state and economy, this approach tends to create a dynamic space, an arena for conflict and co-operation, connecting the established world of policy and management with the world of social movements. Within this context, the contention between incremental and radical approaches may be expected to have results that no single party could predict or control.

Notes

1. A version of some material in this chapter was presented to the New York Academy of Sciences, New York City, 5 January 1994 (and some part appeared in Torgerson, 1994). I am grateful to the participants at the session for a useful discussion. For his advice on the preparation of this chapter, I especially thank Frank Fischer. I also thank the following people for helpful responses to versions of the material: John Bishop, Michael Black, Jonathan Bordo, David B. Brooks, Leanne Burney, Maarten Hajer, Eric Helleiner, David Holdsworth, Richard Norgaard, Andreas Pickel and John Wadland.

2. The concept of the ideology of industrialization presented here relies on an earlier, more extensive discussion (Torgerson, 1980, Ch. 2) and draws particularly upon the work of Leiss (1974; 1990). The term itself is derived from Dickson (1974), who uses it in a different yet largely complementary manner. Merchant (1980) draws attention to the significance of gender in this context. For a critique of the technocratic orientation in public discourse, see Fischer (1990).

3. On the concept of a rationalized myth, see Meyer and Rowan (1977); for an incisive case study of a rationalized myth in contemporary management practices, see Quaid (1993, esp. Ch. 10). My point is not to deny that human discourses may necessarily exhibit mythical, or at least fictional, features, but to indicate that the ideology of industrialization is based on this denial.

4. See Hays (1975, esp. p. 265): 'The broader significance of the conservation movement stemmed from the role it played in the transformation of a decentralized, nontechnical, loosely organized society, where waste and inefficiency ran rampant, into a highly organized, technical and centrally planned and directed social organization which could meet a complex world with efficiency and purpose' (see also Hofstader,

1955; Haber, 1964; Merkle, 1980; Rodman, 1976; 1983). For a key passage linking the scientific management and conservation movements, see Taylor (1972, pp. 5–6). While the discussion here of course focuses on the American context, similar – though perhaps less dramatic – patterns would seem to hold in other advanced industrial countries at the intersection of social movements and the administrative sphere (see, e.g. Allison, 1975).

    5.   Produced by the BBC, the film was used by environmental groups in the 1970s.

    6.   While radical environmentalism is, of course, a fragmented field, coherent features have been noted both by those who are sympathetic and those who are not (e.g. Eckersley, 1992; Lewis, 1992; Merchant, 1992).

References

Allison, L. (1975) *Environmental Planning*. Allen & Unwin, London.

Bordo, J. (1992) 'Ecological peril, modern technology and the postmodern sublime,' in P. Berry and A. Wernick (eds) *Shadow of Spirit: Postmodernism and Religion*. Routledge, London.

Brooks, D.B. (1992) 'The challenge of sustainability: is integrating environment and economy enough?' *Policy Sciences*, Vol. 26, no. 4, pp. 401–8.

Bruton, J. and Howlett, M. (1992) 'Differences of opinion: round tables, policy networks, and the failure of Canadian environmental strategy,' *Alternatives: Perspectives on Society, Technology and Environment*, Vol. 19, no. 1, pp. 25–8, 31–3.

Bury, J.B. (1955) *The Idea of Progress*. Dover, New York.

Carroll, W.K. (ed.) (1992) *Organizing Dissent: Contemporary Social Movements in Theory and Practice*. Garamond Press, Toronto.

Cole, H.S.D., Freeman, C., Jahoda, M. and Pavitt, K.L.R. (1973) *Thinking about the Future: A Critique of the* Limits to Growth. Chattos & Windus, London.

Daly, H.E. (ed.) (1973) *Toward a Steady State Economy*. W.H. Freeman, San Francisco, Calif.

Davis, J. (1991) *Greening Business: Managing for Sustainable Development*. Basil Blackwell, Oxford.

Dickson, D. (1974) *Alternative Technology and the Politics of Technical Change*. Fontana, Glasgow.

Dryzek, J.S. (1987) *Rational Ecology: Environment and Political Economy*. Basil Blackwell, London.

Dryzek, J.S. (1990) *Discursive Democracy: Politics, Policy and Political Science*. Cambridge University Press.

Eckersley, R. (1992) *Environmentalism and Political Theory: Toward an Ecocentric Approach*. SUNY Press, Albany, NY.

Fischer, F. (1990) *Technocracy and the Politics of Expertise*. Sage, Newbury Park, Calif.

Fischer, F. (1993) 'Citizen participation and the democratization of policy expertise: from political theory to practical cases,' *Policy Sciences*, Vol. 26, no. 3, pp. 165–87.

Gibson, R.B. (1992) 'Respecting ignorance and uncertainty,' in E. Lykke (ed.) *Achieving Environmental Goals*. Belhaven Press, London.

Haber, S. (1964) *Efficiency and Uplift: Scientific Management in the Progressive Era, 1890–1920*. University of Chicago Press, Chicago, Ill.

Hajer, M. (1992) 'The politics of environmental performance review: choices in design,' in E. Lykke (ed.) *Achieving Environmental Goals*. Belhaven Press, London.

Hajer, M. (1995a) 'Ecological modernisation and social change,' in S. Lash, B. Szersynski and B. Wynne (eds) *Risk, Environment and Modernity: Towards a New Ecology*. Sage, London (in press).

Hajer, M. (1995b) *The Politics of Environmental Discourse: A Study of the Acid Rain Controversy in Great Britain and the Netherlands*. Oxford University Press (forthcoming).

Hays, S.P. (1975) *Conservation and the Gospel of Efficiency: The Progressive Conservation Movement, 1890–1920*. Atheneum, New York.

Hays, S.P. (1989) *Beauty, Health and Permanence: Environmental Politics in the United States, 1955–1985*. Cambridge University Press, Cambridge, England.

Hofstader, R. (1955) *The Age of Reform*. Anchor, New York.

Lee, K.N. (1993) *Compass and Gyroscope: Integrating Science and Politics for the Environment*. Island Press, Washington, DC.

Leiss, W. (1974) *The Domination of Nature*. Beacon Press, Boston, Mass.

Leiss, W. (1990) *Under Technology's Thumb*. McGill-Queen's University Press, Montreal and Kingston.

Lewis, M.W. (1992) *Green Delusions: An Environmentalist Critique of Radical Environmentalism*. Duke University Press, Durham, NC.

Majone, G. and Wildavsky, A. (1984) 'Implementation as evolution,' in J. Pressman and A. Wildavsky (eds) *Implementation* (3rd edn). University of California Press, Berkeley, Calif.

March, J.G. and Simon, H.A. (1958) *Organizations*. Wiley, New York.

Meadows, D.H., Meadows, D.L. and Randers, J. (1992) *Beyond the Limits: Global Collapse or a Sustainable Future*. Earthscan, London.

Meadows, D.H., Meadows, D.L., Randers, J. and Behrens, W.W. (1972) *The Limits to Growth: A Report for the Club of Rome's Project on the Predicament of Mankind*. Universe Books, New York.

Merchant, C. (1980) *The Death of Nature: Women, Ecology, and the Scientific Revolution*. Harper & Row, San Francisco, Calif.

Merchant, C. (1992) *Radical Ecology*. Routledge, London.

Merkle, J. (1980) *Management and Ideology: The Legacy of the International Scientific Management Movement*. University of California Press, Berkeley, Calif.

Meyer, J.W. and Rowan, B. (1977) 'Institutionalized organizations: formal structure as myth and ceremony,' *American Journal of Sociology*, Vol. 83, pp. 340–63.

Mill, J.S. (1965) *Principles of Political Economy* (1848), in *The Collected Works of John Stuart Mill, Vols 2–3*. University of Toronto Press.

Norgaard, R.B. (1994) *Development Betrayed: The End of Progress and a Coevolutionary Revisioning of the Future*. Routledge, London.

O'Riordan, T. (1988) 'The politics of sustainability,' in R.K. Turner (ed.) *Sustainable Environmental Management*. Belhaven Press, London.

Paehlke, R. (1989) *Environmentalism and the Future of Progressive Politics*. Yale University Press, New Haven, Conn.

Paehlke, R. (1992) 'Eco-history: two waves in the evolution of environmentalism,' *Alternatives: Perspectives on Society, Technology and Environment*, Vol. 19, no. 1, pp. 18–23.

Paehlke, R. and Torgerson, D. (1990) 'Environmental politics and the administrative state,' in R. Paehlke and D. Torgerson (eds) *Managing Leviathan: Environmental Politics and the Administrative State*. Broadview Press, Peterborough, Ontario.

Pearce, D., Markandya, A. and Barbier, E.B. (1989) *Blueprint for a Green Economy*. Earthscan, London.

Plant, C. with Albert, D.H. (1991) 'Green business in a gray world – can it be done?' In C. Plant and J. Plant (eds) *Green Business: Hope or Hoax? Toward an Authentic Strategy for Restoring the Earth*. New Society Publishers, Philadelphia, Pa.

Quaid, M. (1993) *Job Evaluation: The Myth of Equitable Assessment*. University of Toronto Press.

Redclift, M. (1987) *Sustainable Development: Exploring the Contradictions*. Methuen, London.

Rodman, J. (1976) Four forms of ecological consciousness, part one: resource conservation. Paper given at the annual meetings of the American Political Science Association, Chicago, Ill., 2–5 September.

Rodman, J. (1983) 'Four forms of ecological consciousness reconsidered,' in D. Scherer and T. Attig (eds) *Ethics and the Environment*. Prentice-Hall, Englewood Cliffs, NJ.

Rosenbluth, G. (1976) 'Economists and the growth controversy,' *Canadian Public Policy*, Vol. 11, no. 2, pp. 225–39.

Salsman, R.M. (1993) 'Corporate environmentalism' and other suicidal tendencies, in J. Woiceshyn (ed.) *Environmentalism: What Does It Mean for Business?* University of Calgary, Faculty of Management.

Taylor, F. (1972) *The principles of scientific management (1911)*, in *Scientific Management*. Greenwood Press, Westport, Conn.

Torgerson, D. (1980) *Industrialization and Assessment: Social Impact Assessment as a Social Phenomenon.* York University, Toronto.

Torgerson, D. (1990) 'Limits of the administrative mind: the problem of defining environmental problems,' in R. Paehlke and D. Torgerson (eds) *Managing Leviathan: Environmental Politics and the Administrative State.* Broadview Press, Peterborough, Ontario.

Torgerson, D. (1994) 'Strategy and ideology in environmentalism: a decentred approach to sustainability,' *Industrial and Environmental Crisis Quarterly*, Vol. 8, no. 4, pp. 295–321.

Torgerson, D. and Paehlke, R. (1990) 'Environmental administration: revising the agenda of inquiry and practice,' in R. Paehlke and D. Torgerson (eds) *Managing Leviathan: Environmental Politics and the Administrative State.* Broadview Press, Peterborough, Ontario.

Turner, R.K. (ed.) (1988) *Sustainable Environmental Management*, Belhaven, London.

Vargish, T. (1980) 'Why the person sitting next to you hates "Limits to Growth",' *Technological Forecasting and Social Change*, Vol. 16, pp. 179–89.

Weiss, A. and Woodhouse, E. (1992) 'Reframing incrementalism: a constructive response to the critics,' *Policy Sciences,* Vol. 25, no. 3, pp. 255–74.

Woiceshyn, G. and Woiceshyn, J. (1993) Commentary: 'Corporate environmentalism' and other suicidal tendencies, in J. Woiceshyn (ed.) *Environmentalism: What Does It Mean for Business?* University of Calgary, Faculty of Management.

World Commission on Environment and Development (1987) *Our Common Future.* Oxford University Press.

2

Sustainable development as a power/ knowledge system: the problem of 'governmentality'

TIMOTHY W. LUKE

Virginia Polytechnic Institute and State University

This chapter questions the ideas and actions of one of the most unquestioned environmental movements now operating all over the world, namely, groups supporting the goal of 'sustainable development'. One must wonder about concepts like sustainable development. Some will take sustainable development to mean ecologically sustainable.[1] Others can just as rightly see it as economically sustainable, technologically sustainable or politically sustainable.[2] Consequently, chambers of commerce and ministries of industry in the 1990s glibly appropriate sustainable development discourse as their own: this dam, that factory, these highways, those powerlines must be built to sustain, not nature, but job creation, population growth, industrial output or service delivery, because such elements improve human life and enhance its eco-systems' carrying capacities. This construction, however, clashes with more ecological interpretations of sustainability in which humans allegedly are seeking 'social and material progress within the constraints of sustainable resource use and environmental management' and, as a result,

> renewable resources (plants, trees, animals and soil) will be used no faster than they are generated; non-renewable resources (such as fossil fuels and metals) will be used no faster than acceptable substitutes can be found; and pollutants will be generated no faster than can be absorbed and neutralized by the environment.[3]

As a social goal, then, sustainability is fraught with unresolved questions. Sustainable for how long: a generation, one century, a millennium, ten millennia? Sustainable at what level of human appropriation: individual households, local villages, major cities, entire nations, global economies? Sustainable for whom: all humans alive now, all humans that will ever live, all living beings living at this time, all living beings that will ever live? Sustainable under what conditions: for contemporary transnational capitalism, for low-impact Neolithic hunters and gatherers, for some future space-faring global empire?

Sustainable development of what: personal income, social complexity, gross national product, material frugality, individual consumption, ecological bio-diversity? For the most part, few of these questions are even being adequately conceptualized, much less thoroughly addressed in the debates over sustainable development. Therefore, in this critique of sustainability, I borrow insights from Michael Foucault to re-examine the operational disposition of sustainable development discourses, highlighting the continuing tension in the sustainability debate between the contradictory operational objectives of 'preserving nature' and the practical ends of 'maintaining the economy'.[4] While some sustainability theorists do present their visions of development in nature preservation terms, many other sustainability advocates are much more firmly committed to maintaining economic growth (albeit with an environmental overlay) as their yardstick for judging the sustainability of many public policies. Most importantly, this analysis argues that perhaps there really is no contradiction between ecology and economy in sustainable development discourses. Instead, this contradictory devotion to 'economically sustainable environmentalistic development' is the inescapable by-product of sustainable development becoming entwined in the webs of governmentality running through much of modern environmentalist reasoning.

Origins and orientations

Sustainable development discourse emerges at an historically particular conjuncture in recent history: the early 1970s. At this time, the popular fascination with ecological concerns after the first Earth Day celebrations in 1970, the élite preoccupation with resource scarcities in the midst of OPEC's manipulation of oil prices and supplies during 1971–3, and the apparent abatement of superpower competition in US/USSR detente around 1972 to 1975 permitted new global agendas to be advanced above and beyond cold-war debates fixed on images of some unending east/west rivalry. In these more north/south centred discussions, questions were raised about the survivability of contemporary industrial civilization in the light of tremendous material waste in the overdeveloped north's economies of affluence, which could be seen as including some state socialist societies, as well as pressing material shortages stemming from the underdeveloped south's population explosions, which also countered some state socialist systems in their ranks. Even though they are crudely formulated, these preoccupations are captured in *The Limits to Growth* report of the Club of Rome in 1972:

> If the present growth trends in world population, industrialization, pollution, food production, and resource depletion continue unchanged, the limits to growth on this planet will be reached sometime within the next one hundred years. The most probable result will be a rather sudden and uncontrollable decline in both population and industrial capacity.[5]

Such conclusions, despite their methodological murkiness, drew the attention of many. Sustainable development thinking, in turn, has been one response to the globalistic perspectives of 'the limits to growth' school, but sustainable development reasoning often does little more than assume that the limits to growth might be far more flexible. Indeed, a commitment to sustainable growth is anticipated by envisioning a much more complex global system with many contradictory trends working simultaneously in favour of conservation and waste, ecological care and anti-environmental neglect, social change and institutional inertia.[6] Instead of detecting a single inexorable push by the whole world up against one set of uniform limits to growth in a single catastrophic collapse, sustainable development analysis argues that real ecological damage occurs daily on a piecemeal basis at gradually varying rates. The advocates of sustainable development, in turn, want to problematize these anti-ecological tendencies, while presenting new governmental tactics and moral values to mitigate or eliminate them by taking alternative paths towards continuing economic growth.

In the light of these tendencies, the definition of sustainable development advanced by the World Commission on Environment and Development in its 1987 report, *Our Common Future*, is very instructive:

> Humanity has the ability to make development sustainable – to ensure that it meets the needs of the present without compromising the ability of future generations to meet their own needs. The concept of sustainable development does imply limits – not absolute limits but limitations imposed by the present state of technology and social organization on environmental resources and by the ability of the biosphere to absorb the effects of human activities but technology and social organization can be both managed and improved to make way for a new era of economic growth.[7]

With this declaration, one high-profile group of environmental, governmental and scientific experts (who are answering a call by the General Assembly of the United Nations) begin using the powers delegated to their special, independent commission to refocus the discourses of knowledge generation in environmental affairs. As the commission's chairperson, Gro Harlem Brundtland, declares in the report's Foreword,

> the environment does not exist as a sphere separate from human actions, ambitions, and needs, and attempts to define it in isolation from human concerns have given the very word 'environment' a connotation of naivety in some political circles . . . but the 'environment' is where we all live; and 'development' is what we all do in attempting to improve our lot within that abode. The two are inseparable.[8]

Deep ecologists, ecofeminists, Bhuddist economists, bioregionalists and other nature preservationists might well argue that a life of material simplicity beyond economic growth, or perhaps even poverty, is morally desirable for the earth to survive.[9] The commission, on the other hand, believes that safeguarding the environment actually can sustain economic development:

> widespread poverty is no longer inevitable. Poverty is not only an evil in itself, but sustainable development requires meeting the basic needs of all and extending to all the opportunity to fulfil their aspirations for a better life. A world in which poverty is endemic will always be prone to ecological and other catastrophes.[10]

Humanity must not choose to live in the poor house by opting not to improve its economic lot. Such moves would be evil itself; the world must instead be

constantly redeveloped economically and environmentally to evade ecological
disasters through qualitatively enhanced economic growth.

In advancing this agenda, the Brundtland Commission asssumes that everything it stipulates can be known about the earth's environment – how to define
aspirations for a better life, what constitutes basic needs, when to manage
economic growth, why to improve technology, where to organize environmental resources, how to judge the ability of the biosphere to absorb human
pressures – actually is known. Since these knowledges exist, all that is necessary is the mobilizing of that moral-political will needed to change how systems
of ecological order and economic power work: forcing the rich to become
frugal, transferring resources to the poor, enhancing citizen participation in
collective decision-making, slowing population growth everywhere, creating
harmony between the ecology and the economy of the environment where
humanity lives.

Sustainability as power/knowledge

Such ideas, as they are advanced by sustainability discourses, seem quite in-
triguing. And if they were implemented in the spirit their originators intended,
then the ecological situation of the earth might well improve. Yet even after
two decades of heeding this theory and practice, sustainable development
mostly has not happened, and it most likely will not happen, even though its
advocates continue to be celebrated as visionaries. Perhaps these discursive
formations should be reinterpreted as another combination of strategic moves
in the larger ongoing project of what Foucault defines as 'governmentality'.

As Foucault sees the arts of government, they essentially are concerned with
how to introduce economy into the political practices of the state. Government
becomes in the eighteenth century the designation of a 'level of reality, a field
of intervention, through a series of complex processes' in which 'government is
the right disposition of things'.[11] Governmentality, then, applies techniques of
instrumental rationality to the arts of everyday management exercised over the
economy, society or, in this case, the environment. It evolves as an elaborate
social formation, which articulates itself administratively as 'a triangle,
sovereignty–discipline–government, which has as its primary target the population and as its essential mechanism the apparatuses of security'.[12]

Most significantly, Foucault sees state authorities mobilizing governmentality to bring about 'the emergence of population as a datum, as a field of
intervention and as an objective of governmental techniques, and the process
which isolates the economy as a specific sector of reality'[13] so that now 'the
population is the object that government must take into account in all its
observations and *savior*, in order to be able to govern effectively in a rational
and conscious manner'.[14] The networks of continuous, multiple and complex
interaction between populations (their increase, longevity, health, etc.), territory (its expanse, resources, control, etc.) and wealth (its creation, productivity, distribution, etc.) are sites of governmentalizing rationality to manage the
productive interaction of these forces.[15] What begins as a concern only for

human populations in national territories pursuing agricultural wealth in an era of physiocratic mercantilism now can reshape itself as interventions for any biotic population of global ecosystems sustaining the developed capitalist world system. Encircled by grids of ecological alarm, sustainability discourse often tells us that today's allegedly unsustainable environments can be disassembled, recombined and subjected to the disciplinary designs of its organizationally embodied expert management.

Enveloped in such governmentalized interpretive frames, any environment could be redirected to fulfil the ends of other economic scripts, managerial directives and administrative writs denominated in sustainability values. Sustainability, then, also engenders its own code of 'environmentality', which would embed alternative instrumental rationalities beyond those of pure market calculation in the policing of ecological spaces.[16] This interpretation of sustainable development provisionally reframes it in the practices of what Foucault treats as 'power/knowledge' systems. Foucault's efforts to explain the workings of power in the highly developed bureaucratic settings of modern Europe led him to propound a genealogical theory of power creation and application.[17] Power instead of being the active product of sovereign agencies marking their force on the bodies of subjects, as it often was prior to the eighteenth century, becomes more discursively mediated after the Enlightenment by professional workers using social scientific surveillance techniques to normalize human behaviour. Knowledge systems, working in terms of formal disciplinary discourses, increasingly become the mediations of this sort of normalizing power, moving Foucault to look at power/knowledge systems as mediations of governmentality rather than the coercive actions of governments to explain how authority actually might operate in modern societies.

Initially, one can argue that the modern regime of biopower formation described by Foucault was not especially attentive to the role of nature in the equations of biopolitics.[18] The controlled tactics of inserting human bodies into the machineries of industrial and agricultural production as part-and-parcel of strategically adjusting the growth of human populations to the development of industrial capitalism, however, did generate systems of biopower. Under such regimes, power/knowledge systems bring 'life and its mechanisms into the realm of explicit calculations', making the manifold disciplines of knowledge and discourses of power into new sorts of productive agency as part of the 'transformation of human life'.[19] Once this threshold was crossed, some observers began to recognize how the environmental interactions of human economics, politics and technologies continually placed all human beings' existence as living beings into question.

Foucault can be read as dividing the environment into two separate, but still completely interpenetrating, spheres of action: the biological and the historical. For most of human history, the biological dimension, or forces of nature acting through disease and famine, dominated human existence with the ever-present menace of death. Developments in agricultural technologies as well as hygiene and health techniques, however, gradually provided some relief from starvation and plague by the end of the eighteenth century. As a result, the historical dimension begins to grow in importance as 'the development of the different fields of knowledge concerned with life in general, the improvement of agricultural techniques, and the observations and measures relative to man's life and survival contribute to this relaxation: a relative control over life averted some of the imminent risks of death'.[20] The historical then begins to envelope, circumscribe or surround the biological, creating interlocking disciplinary expanses for 'the environmental'. And these environmentalized settings quickly dominate all forms of concrete human reality: 'in the space of movement thus conquered, and broadening and organizing that space, methods of power and knowledge assumed responsibility for the life processes and undertook to control and modify them.'[21] While he does not explicitly define these spaces, methods and knowledges as such as being 'environmental', such manoeuvres are the origin of many projects all feeding into environmentalization. As the conditions underpinning all of earth's biological life are refracted through humanly controlled systems for organizing economic, political and technological existence, 'the facts of life' pass into fields of economic control for ecoknowledge and spheres of ecological intervention for geopower.

Foucault recognizes that these transformations implicitly raise ecological issues to the degree they disrupted and redistributed the understandings provided by the classical episteme for defining human interactions with nature. Living became environmentalized as humans, or 'a specific living being, and specifically related to other living beings',[22] began articulating their historical and biological life in profoundly new ways from within artificial cities and mechanical modes of production. Environmentalization arises from 'this dual position of life that placed it at the same time outside history, in its biological environment, and inside human historicity, penetrated by the latter's techniques of knowledge and power'.[23] Strangely, even as he makes these linkages, Foucault does not develop his environmental insights, suggesting 'there is no need to lay further stress on the proliferation of political technologies that ensued, investing the body, health, modes of subsistence and habitation, living conditions, the whole space of existence'.[24]

None the less, here is one essential conjunction needed for the emergence of 'the environment' as a knowledge formation and/or a cluster of power tactics. As human beings begin consciously to wager their life as a species on the products of their biopolitical strategies and technological systems, a few recognize how they also are now wagering the lives of many other, or all, species as well. While Foucault regards this shift as just one of many lacunae in his analysis, everything changes as human biopower systems interweave their operations in the biological environment, penetrating the workings of many ecosystems with the techniques of knowledge and power. Once human power/ knowledge formations become the foundation of industrial society's economic development, they also become a major factor in all terrestrial life forms' continuing the conditions of their physical survival. Ecological analysis thus becomes one more productive power formation, disciplinary knowledge system or strategic political technology that reinvests human bodies – their means of health, modes of subsistence and styles of habitation integrating the whole space of existence – with biohistorical significance, and then reframes them within their biophysical environments, which are now also filled with various animal and plant bodies positioned in geophysical settings as essential elements of the human ecosystem's carrying capacity. The immanent biological designs of nature, when and where they are 'discovered' historically in geophysical sites grasped bureaucratically and scientifically as environments, closely parallel the arts of government. In sustainable development discourse, the two merge in another geopower/ecoknowledge system.

With his notions of governmentality, Foucault invites social theorists not to reduce the complicated ensembles of modernizing development to the actions of 'the state', operating as an expansive set of managerial functions that register their effects in the development of productive forces, the reproduction of relations of production or the organization of ideological superstructures.[25] Instead he argues in favour of investigating the 'governmentalization' of the economy and society. With this interpretation, individuals and groups are enmeshed within the tactics and strategies of more complex forms of biopower whose institutions, procedures, analyses and techniques loosely manage mass populations and their surroundings in a highly politicized symbolic and material economy. While it is still an inexact set of bearings, Foucault asserts:

> This governmentalization of the state is a singularly paradoxical phenomenon, since if in fact the problems of governmentality and the techniques of government have become the only political issue, the only real space for political struggle and contestation, this is because the governmentalization of the state is at the same time what has permitted the state to survive, and it is possible to suppose that if the state is what it is today, this is so precisely thanks to this governmentality, which is at once internal and external to the state, since it is the tactics of government which make possible the continual definition and redefinition of what is within the competence of the state and what is not, the public versus the private, and so on; thus the state can only be understood in its survival and its limits on the basis of the general tactics of governmentality.[26]

Because governmental techniques are always the central focus of political struggle and contestation, the interactions of populations with their natural surroundings in highly politicized economies compel states constantly to redefine what is within their competence throughout the modernizing process.[27] To survive after the 1960s in a world marked by decolonization, global industrialization and nuclear military confrontation, it is not enough for territorial states merely to maintain legal jurisdiction over their allegedly sovereign territories. As ecological limits to growth are either discovered or defined in sustainability discourses, states are forced to make good upon an almost impossible obligation, namely, guaranteeing their populations' fecundity and productivity in the global setting of a world political economy by becoming 'environmental protection agencies'.[28] To develop these protected environments and their increasing populations, economic growth must not remain defined as unlimited quantitative increases of output continuing infinitely, but rather it must become seen as sustainable qualitative improvements in everyday life.[29]

Governmental discourses methodically mobilize particular assumptions, codes and procedures in enforcing specific understandings about the economy and society. They generate truths or knowledges, like those embedded in notions of sustainabilty or development, that also constitute significant reserves of legitimacy and effectiveness. Inasmuch as they classify, organize and vet larger understandings of reality, such discourses can authorize or invalidate the possibilities for constructing particular institutions, practices or concepts in society at large. They simultaneously frame the emergence of collective subjectivities – nations as dynamic populations – and collections of subjects – individuals as units in such nations.[30] Individual subjects as well as collective subjects can be re-evaluated as 'the element in which are articulated the effects of a certain type of power and the reference of a certain type of knowledge, the machinery by which the power relations give rise to a possible corpus of knowledge, and knowledge extends and reinforces the effects of this power'.[31] Therefore, an environmentalizing power/knowledge formation, like those produced by sustainable development experts and expertise, must advance its ecoknowledges to activate managerial command over processes of economic growth as well as to operationalize its vision of governmentality as environmentality. Like governmentality within nation-states, the disciplinary articulations of sustainability and development for a global ecosystem must centre on establishing and enforcing 'the right disposition of things' between humans and their environment.

Sustainability as green governmentality

The categories of sustainable development reconstitute nature – through their recognition of the encirclement of space and matter by national as well as global economies – as a system of systems that can be dismantled, redesigned and assembled anew to produce 'resources' efficiently and in adequate amounts when and where needed in the modern market-place without seeing a degradation in carrying capacity. As a cybernetic system of biophysical systems, nature's energies, materials and sites are redefined by the ecoknowledge of sustainability as manageable resources for human beings to produce large quantities of material 'goods' for sizeable numbers of some people.

Sustainable development in this conceptual register follows from assumptions that nature somehow can be regarded as normal or subjected, at least, to normalizing criteria that will reveal year-in and year-out predictable levels of rain, soil creation, timber growth, fish population, agricultural output or human settlement. Once these factors have all been identified and tracked, ecological monitors can watch all these variables and manage the global ecosystem. Yet nature is often far more chaotic, much less unpredictable and plainly not as normal as many scientists hitherto have believed. As a result, technocratic efforts to track its many elements in normalizing models, which often do artlessly assume levels of docile predictability and stable replicability in ecological dynamics, can render many bureaucratic efforts to administer nature's workings highly problematic.

Plainly, sustainable development discourses can be reread as a new power/knowledge formation, aiming at accumulating power for comparatively powerless subnational and supranational agencies through the mobilization of new knowledges about the performance of essentially national economies and states that exert their authority to foster development at any cost. Rather than sovereign territories, these discourses look at subnational and transnational domains for sustainable ecosystems (in both their simple ecological and more complex economic articulations) to reconfigure the circuits of biopower generation and utilization.[32] The environmentalization of national territories reconfigures their existing boundaries, bringing new forces and agents inside even as old forces and agents are put aside or even outside. Attaining national growth alone no longer is enough, national growth must also not degrade transnational ecological carrying capacity or subnational ecosystem survival. National bureaucrats typically do not, and perhaps will not, engage in such calculations, but would-be sustainable development ecocrats can make both of these moves through knowledge constitution to acquire new powers. The powers may not be extensive, but they are real inasmuch as sustainability criteria begin to constrain international protocols on whaling, logging, manufacturing or even set national policies for fishing, land use and forests to preserve localized concentrations of a whale species, old-growth trees or ozone density.

In the last analysis, these apparently well intentioned programmes for sustainable development mostly point towards maintaining the economy rather than sustaining nature as their central premiss. In many ways, as the work of the Worldwatch Institute or the Nature Conservancy illustrates, it is difficult to differentiate their practices from more traditional grow-minded 'conservationist' agendas for contemporary development policies.[33] The representation of the world rendered by sustainable development experts is that of a closed totality with almost cybernetic circuits of ecological interaction, which will disclose transparently most of its logics, interconnections and operational ties to correctly informed analysts, who want to conserve resources to sustain turnover.[34] This conceptual construction of the world also reveals the material relations of many sustainable development advocates' actual engagement to the world as such; they sit above, outside, beyond the sites of greatest crisis as analytical ecocrats.

Sustainable development discourse, therefore, might also be seen as an ideological power/knowledge formation of general theories and specific practices of/by/for contemporary NGO experts. Its backers place a great deal of faith in multinational scientific conferences, special emergency organizations and existing international institutions, like the World Bank or the United Nations, to solve the world's economic and/or ecological crises. Indeed, sustainable development is largely an idea forged for and vended at such NGO venues. Like the analyses of so many of these institutions, however, such discussions ignore how far unsustainable environmental destruction already has advanced under the attentive eyes of global NGOs. These actors and institutions basically must accept the world as it exists, even though it now works at serious suboptimal efficiencies, because they have little or no political power to change it apart from cajoling the leadership élites of existing nation-states and/or subnational civil administrations to do something on their behalf. They want development to work more efficiently or ecologically; and, indeed it would, if only they could design its operations. The NGOs hold that the existing flows of energy, information and resources are not wrong as such, only that the business and administrative élites of nation-states are mismanaging their volumes, rates and levels, which shrewd ecological management provided by sustainable development ecocrats could provide at a local level or from global NGO headquarters.[35]

This NGO approach would not necessarily change the technoeconomic order of the status quo, but it might make it more sustainable for those populations currently trapped in its lower loops of cost and benefit. Developing zones in the second, third and fourth world inasmuch as they are already ensnared within the transnational cycles of global industrialization might advance, but vast regions in the periphery – now largely still left behind – would arguably remain shut out of the sustainable industrial lifestyle as well – even if the environmental initiatives of global NGOs succeed – simply because their present resource base may not support it.

Most sustainable development discourses are extremely conflicted. As discourses of a green governmentality, they are often little more than a bureaucratic conceit, indulging the empire-building of professional would-be ecocrats in the global not-for-profit sector, transnational environmental groups and international organizations, who believe they can effectively monitor global environmental processes in tandem with artfully cultivated national plans for economic development. In the time-space compression of postmodern informational capitalism, many businesses are also willing to feed these delusions with images of environmentally responsible trade, green industrialization or ecologically sustainable commerce in order to create new markets for new products. In some sectors or at a few sites, ecologically more rational participation in some global commodity chains may well occur as the by-product of sustainable development. Overlogged tropical forests might be saved for biodiversity-seeking genetic engineers; overfished reefs could be shifted over to ecotourist hotel destinations; and overgrazed prairies may see bison return as a meat-industry animal.

All of these advances should be supported for their progressive dimensions. None the less, do they really contribute to ecologically sustainable development? Or do they simply shift commodity production from one fast track to another slower one, increasing value-added for local people to gain more income to buy more commodities that further accelerate transnational environmental degradation? And do they empower a new group of outside experts to intervene in local communities and cultures, not unlike how it has occurred over and over again during cold-war era experiments at inducing agricultural development, industrial development, community development, social development and technological development? In other words, now that the cold war is over, does the environment become the substitute for communism as a source and site of strategic contestation, justifying rich/powerful/industrial states' intervention into poor/weak/agricultural regions to serve the interests of those outsiders? Realizing new systems for ecological sustainability is a pressing imperative, but one must wonder if sustainable development discourses and consultants actually have any workable solution for its challenges or a convincing analysis of its complexities beyond the perpetual articulation of their discursive codes for a green governmentality.

Notes

A longer version of this chapter originally was presented at the annual meeting of the American Political Science Association, August 30–September 4, 1994.

1.   See, for example, the annual reviews of the Worldwatch Institute, such as L.R. Brown *et al.*, *State of the World 1994*. (New York: W.W. Norton, 1994) as well as the previous 1984–93 editions; M.R. Redclift, *Sustainable Development: Exploring the Contradictions* (London: Methuen, 1987); or IUCN, *World Conservation Strategy* (Gland, Switzerland: International Union for the Conservation of Nature, 1980).
2.   J. Makower, *The E-Factor: The Bottom-Line Approach to Environmentally Responsible Business* (New York: Times Books, 1993); B. Piasecki and P. Asmus, *In Search of Environmental Excellence: Moving Beyond Blame* (New York: Simon & Schuster, 1990); and A. Gore, *Earth in the Balance* (Boston, Mass.: Houghton Mifflin, 1992).
3.   D.J. McMichael, *Planetary Overload: Global Environmental Change and the Health of the Human Species* (Cambridge University Press, 1993), p. 309.
4.   For a discussion of Foucault's intellectual project, see J. Miller, *The Passion of Michel Foucault* (New York: Simon & Schuster, 1993); and J. Rajchmann, *Michel Foucault: The Freedom of Philosophy* (New York: Columbia University Press, 1985).
5.   D.H. Meadows *et al.*, *The Limits to Growth* (New York: Unicorn Books, 1972), p. 27.
6.   See L. Brown, C. Flavin and S. Postel, *Saving the Planet: How to Shape an Environmentally Sustainable Society* (New York: Norton, 1991).
7.   World Commission on Environment and Development, *Our Common Future* (Oxford University Press, 1987), p. 8.
8.   *Ibid.*, p. xi.
9.   See M. Zimmerman, *Contesting Earth's Future: Radical Ecology and Postmodernity* (Berkeley, Calif: University of California Press, 1994).
10.   World Commission, *Our Common Future*, p. 8.
11.   M. Foucault, 'Governmentality,' in *The Foucault Effect: Studies in Governmentality*, eds G. Burchell, C. Gordon and P. Miller (Chicago, Ill.: University of Chicago Press, 1991), p. 93.
12.   *Ibid.* p. 102.
13.   *Ibid.*
14.   *Ibid.* p. 100.
15.   The statistical surveillance regime of modern bureaucratic states, as Foucault maintains, emerges alongside monarchical absolutism during the late seventeenth century. Intellectual disciplines, ranging from geography and cartography to statistics and civil engineering, are mobilized to inventory and organize the wealth of populations in territories by the state. For additional discussion, see Burchell, Gordon and Miller, *The Foucault Effect*, pp. 1–48.
16.   See T. Luke, 'Green hustlers: a critique of eco-opportunism,' *Telos*, Vol. 97, Fall, 1993, pp. 141–54.
17.   These topics are addressed in M. Foucault, *Power/Knowledge: Selected Interviews and Other Writings, 1972–1977*, ed. C. Gordon (New York: Pantheon, 1980); and H.L. Dreyfus and P. Rabinow, *Michel Foucault: Beyond Structuralism and Hermenentics,* 2nd edn (Chicago, Ill.: University of Chicago Press, 1983).
18.   M. Foucault, *The History of Sexuality, Vol. I: An Introduction* (New York: Vintage, 1960), pp. 138–42.

19. *Ibid.* p. 143.
20. *Ibid.* p. 142.
21. *Ibid.*
22. *Ibid.* p. 143.
23. *Ibid.*
24. *Ibid.* pp. 143–4.
25. Foucault, 'Governmentality,' pp. 96–8.
26. *Ibid.* p. 103.
27. See T.W. Luke, 'Placing powers/siting spaces: the politics of global and local in the new world order,' *Environment and Planning D: Society and Space*, Vol. 12, no. 5, pp. 613–28. 1994; and T.W. Luke, 'Worldwatching at the limits to growth,' *Capitalism, Nature, Socialism*, Vol. 18, June, 1994, pp. 43–63.
28. See, for more discussion of this tendency, International Union for the Conservation of Nature, United Nations Environmental Project and World Wildlife Fund, *Caring for the Earth: A Strategy for Sustainable Living* (Gland, Switzerland: Earthscan, 1991).
29. For a typical expression of sustainability discourse as a legitimation code, see J. Young, *Sustaining the Earth* (Cambridge, Mass.: Harvard University Press, 1990).
30. See T.W. Luke, 'Discourses of disintegration, texts of transformation: re-reading realism in the new world order,' *Alternatives,* Vol. 13, 1993, pp. 229–58.
31. M. Foucault, *Discipline and Punish: The Birth of the Prison* (New York: Vintage, 1979), p. 29.
32. See, for example, I. Sachs, 'Ecodevelopment: a definition,' *Ambio*, Vol. 8, 1978, p. 11. Also see I. Sachs, 'Developing in harmony with nature: consumption patterns, time and space uses, resource profiles, and technological choices,' *Ecodevelopment: Concepts, Projects, Strategies*, ed. B. Glaeser (New York: Pergamon Press, 1984), p. 211; M.R. Redclift, *Development and the Environmental Crisis: Red or Green Alternatives* (London: Methuen, 1984), p. 34; R.F. Dasmann, 'Achieving the sustainable use of species and ecosystems,' *Landscape Planning*, Vol. 12, 1985, p. 215; or R. Riddell, *Ecodevelopment* (London: Gower, 1981), pp. 8–9.
33. See P. Bartelmus, *Environment and Development* (London: Allen & Unwin, 1986); and R.F. Dasmann, *The Conservation Alternative* (London: Wiley, 1975).
34. See L.R. Brown, *Building a Sustainable Society* (New York: W.W. Norton, 1981) as well as the Worldwatch Institute's latest series of surveillance reports beginning in 1992 or, most recently, L. Brown *et al.*, *Vital Signs: The Trends that are Shaping our Future* (New York: W.W. Norton, 1994) for more illustration.
35. These possibilities are explored in L.W. Milbrath, *Envisioning a Sustainable Society: Learning our Way out* (Albany, NY: SUNY Press, 1989); and G. Hardin, *Living Within Limits: Ecology, Economics, and Population Taboos* (Oxford University Press, 1993).

3

Towards a sustainable future: the organizing role of ecologism in the north–south relationship

HECTOR R. LEIS and EDUARDO J. VIOLA
Federal University of Santa Catarina, Brazil

The global disorder of the biosphere

Today, the rapid growth of world populations endangers the earth. There are now five billion people on the planet and it is impossible to feed, house, educate and give jobs to most of those people according to the minimal requirements (World Commission, 1987). The root of the problem is not only a matter of a population boom but it is also a boom of consumption: a billion people (one-fifth of the world population) can afford to have an 'excellent' lifestyle, which imposes a tremendous and unnecessary burden on the planet's ecosystem. Another billion people enjoy moderate levels of consumption, with enough to satisfy their basic material needs without superfluous consumption (although a great number of these people expect to reach the same level of conspicuous consumption as the privileged one-fifth). Finally, there are three billion people (three-fifths of the earth's total) who cannot afford to satisfy even their most basic material needs and live in abject poverty. Worst of all, because of the spread of global media, a large part of this impoverished population aspires to adopt the same predatory types of consumptive behaviour as the privileged minority. Considering the present state of the disorder of the biosphere, we easily realize that it is most unfeasible for the world population as a whole to achieve the high levels of 'affluent squalour' (Sprout and Sprout, 1971) of the privileged one-fifth.

Consumerism (the essence of a materialistic conception of life) became the predominant ideology in the second half of the twentieth century (Ophuls, 1977). Save for a few marginal exceptions, all over the planet economic growth has become a principle means of legitimacy for nation-states. The biological foundations (nature) underpinning that growth was thought to be inexhaustible, both from the point of view of 'resources' and of pollution. Such a hyperdevelopmentalist position was based on a highly materialistic system of

---

values: it assumes that the goal of human existence is an ever-increasing accumulation of goods (which implies an equally increasing consumption of energy). It likewise valourizes the human ability to build artificial niches. It also assumes that technology is intrinsically positive and is able to correct *ad infinitum* any disturbance caused by human activities. The extreme manifestations of such a hyperdevelopmentalistic position are the superpowers' military-industrial-scientific complexes, which are voracious consumers of resources, energy and highly skilled labour.

Consumerism is propelled by the rapid expansion of technological advancement, which requires more and more elements of the living and non-living world. Yet we do not think we are faced with either a demographic crisis or a crisis in natural resources but rather with a crisis of 'civilization' in the biosphere (Herrera, 1982; Myers *et al.*, 1987). The contemporary socioecological imbalance does not occur in the same way all over the planet: most of the population of the first world has sumptuous consumption habits while the third-world majority is impoverished. In the first world, there is a concentration of 'wealthy pollution': nuclear plants, acid rain, sumptuous consumption, dumped garbage and illnesses caused by the excessive consumption of food, alcohol and drugs. 'Poor pollution' exists in the third world: malnutrition, inadequate sewage and water treatment systems, open-air deposits of rubbish or no rubbish collection at all, deficient health care and excessive consumption of drugs and alcohol. In the first world, therefore, one can detect a gradual loss of the real meaning of life because of a one-sided materialistic conception of human life. In the third world, general degradation derives from inequalities and bad distribution of wealth. Wealth that does exist is concentrated in the hands of a few, which allows for no prospective changes to benefit the poor majority. Hence there is generalized social violence, little public space and few conditions for democratic self-determination (Lasch, 1986).

A good example of extreme sociopsychoenvironmental degradation that occurred during the 1980s is the north-south drug problem (encompassing production, trafficking and consumption). On the one hand, there is high demand for drugs in the wealthier cities of the north, where many people are wealthy in material terms but poor in spiritual ones. On the other hand, in the south there exists a vast political-economic-military underground network that sometimes is as powerful as the states themselves and which devastate forests and disseminate the use of drugs in cities of the south (for example, many areas of the Bolivian, Columbian and Peruvian Amazon, and the cities of Medellin and Rio de Janeiro).

Western Europe has been the centre of power since the sixteenth century (Spain, sixteenth century; Holland, seventeenth century; England from the eighteenth century until the first world war). This concentration of power has derived from a European imperialism that was observed in all four spheres of domination: biological, economic, political and cultural. The effects of Europe's ecological imperialism have not been investigated as much as the other spheres but it has certainly been responsible for several crucial processes including the exportation of the European flora and fauna to the rest of the world; the infestation of the rest of the world by European populations and micro-organisms (which sometimes had devastating effects on the local population in the form of epidemics); and the productive activation of non-European natural resources (such as farmland, mineral deposits and forests) to serve European economic interests which simultaneously provoked an increase in the value of these resources as well as their depletion in the long run (Crosby, 1986).

Contemporary ecological changes were compounded starting in the late 1960s when the countries in the first world began to export a costly commodity called 'pollution' into third-world countries. In the 1970s the 'dirty' industries were exported primarily to newly industrializing countries (NICs). In the 1980s, industrial and urban toxic waste was exported (mainly to Africa and central America). Large areas in Africa were affected in the 1980s by serious socioecological calamities which characterize this kind of ecological imperialism – desertification of areas, drought, floods, famine, refugees, epidemics and a proliferation of toxic waste-dumping sites (Dumont, 1989).

After the second world war, anthropogenic ecological calamities accelerated (Hewitt, 1983). The first environmental problems confronted by the first-world states in the 1950s were on regional and national scales. Areas where there was a high concentration of industry consequently suffered an adverse impact on water and air. Swift erosion of farmland areas resulted, due to destructive land-use practices. Generalized ecosystem degradation was caused by energy and mining projects. In the 1970s, environmental problems were no longer regional or national but became global and the use of the concept of biosphere was disseminated among scientists and technical experts working on these issues. Increasingly, previously isolated environmental problems came to be viewed as international problems. A group of cumulative crises were responsible for this shift from regional to planetary scale: the threat of nuclear war, hypothetical and irreversible changes in the world's climate because of the 'greenhouse' effect and the weakening of the earth's ozone layer, the exponential growth of water, air, soil and food-chain poisoning, and an unbearable demographic boom.

The first-world countries, which redefined the terms of national environmental policy in the early 1970s, have since sought to redeploy the problems caused by depletion of natural resources and pollution within their national boundaries to other areas (mainly third-world countries) without confronting the high consumption levels of their population. Thus their policies have brought about contradictory consequences – the improvement of the local first-world environment and the acceleration of environmental degradation among those least equipped to confront the problem (especially in the third world). Therefore, the net effect of those national environmental policies on the biosphere as a whole is to maintain the present levels of environmental degradation. It is most likely, however, that those policies will be short lived for two reasons. First, because the cycles of the biosphere are fluid, the environmental degradation cannot be contained within traditional national boundaries. Second, because of a rising environmental awareness, third-world countries have also started to outline their own environmental policies, thereby reducing the space for depletion of natural resources and pollution.

The socioenvironmental situation in Latin America

Latin America's socioenvironmental problems derive from a region dominated by transnational capital, which generates a kind of development orientated to the needs of the centres of international power (even though it has not prevented Brazil, for instance, ascending in the hierarchy of world power). This kind of development is characterized by sharp inequities, which are maintained by élites who have deeply incorporated exogenous patterns of consumption and that have as a counterpart the present state of poverty of the majority of the people. The dominant technological pattern is either imposed by or imported from those distant centres of power and it frequently proves to be unsuitable for optimal use of the environmental potentialities of the region. Such trends culminate in the degradation of the ecosystem, demographic concentrations and a general biological deterioration of the populations. International financial mechanisms have also been generating dramatic effects in the area. The huge external debt, produced by pay-back schemes, leads cash-starved countries to adopt exportation policies which have their natural resources as a guarantor for the high interest rates of the debt (one such example is the Brazilian Amazonian project 'Carajas').

In the 1980s in particular, the structural crisis in Latin American has become more dramatic since the region still follows the same old pattern of development. The main characteristics of this postwar developmental style are well known: capital-intensive technological patterns of mass production and intensive energy consumption driven by cheap hydrocarbons that valourize automation. Expanded to a worldwide scale this technological pattern has produced notorious effects in Latin American including severe blockage of the processes of industrialization in most of the region's countries (without offering alternative patterns which could absorb the displaced labour force) and a consequent increase in the vulnerability of the area to natural disasters (Caputo *et al.*, 1985). Furthermore, the technological débâcle is being accelerated by a new and very 'efficient' technoproductive paradigm which is based on the control of information through microelectronic processes, telecommunications and a new philosophy governing the organization of worldwide productive units. This new informational pattern will substantially modify the economic system of the ruling centres and will continue to have contradictory repercussions throughout Latin America. It will likely accelerate existing boom/bust cycles in the region because other global suppliers (from the north or the south) will be available to provide the north's buyers with what they want, thus provoking further deterioration or transformation of the present style of development.

The Latin American environmental crisis has worsened in the last two decades because some highly polluting industries (such as chemical and petrochemical concerns) and energy-intensive industries (such as aluminum) have been transferred to some countries of the region. Moreover, to fuel this pattern of growth, some nuclear plants have been built in Argentina, Brazil and Mexico.

Another crucial component of Latin America's socioenvironmental crisis is militarism. This militarism (which does not necessarily mean its final product is a military regime) channels a significant part of the national budgets into the armed forces. In countries like Argentina, Brazil, Chile, Cuba and Peru, the bulk of production, technological research and scientific research has served military interests and needs until the late 1980s. In Argentina and Brazil this militaristic logic has been responsible for the construction of nuclear plants, using up important financial resources in a context characterized by monetary scarcity. Furthermore, it seriously threatens the environment as an irrational energy alternative for these countries if we consider there are other energy possibilities available more appropriate to their ecological balance (Girotti, 1984; Pingueli Rosa, 1985).

Another important problem is the market's artificial intervention in the natural ecosystems of Latin America. In the last three decades, most of these ecosystems have been converted into mechanized agribusiness strongholds which use large quantities of oil and oil-derived fertilizers and pesticides (Cepal-Pnuma, 1985). This process of transforming fossil fuel into food also erodes the soils, culminating in gradual salinization and sedimentation of waterways. This total or partial obstruction of rivers was the primary cause of the catastrophic floods of the 1980s. Add to this the rapid devastation of humid tropical forests in the last decade and one can grasp the problem (Gallopin, 1987; Bedoya, 1989; Sawyer, 1989).

The so-called 'green revolution' has been responsible for negative consequences throughout rural areas of Latin America and has resulted in marginal existence and expulsion of the rural populations, soil erosion, destruction of native flora and water pollution. Within such a system, the disadvantages outnumber the advantages by producing a limited increase in food production for domestic markets. Exacerbating the problem is an attempted imposition of a technological-agricultural pattern designed for mild regional temperatures and not for the tropical Latin American climate, thereby ignoring the ecological principles for agricultural production (Lutzenberger, 1980; Bautista Vidal, 1987; Prudkin, 1989). The widespread use of herbicides, insecticides and fungicides (many of which are banned in the USA) by farm workers with no training on how to handle these poisonous substances has had dramatic results – thousands of seriously ill agricultural workers as well as contaminated water and food supplies.

In the last two decades several big energy-mining projects have been settled, particularly in Brazil, Venezuela and Mexico. These projects occupy huge spaces, devastating people and environment on a vast scale. These projects were arrived at without initial evaluation and, many times, their technological patterns were already obsolete in the first world. In most of these cases, the raw materials produced by these big projects are consumed by industries from the dominant northern-tier countries.

Last but not least, we should consider the present process of accelerated and chaotic urbanization which began in the 1950s and is now the main cause of this ecological crisis. More than one-fourth of the population of Latin America now lives in the large metropolises. Large-scale industrialization and urbanization coincided with increased consumption of energy. The new patterns of high consumption caused a waste of energy because of the large variety of superfluous electric appliances sought. The process of urbanization has increased commercial and financial activities. Building construction in turn has created problems in the transportation and communication arenas. Noise, garbage, fouled air and water pollution were the results of a deepening environmental crisis.

In fact, this process of urbanization is the counterpart to the 'modernization' of agriculture. The millions of farm workers and peasants expelled from their land became concentrated in the belts of poverty which surround the big cities. Most of these people are either employed in industries characterized by highly exploitative and precarious working conditions or they are underemployed in odd or temporary jobs. The big Latin American metropolises are the best expression of socioenvironmental degradation – most of the population drinks contaminated water, has no sewer system, breathes polluted air, has enough to eat only infrequently and is vulnerable to epidemics and natural disasters such as floods and earthquakes. This runaway urbanization fuels the collapse of the existing public services (water, sewage, transportation, education, health). Municipal administrations are faced with insoluble infrastructure problems because of the grand scale on which they have to operate. The metropolitan areas depend on a vast surrounding ecosystem, which means long distances for entrance (the collection of natural resources necessary for life in the cities) and to exit (deposits of liquid and solid wastes). Due to their irrational occupation of space, Latin American metropolises have created a situation of generalized impermeability of the soil and are therefore very vulnerable to rains (which repeatedly result in catastrophic floods, as have occurred in Rio de Janeiro, Sao Paulo and Mexico).

Reports on the environment, development and the north–south relationship

The World Commission report on the environment and development (World Commission, 1987) is the most recent in a series of important international works (important because of their origin and/or scope) concerned with the socioenvironmental degradation of our planet. Prior to this report, other reports originated from the Stockholm Conference on the Human Environment (Ward and Dubos, 1972), the Club of Rome (Meadows, 1972), the Bariloche Foundation (Herrera *et al.*, 1977), the Brandt Commission (Comision Independiente, 1981) and the Worldwatch Institute (from 1984 onwards; Brown *et al.*, 1984). All the reports, but especially the first one (which is also known as the Brundtland report) represent an urgent appeal to international society for co-operative action which could arrest and reverse the present course of action. Towards this end, the report advanced the concept of 'sustainable development'.

Despite some differences in the areas of focus and on their approaches, all the documents agree on the point that there is increasing interdependence among nations in the context of a global ecological crisis. The reports also call for changes and/or reforms in the international order. We believe that there is no 'invisible hand' in the world which would magically transform the pursuit of private interest into the 'common good'. Further, if there is not conscious and decisive intervention which would change the behaviour of the traditional international actors (states, international agencies and transnational companies), the degradation of the biosphere would tend to continue. Who would be the protagonists in such an intervention and how such a new order would be achieved are questions which, unfortunately, the authors of these documents left unanswered.

Perhaps the most important aspect of the reports is the hierarchization of the north–south relationship, as far as the effects of the crisis are concerned – the further apart in their interests the hemispheres become, the more severe the ecological degradation becomes. However, the most acute problem may be the fact that these documents have not really considered that there are contradictions between the alternatives they offer and our present economic and political course. In some of the documents (the Brundtland report, for example), a concensual solution is technically impossible because of the heterogeneous political origins of the authors (World Commission, 1987, xii–xiii). The problem, however, is not technical but, rather, theoretical. The reports are centred on a materialistic conception of human needs. For this reason, the actors and policies favouring the reallocation of resources on local and international levels continue to reproduce the essential traits of the present system, making it more difficult to think our way out of the crisis.

The policies for the sustainable management of resources offered in the reports follow a utilitarian logic by reducing the ecological proposal to a subset of greater political and economic efficiency. The reports reduce the importance of an option for self-limitation and constraint, provided by a redefinition of human needs (Sachs, 1988). It is obvious that there is a problem in the administration of resources on our planet. It is also true that the present mismanagement affects the dynamics of real economic development. Once the focus is placed solely on the economic growth question, it legitimates the dominant position of economics in our society. This, in turn, works against the emergence of any policies that might tend to introduce an alternative. A real management of global resources should not only aim to find environmental limits for the productive system but also to find cultural boundaries for the predominance of production (*ibid.*).

Yet the response given by the Bariloche Foundation to the model presented by the Club of Rome is a valid one. According to the so-called 'Latin American paradigm', the true limits to development are not determined by the shortage of either natural resources or capital, but by the unpredictability of élites and by social injustices (Herrera *et al.*, 1977). We should recognize that the élites are part of the problems we are trying to solve. In other words, we should not hope for any kind of sustainable development which is not backed on local and global levels at one and the same time. The strongest hypothesis of this chapter amounts to this: given our planetary ecological disorder and the sharp increase in the interdependence of productive and communication systems, management of the serious problems we now face must be shifted from the nation to the transnational level. Today, the 'dramas' seem to be suffered in national scenarios but the real theatre, complete with protagonists and solutions, are at the local and/or global levels. According to the Brundtland report, both sustainable development and the welfare of humankind depend on achieving a global ethic for their success. In addition, this ethic should be inspired by both spiritual and ecological values. If there is not a moral reformation which enables the inner development of people, there will be no accompanying lasting social development. Hence, global disorder of the biosphere is a very important question from the normative point of view.

The strategies for any possible solution should not place too much emphasis on its purely technical aspects. It is irrefutable that what is bad for the atmosphere will hardly benefit humankind. If one tries to cure these ills by using make-believe, politically neutral technological strategies, they will not produce healing effects because shallow fixes will never solidify to become politically right decisions. For both cultural and social reasons, environmentalism in the north has certain characteristics which cannot be reproduced in the south (Redclift, 1984). The north's environmental perspective (which permeates all the reports to a greater or lesser extent) transforms the urgent need for a north–south dialogue into a quasi-solipsistic monologue. The Brandt report, for instance, correctly concludes that the present process of development is rapidly destroying the ecosystems of the south (Comision Independiente, 1981, p. 133). However, it erroneously proposes that the main problems between north and south could be solved if the north would somehow help the south become richer by increasing commercial trade and the demand for industrial goods. This is based on the assumption that both hemispheres have similar crises of underproduction and underconsumption of luxury goods on the one hand and of basic goods on the other (Redclift, 1984). Even though such a proposal seeks co-operation between the hemispheres, it still overlooks the obvious – the north–south relationship derives from the one-sided process of northern industrialization and, therefore, unless we understand the problem to be a result of hyperindustrialization and consumption of resultant goods, it will be all but impossible to halt, much less arrest, the ongoing environmental destruction in the Southern Hemisphere.

The guidelines of the Brandt and Brundtland reports were partially drawn from a 'developmentalist' and 'modernizing' conceputalization which become prominent in the postwar years. After an impasse because of the emergence of the fascist, national socialist and communist-Stalinist totalitarian systems, the second half of this century has recovered a developmental 'optimism' which has even influenced those radical segments (such as the theorists of dependency in the 1960s) that were initially against the 'modernizing' paradigm (Cardosos and Faletto, 1969). The essence of that theory was that the existence of external obstacles to development resulted from a 'dependence' which transferred resources from the periphery to the core of the international economic system. Contrary to the commonly prescribed ways to solve such a crisis, dependency theorists stated that a peripheral country should not submit itself to the international division of labour but should, instead, seek ways to develop itself in an independent manner. Considering exogenous and endogenous factors, economic growth was understood as the 'only way out' in both ways of thinking (Friberg and Hettne, 1984).

During the 1960s and 1970s, an examination of developmental rhetoric would reveal the thinking that privileged economic growth among political élites would somehow bring about solutions to social injustice and other problems. In the 1980s, because of the emergence of environmental criticism, such developmental conceptions were attenuated although their materialistic ideological nucleus was left untouched as the axial element of the historical dynamic. Today, the main actors of the international community remain the nation-states and the transnational economic groups. There should be no illusion as to whether these actors alone can provide the urgent policies invoked by these reports.

The role of ecologism on a co-operative north–south horizon

The creation of an alternative ecological world requires a community of co-operative nations to abandon existing developmental shibboleths. The ecological perspective is the result of a thorough critique of the dynamics of industrial society over the past two decades (although its origins go back at least a century and a half). It is based on a system of postmaterialistic values which views human development as a harmonious combination of material development and spiritual evolution (Inglehart, 1976; Galtung, 1980; Capra, 1986; Souza, 1986). The undergirding of broad ecological consensus includes the following premises: natural resources and the biosphere's capacity to absorb pollution are finite; technological development has a contradictory nature, both negative and positive; and humans should develop technologies with mild or minimal environmental impact, centred on efficient social management, and oriented to prudence as far as technological development is concerned (Georgescu-Roegen, 1976; Daly, 1977).

In the context of dramatic social and environmental degradation on a planetary scale, we see the need for a new ethically based ecological orientation, or what we call 'ecologism'. Ecologism refers to an imaginative combination of deep understanding of ecological processes together with an expansion of human consciousness. Ecologism proposes a new system of values which are supported by dynamic ecological equilibrium, social justice, active non-violence and solidarity with future generations. In ecologism, the environment becomes the fundamental dimension of development, following the generative idea of ecodevelopment or sustainable development. While the problems of environmental degradation confronting ecologists in the first and third worlds are similar, the problems of social degradation are dramatically divergent. In the first world, most people can satisfy their material needs. In the third world, most people live at or near the threshold of pauperization, thereby making the problems of socioenvironmental degradation more serious in the third world than the first world. Within the third world, the state, the local bourgeoisie and multinational companies are as predatory in relation to the environment as they are towards the workforce.

The ecologistic hope in the first world is for a generalized cultural transformation (which implies a process of deep restructuring of power in first-world societies). Such a renaissance might make possible the incorporation of post-materialistic values by the great majority of the population and the consequent emergence of constraints on material needs. In the third world, the hope is for a process of development which is as ecologically sustainable as it is socially just. The requirement is to raise the low levels of material consumption for the majority and, simultaneously, to stem and ration the levels of consumption of the middle classes (as well as to reduce levels of consumption in the upper classes). This pattern of 'dedevelopment' demands a more drastic restructuring of power in the third world than in the first world. In the third world, an increase in ecological consciousness should correspond to a generalized dissemination of postmaterialistic values among the people (with differentiated characteristics involving modification of the habits of overconsumption among the middle and upper classes, elimination of predatory components in the consumption expectations among the poorer classes and stopping everyone's demographic boom).

In summary, this ecologistic approach proposes a dramatic reorientation of the present course of development all over the world. It calls for a redefinition of global economic growth within the physical, thermodynamic and ecological limits of the biosphere (Myers *et al.*, 1987). Such global harmony between environment and development requires a new international order that, among other things, stanches both the flow of wealth from the Southern Hemisphere to the Northern Hemisphere and the flow and pollution and depletion of resources from the north to the south. It also presumes a transfer of part of the excess of accumulated material wealth from the north to the south. This approach implies a process of drastic redistribution of wealth and power on a worldwide scale which, in turn, implies the formation of a vast worldwide coalition of groups committed to ecologism. Within such a coalition, ecologists become important players and include representatives of the third world as well as those peoples of the first and third worlds who are sympathetic towards resolving the global problems of the biosphere.

We believe, however, that such a new order will face strong opposition from existing international power structures. In fact, it will be nearly impossible to implement the new order if some restrictions on national sovereignty are not intentionally set. The ecologism project presupposes an institutional organizational structure on top of and from beneath the current nation-state system. This coalitional order would administer important parts of the sovereignty now claimed by the state. Because such a transformation is multidimensional and on a large scale, it assumes that ecologism should be considered as a 'historical' movement. Such a characterization cannot be minimized or neglected when the long-run strategies to resolve the global disorder of the biosphere are laid bare. A fundamental merit of ecologism in the present international situation is that of having broken with the idea of possessing one solution to the crisis (Touraine, 1980). It claims that there is not one single rational way to view development but, rather, a plurality of strategies for each community, society and region of the planet to choose from. These strategies are based on criteria which are not only technical and economic but also social and cultural.

The need for transformations on a large scale is always accompanied by the birth of new social and political actors, as we have seen over the last decade (Nerfin, 1986; McCormick, 1989; Paehlke, 1989). On a local and international scale, thousands of new non-governmental organizations are being founded all over the planet. These organizations do not seek to have political or economic power. Despite their diversity, they share a common denominator which is to provide answers to the problems which threaten the future of the planet (Offe, 1985). The solution to the north–south impasse has started to germinate because of the dialogue these actors indefatigably offer, multiplying their potential for action, infiltrating the power of the state and actually restricting its sovereignty.

Yet the state is, and will remain for some time, an important actor in the international political arena. Meanwhile, mainstream social sciences will be disorientated in understanding transnational phenomena and theatres outside the traditional economic sphere (Ophuls, 1977; Falk, 1987; Lowe and Rudig, 1987). Peering beyond the edge of the system of nation-states and multinational corporations, many social scientists see only the possibility of 'Utopia' and all modifications of that given order are viewed as eventual changes in the behaviour of those actors. As a result, little conceptual attention has been given to the interaction between the new social movements and the international order (Falk, 1987). This goes on despite the impact of some distinct non-governmental organizations on very important issues (such as the actions of Greenpeace against ocean pollution or those of the World Wildlife Fund concerning third-world external debt).

In recent years, ecologism has begun to open up important transnational public spaces, a *sine qua non* condition for the development of co-operative relations between the north and the south (just as the peace movements have been opening up similar spaces in east–west relationships in the last decades). The influence of the peace movements does not mean western governments have lost their military capacity but they have lost their capacity to monopolize the processes of decision-making on security. Security has become subject to public discussion outside the limits of the state military system. A transnational forum was created which governments cannot possibly ignore. This forum includes a new ethic that assumes national defence is a planetary question (Hegedus, 1987). The peace movements have influenced not only concrete policies themselves but also the way those policies may be achieved. In effect, non-governmental organizations actually curbed the sovereignty of the state and created better conditions for agreements on disarmament between nations. In very much the same way, ecologism is promoting a debate about all the issues of biospheric disorder, transcending any kind of sectorial or national interest, and creating ethical, communicative and material conditions for the mutual responsibility of the 'developed' Northern Hemisphere and the 'under-developed' Southern Hemisphere. This fact alone makes true co-operation between the north and the south possible.

Long-term lasting co-operation between the north and the south requires a common ecological-ethical framework. Unfortunately, in the contemporary world, politics is not subordinated to ethics (and it is even less so in international politics). It is then of little help to appeal for a global ethic if we do not consider the real preconditions for its creation. Two very concrete and important requirements to produce an ethic for the relationship of north and south are 1) a drastic increase in the global disorder of the biosphere as a result of the character of the present relationship; and 2) a quantitative and qualitative growth of ecologism in both hemispheres orientated to the establishment of a powerful network between the continents (in this way, a transnational public space opens to everyone). North–south co-operation is possible because it is necessary. Because it is necessary, it is possible to speculate about its mechanisms and conditions.

A new international co-operative order should have as its starting-point a process of differentiated self-constraint of consumption of material goods and resources in both hemispheres in order to promote the balance in the biosphere. Each region will have to surrender something on behalf of the whole. For everything not degraded or consumed, there should be a compensatory gain in the global control of the whole (Offe, 1987). Such a Rousseauian trade is not new and is the basis for most existing intergovernmental organisms with supranational aspirations.

Since its inception, the United Nations has not effectively accomplished its proposed goals. The United Nations should represent an international contractual agreement encompassing moral and physical means. Its original guidelines should be recovered and enlarged so that the agency could become an institutional vehicle promoting the required trade-offs between differentiated self-limitations and global responsibilty to impede free riders. The United Nations should therefore prioritize its transnational issues and reduce its focus on intergovernmental issues. Any institution that aims at more rationally administering an international order should downplay dominant political representation by nation-states (Mische, 1977). This is due not only to governments' failures to represent their peoples but also principally because the problems posed by global biospheric disorder are multidimensional and complex, requiring interdisciplinary and transcultural approaches which national political élites can seldom provide.

The historical character of ecologism is clearly evident in its rapid and vast process of global dissemination. In the third world, ecologism is very heterogeneous. Brazil, India and Malaysia are the leading countries in the group, but the characteristics of their respective ecologism movements differ because of the particularities of each country's social structures and cultural history. The Chipko Andolan movement (the 'hug a tree' movement), born in the north of India in 1974 and extended into several regions, is the best example of the potential capacity of this people for the ecological struggle (Shiva, 1987). Clearly a popularly based movement, the Chipko is inspired by a cultural tradition that emphasizes the balance between human and nature, promoting the preservation of natural resources in seeking survival. Thus it makes claims directly and indirectly for a type of development which could be an alternative to the present path of 'modernization'. In India, just as in other Afro-Asian countries with essentially rural social structures (such as Sri Lanka, Thailand, Kenya and Tanzania), the ecological movement has a clearly popular profile and has had some significant experiences of sustainable development, albeit on a small scale (Centre, 1985; Harrison, 1987). However, this presence does not always mean political representation nor the existence of green parties or other similarly organized political power.

In Brazil, as in other Latin American countries (Venezuela, Chile, Costa Rica and Mexico), the ecological associations were mainly born in the cities and have university-educated leaders. Unlike the Afro-Asian groups, the movements in Latin America have political representation (especially in Brazil). This representation has reached the middle and popular sectors of the society. A small Brazilian green party has existed since 1986 (Viola, 1987).

In Malaysia, the ecological movement is strong, both in urban and rural areas, with membership derived from popular and middle sectors. Malaysian ecologism is strongly related to its British counterpart, and has been largely successful in addressing a wide range of issues, from occupational health to the devastation of the rain forest. Their ecologism movement has the capacity to influence public policies although this capacity has not yet reached into traditionally established politician parties.

Thus far we have described ecologism by focusing on its unity. It is now necessary to discuss its internal diversity and complexity. At first glance, one can identify at least five major different sectors in the international panorama. The first is the conservationist-environmentalism movement, which seeks environmental preservation and recuperation compatible with a capitalist system (mainly such entities as the Sierra Club, National Wildlife Federation, Nature Conservancy, Audubon Society, Environmental Defence Fund, Wilderness Society and national parks and conservation associations). This sector has its origins in North America but has been growing rapidly in western Europe, Asia and Latin America.

Second is the radical ecologism of direct action, represented by such organizations as Greenpeace and Earth First! These organizations attack both capitalist and socialist systems' vulnerable points, from a perspective which appeals to mass consciousness-raising. This sector is active mostly in the Northern Hemisphere.

The next sector is green politics, which is made up of a vast constellation of ecological associations (a network of informal organizations and green parties), which aim for parliamentary influence on local, national and supranational levels in order to 'ecologize' existing cultural policy. With favourable conditions, some of these coalitions even take active part in governments. This sector is flourishing in western Europe, eastern Europe and in Brazil.

The fourth sector is rural ecologism, which values highly the systems and *modus vivendi* of the rural areas. This sector consists of community networks aiming at the developing of suitable technologies of low environmental impact. This sector predominates in Asia but it is also observed in some areas of Latin America (for example, Bolivian and Ecuadorian communities, Brazilian Amazonian communities and in central Brazilian areas).

Last is the sector of global action ecologism, which is strongly science based and orientated towards building a planetary paradigm able to diagnose and suggest possible alternatives. Examples in this sector include the Society for General Systems Research, the Club of Rome and the Worldwatch Institute. Global action is directed at decision-makers at all levels (not only in the political arena) and focuses on the urgent need to form a worldwide authority in order to address environmental problems (problems including security, food, energy and population issues). This group consists mainly of scientists, politicians and other persons who have a broad understanding of the planetary nature of the present ecological crisis.

An exploration of ecologism shows that, with the exception of China, it has been established in all the most important and powerful countries of the world. This circumstance is quite relevant because, through those leading countries, bridges of influence can be extended into the rest of the world. Ecological organizations can promote agreements between governments and networks of social movements. In short, these organizations produce a transnational public space whose scope of action is global. However, the present scenario is also characterized by highly unequal levels of development and influence in the ecologism movements of the first and third worlds. Such differences are particularly evident when we compare the ecological movements of North America, northwestern Europe, Australia and New Zealand with the movements of the rest of the world. This uneven distribution calls for the expansion of the actions and organizational structures of the movements from North America to numerous countries in the third world. It is well known that the ecological movements in North America contribute greatly to the world struggle against the degradation of the global environment. However, it is important to point out that there may be undesirable effects of such an expansion if those organizations do not respect the development of local and autonomous movements. The ecological culture of the north (especially the USA) emerges from the point of view of highly advanced capitalist societies and it would be a mistake simply to transfer it to the south without mediation (Redclift, 1984; Regidor, 1988). Northern culture has a conservative view of the present situation in the third world, where it emphasizes environmental preservation by often overlooking accompanying sociopolitical crises and the cultural roots of each country. Ecologism in the third world must develop its own autonomous structure and enrich itself through its own experiences as well as, where appropriate, to borrow from international ecologism.

We believe that this process of globalization of ecologism is irreversible (though the scenarios are not wholly defined). Three basic alternatives may be posed. First, a scenario which is shaped predominantly by the organizations and culture of the north. Second, a scenario which results from the significant development of an autonomous ecological organization in the south but with continuing hegemony of the north. Third, a scenario in which there is a pluralistic balance and a rich intermingling between organizations and culture of both north and south.

It is still too early to evaluate the first two alternatives presented, but the third seems to be highly improbable, given current world tendencies. However, the possibility for construction of a real transnational public space and a co-operative north–south relationship largely depends on the third alternative (or, at least to a smaller extent, on the second alternative presented). Within the framework of the first alternative, no conditions would exist for a significant change of international relations.

It is also useful to describe a broader spectrum of questions which are hypothetically implied in each of the previously mentioned scenarios. The first one (predominantly marked by the north) would increase the ecological component of imperialism. This would in fact mean a failure of the organizing role of ecologism because of its association with authoritarian forces, at both national and international levels. This scenario would imply an internal agreement between the élites of powerful countries, freezing the present international structure of wealth and quality of life and embracing a double standard of ecological restrictions on productive systems in both the north and south. It would also imply a growing dissociation between the problems of social injustice and ecological disorder, including the demographic boom.

The second scenario, with autonomous ecologistic organizations in the south but with the hegemony of the north, would imply a combination of relative organizational success of the ecologism movement with the establishment of top-down controls by a global environmental technocracy. This scenario would presuppose a trend towards global agreements for increasing equity in international relations and equitable standards of ecological restrictions but, nevertheless, retaining the present north–south asymmetries. It would also imply some degree of environmental political coercion against the south (though not as significant as in the first scenario).

The last scenario with its balance and intermingling between organizations and cultures of both the north and south would imply a global, self-governing eco-organization. Such a strategy means achieving the organizing goal of ecologism, because it would constitute a radical rupture with the mainstream of our civilization and even with the historical biopsychosocial human nature. This scenario would be bound with a balance between top-down and bottom-up political processes and between centralization and decentralization trends. It would allow for the vast diversity of cultural traits while eliminating asymmetries between north and south. It would seek to promote democratic solutions to ecological problems as well as to seek a decrease in world population trends.

Considering what has been outlined in this chapter, we highly recommend that ecologism from the first world and the third world realizes the importance of mutually co-operative partnerships. Both first-world and third-world environmental groups need to increase their solidarity and discover ways to promote better performance by autonomous organizing structures (especially in the third world). Each group needs to preserve their independence while learning to respect unique cultural particularities and objectives. The power of an emergent global ecologism may result in a better understanding of north–south issues and provide each player with a realization of the benefits which would be derived from accelerated co-operation. We not only know that this *can* be done but also that it *must* be done. If we swiftly undertake such heroic change, a new global governance may be born, one with no need for reforms to be reconciled with the principles of democracy.

Note

An earlier version of this chapter was presented at a conference in Brazil in 1989.

References

Bautista Vidal, I.W. (1987) *De Estado Servil a Nacão Soberana. Civilzacao Solidaria dos Tropicos*. Editora de Universidade de Brasilia, Brasilia.

Bedoya, E. (1989) 'Las Estrategias Productivas Familiares y el Deterioro Ambiental en la Selva Alta,' in C. Reboratti (ed.) *Poblacion y Ambiente en America Latina*. Grupo Editor Latinoamericano, Buenos Aires.

Brown, L.R. *et al.* (1984) *State of the World 1984*. W.W. Norton, Washington, DC.

Capra, F. (1986) *O Ponto de Mutacao*. Cultrix, Sao Paolo.

Caputo, M. *et al.* (1985) *Desastres Naturales y Sociedad en America Latina*. Grupo Editor Latinoamericano, Buenos Aires.

Cardoso, F.H. and Faletto, E. (1969) *Dependencia y Desarrollo en America Latina*. Mexico, Siglo XXI.

Centre for Science and Development (1985) *The State of India's Environment 1984– 1985*. CSE, New Delhi.

Cepal-Pnuma (1985) *Avances en la Interpretacion Ambiental del Desarrollo Agricola de America Latina*. Cepal, Santiago de Chile.

Comision Independiente sobre Problemas Internacionales del Desarrollo (1981) *Dialogo Norte-Sur*. Mexico, Nueva Sociedad.

Crosby, A. (1986) *Ecological Imperialism: The Biological Expansion of Europe 900– 1900*. Cambridge University Press.

Daly, H. (1977) *Steady State Economics*. W.H. Freeman, San Francisco, Calif.

Dumont, R. (1989) *Um Mundo Intoleravel*. Revan, Rio de Janeiro.

Falk, R.A. (1987) 'The state system and contemporary social movements,' in S.H. Menlovitz and R.B.J. Walker (eds) *Towards a Just World Peace*. Butterworths, London.

Friberg, M. and Hettne, B. (1984) 'El Giro del Mundo Hacia el Verde. Hacia un Modelo no Determinista de los Procesos Globales,' in M. Friberg *et al.* (eds) *Adonde Vamos? Cuatro Visiones de la Crisis Mundial*. Fundacion Bariloche, Rio Negro.

Gallopin, G. (1987) 'Prospectiva ecologica en America Latina,' *Realidad Economica*, no. 78, Buenos Aires.

Galtung, J. (1980) *The True Worlds: A Transnational Perspective*. Free Press, New York.

Georgescu-Roegen, N. (1976) *Energy and Economics Myths*. Pergamon Press, New York.

Girotti, C. (1984) *Estado Nuclear no Brasil*. Brasiliense, Sao Paolo.

Harrison, P. (1987) *The Greening of Africa*. Penguin Books, Harmondsworth.

Hegedus, Z. (1987) 'The challenge of the peace movement: civilian security and civilian emancipation,' in S.H. Menlovitz and R.B.J. Walker (eds) *Towards a Just World Peace: Perspectives from Social Movement.* Butterworths, London.

Herrera, A. (1982) *A Grande Jornada.* Paz e Terra, Rio de Janeiro.

Herrera, A. *et al.* (1977) *Un Monde Pour Tous.* Presses Universitaires de France, Paris.

Hewitt, K. (1983) 'Calamity in a technocratic age,' in K. Hewitt (ed.) *Interpretation of Calamity from the Viewpoint of Human Ecology.* Allen & Unwin, Boston, Mass.

Inglehart, R. (1976) *The Silent Revolution.* Princeton University Press, Princeton, NJ.

Lasch, C. (1986) *O Minimo Eu. Sobrevivencia Psiquica em Tempos Dificeis.* Brasiliense, Sao Paolo.

Lowe, P. and Rudig, W. (1987) 'Review article: political ecology and the social science: state of the art,' *British Journal of Political Science*, no. 16.

Lutzenberger, J. (1980) *Fim do Futuro? Manifesto Ecologico Brasileiro.* Movimento, Porto Alegre.

McCormick, J. (1989) *Reclaiming Paradise: The Global Environmental Movement.* Indiana University Press, Bloomington, Ind.

Meadows, D.L. (1972) *Os Limites do Crescimento.* Perspectiva, Sao Paolo.

Mische, G. and P. (1977) *Towards a Human World Order.* Paulist Press, New York.

Myers, N. *et al.* (1987) *El Atlas Gaia de la Gestion del Planeta.* Blume, Barcelona.

Nerfin, M. (1986) 'Ni Principe ni Mercader, Cuidadano: Una Introducion al Tercer Sistema.' *Promundo*, Vol. 1, no. 1, Buenos Aires.

Offe, C. (1985) 'New social movements: challenging the boundaries of institutional politics,' *Social Research*, Vol. 52, no. 4, pp. 275–93.

Offe, C. (1987) 'L'Utopia del Opzione Zero,' in A. Giddens *et al.* (eds) *Ecologica Politica.* Feltrinelli, Milan.

Ophuls, W. (1977) *Ecology and the Politics of Scarcity.* W.H. Freeman, San Francisco.

Paehlke, R. (1989) *Environmentalism and the Future of Progressive Politics.* Yale University Press, New Haven, Conn.

Pingueli Rosa, L. (1985) *A Politica Nuclear e o Caminho das Armas Atomicsa.* Zahar, Rio de Janeiro.

Prudkin, N. (1989) 'Medico Ambiente, Recursos y Agricultura,' in C. Reboratti (ed.) *Poblacion y Ambiente en America Latina.* Grupo Editor Latinoamericano, Buenos Aires.

Redclift, M. (1984) *Development and the Environmental Crisis.* Methuen, London.

Regidor, J.R. (1988) 'Ambiente e Sviluppo nei Rapporti Nord-Sud,' *Volontari e Terzo Mondo*, no. 4, pp. 12–17.

Sachs, W. (1988) 'Il Vangelo dell'Efficienz Globale,' *Emergenze*, no. 4, pp. 21–28.

Sawyer, D. (1989) 'Poblacion, Desarrolllo y Medio Ambiente en la Region Amazonica Brasilena: El Papel de las Politicas Oficiales,' in C. Reboratti (ed.) *Poblacion y Ambiente en America Latina.* Grupo Editor Lationoamericano, Buenos Aires.

Shiva, V. (1987) 'People's ecology: the Chipko movement,' in S.H. Menlovitz and R.B.J. Walker (eds) *Towards a Just World Peace: Perspectives from Social Movement.* Butterworths, London.

Souza, L. (1986) 'Secularizacao em Diclinio e Ppotencialidade Transformadora do Sagrado, Religiao e Movimentos Sociais na Emergencia do Homem Planetario.' *16 Congresso Latinoamericano de Sociologia*, mimeo, Rio de Janeiro.

Sprout, H. and Sprout, M. (1971) *Towards a Politics of the Planet Earth.* Van Nostrand Reinhold, New York.

Touraine, A. (1980) *La prophétie anti-nucleaire.* Paris, Sevil.

Viola, E.J. (1987) 'O Movimento Ecologico no Brasil (1974–1986): Do Ambientalismo a Ecopolitica,' *Revista Brasileira de Ciencias Sociais*, Vol. 1, no. 3, pp. 32–41.

Ward, B. and Dubos, R. (1972) *Una Sola Tierra.* Mexico, Fondo de Cultura Economica.

World Commission on Environment and Development (1987) *Our Common Future.* Oxford University Press, London.

PART II

Environmental policy-making: beyond industrial ideology and technocratic strategy

Part II focuses on the corporate-industrial goals and technological strategies that have dominated environmental policy-making. The part opens with a discussion of one of the oldest environmental concerns, natural resource policy. Michael Black examines the ways in which state and federal resource policies have seriously harmed wild salmon and salmon fishing on the Pacific coast of the USA. Instead of reigning in commercial interests that have long profited at the ecosystem's expense, government policy is shown to have systematically or 'serialistically' relied on an array of 'technological fixes' to deal with endangered salmon and their collapsing ecosystems. By opting for engineering over ecology, government policy is stuck in a dead heat between running out of money for technical fixes before we run out of wild fish. Intoning one of the most basic tenets of a green perspective, Black concludes by arguing we must give up our ceaseless search for analytical solutions to what are fundamentally political and moral problems.

Following on the theme of the technological fix, the second contribution turns to the development of clean technologies, in particular the 'green car'. The automobile, as a basis contributor to such environmental phenomena as poor urban air quality, global climate change, the need for oil and the clogging of transportation systems, among others, constitutes one of the most important environmental challenges of our time – or what Vice President Albert Gore has called 'a mortal threat to the security of every nation on earth'. Confronting this vexing technological challenge, Lamont Hempel examines the progress of 'green car' development over the past two decades. He points in particular to the ways that a reluctant US auto industry, in contrast to its Japanese and European counterparts, has routinely sought to stymie green-car technology. More recently, however, California's stringent environmental air-pollution standards have compelled Detroit to explore the possibilities of a safe, non-polluting vehicle. Hempel shows that the technocratic approach to green-car development pursued by both Detroit and Washington must give way to a policy framework capable of addressing the competing and often contradictory goals of air quality, social access and mobility. Towards this end, he calls for a 'wedge strategy' designed to fold together a comprehensive mix of policy tools and goals needed to successfully deal with the automobile's environmental problems.

Derek Churchill and Richard Worthington demonstrate the ways in which international trade and its underlying industrial ideology are on a collision course with environmental protection. Focusing on the congressional debates that led to the passage of the North American Free Trade Agreement, they show how neoliberals and conservatives alike advanced a corporate 'competitiveness' agenda that effectively pre-empted and marginalized environmental opposition to the agreement. Documenting the economic and environmental plight of the lengthy border regions between the USA and Mexico, they argue that the free trade agreement raises serious questions about the sustainability of new growth in the three signatory countries. For Churchill and Worthington, greater public participation is the only means of moving beyond the top-down, élite-driven growth model that treats development as something that must be done *for* people. Sustainable development, they argue, must be directed *by* citizens from the bottom up. Newly-emerging green social movements and grassroots coalitions are seen to constitute the democratic political alternative capable of uniting economic and environmental justice.

Continuing the focus on economic and industrial ideology, the final chapter in this part examines the politics of environmental policy in Chile, seen by many to be the next in line for a free trade agreement with the USA. Reluctant to sacrifice development for environmental protection, as Eduardo Silva writes, the leaders of Chile – as in the developing countries generally – have bought into sustainable development's formula of economic growth with environmental safeguards. Because there is no correct alternative to traditional development paths, however, sustainable development has become a highly politicized issue in these countries. Examining these political-economic tensions in Chile, Silva concentrates on the two competing conceptualizations of sustainable development that stand at the core of the environmental struggles in Chile. He contrasts the dominant 'market-friendly' approach to economic growth and its 'progressive' alternative which seeks to balance growth, social equity and environmental sustainabilty on their own terms. In the process, he attempts to sort out when and how ideas, state institutions, sociopolitical coalitions and external forces such as the World Bank have influenced policy outcomes in the debate over Chile's comprehensive environmental law, as well as the law's specific impacts on the problems of ozone depletion and native forest policy. He concludes by suggesting several lessons that Chile's experience holds out for green politics in other Latin American countries.

4

The unnatural policies of natural resource agencies: fishery policy on the Sacramento River

MICHAEL BLACK
Harvey Mudd College, USA

The reasonable man adapts himself to the world;
the unreasonable one persists in trying to adapt the world to himself.
. . . Therefore all progress depends on the unreasonable man.

(George Bernard Shaw)

Introduction

The collapse of California's salmon stocks and what we do about it is a critical environmental policy issue for our time. Pacific salmon may be one of our most powerful litmus tests for evaluating successful human coevolution with nature. Biologists call them an 'indicator species', for they provide us a window into the viability of landed and aquatic life. As 'fresh water species that have invaded the ocean for part of their lives' (Healey, 1993), Chinook salmon bind together vast ecological regions, from wilderness headwater spawning grounds to downstream wetlands, estuaries and the ocean itself. From Monterey to the Arctic Circle, the main way to define a western river is to say that it is a watercourse frequented by migratory salmon. Salmon respond like exquisitely sensitive barometers to instream swings in water temperature, oxygenation or sedimentation. Their capacity to thrive is undercut by, among others, clear-cutting forests, diminished water flows, destruction of wetlands or urban and agricultural pollution. Throw any of these conditions out of kilter and fish populations plummet.

California's Sacramento River was once a powerhouse for producing enormous numbers of Chinook salmon. Some runs of returning spawning salmon once numbered a million or more fish. Of that river's four returning stocks of anadromous fish, two runs are near extinction.[1] The winter-run *(Oncorhynchus tshawytscha)* and spring-run fish (so named according to the time of year they return upriver to spawn) are listed by the US Fish and Wildlife Service as 'endangered' and 'threatened', respectively. In 1993, the last vestiges

---

of the winter-run salmon numbered a mere 189 fish, down from a late 1960s average of 86,509 fish. The spring-run Chinook salmon, which historically numbered a million or more fish, now total less than a thousand returning salmon. Dwindling numbers of winter and spring-run Chinook salmon remind us that a long-ignored moral, ecological and financial reckoning has become due.

Endangered Pacific salmon are victims of a kind of fleeting success – our desire and capability endlessly to break apart and modify the natural world. We call what has occurred here 'reclamation', a process designed to adapt the wild to suit utilitarian ends. It is here in California, over a century ago, that European descendants began carving out an 'oasis civilization' from an unexplored terrain once called 'the Great American Desert' (Webb, 1957). Aridity is the dominant fact of life here, where an unstable yearly rainfall rarely exceeds 20 inches. Since human settlement and agriculture invariable require the moving of water from where it naturally occurs to where it is desired, the state was drafted to accomplish this feat. In so doing, the rapid alteration of California's hydrology and its landscapes has created a biologically untenable, as well as the largest and most costly, hydraulic experiment in human history.

Western fish and fisheries were among the first victims of water mobilization in California and they remain among the species most endangered today. Environmental historian Arthur McEvoy writes that the last healthy spring-run of Sacramento River Chinook salmon occurred in 1852, just four years after the onset of California's gold rush (McEvoy, 1990). By 1883, so much fishing pressure was placed by cannery interests on these highly prized food fishes that the runs virtually collapsed (*ibid.*). Today biologists W.L. Minckley and Michael E. Douglas report that 122 out of 150 western fish taxa are in some form of basic ecological distress (Minckley and Douglas, 1991, p. 15). Of this total, the west's Pacific salmon are in a particularly grave state of decline.

This chapter recounts a century of failed fishery policy in California, culminating in the impending extinction of Pacific salmon. This history is not only significant for salmon and those who appreciate them but also as an archetype of policy delusion in the face of a growth-driven political economy. I begin by examining the state and federal institutional precedents which contributed to what I come to describe as a century-old environmental policy trap. The next section discusses an interpretive framework I call 'serialistic' policy (after something which occurs in a series, rank or row), to explain why agencies continue to substitute an array of technological fixes to mitigate for endangered salmon and their collapsing ecosystems. The following section profiles an ongoing case in which biologists hope to stave off extinction through technological means. I close by asking what we have learnt in governing human affairs by choosing engineering over ecology.

The institutional trap?

State fish commissions: west to California
In 1857, naturalist George Perkins Marsh issued a report to a worried Vermont governor, Ryland Fletcher, about what his state should do to save an

increasingly 'shorn and crippled nature'. As with much of New England, during the early nineteenth century, Vermont's landscape underwent rapid alteration and industrialization (Marsh, 1857, p. 13; Steinberg, 1991). 'Rivers as open sewers' was one of the many prices paid by civilization. Vermonters were becoming nostalgic for what they had lost, including bountiful stocks of Atlantic salmon (*Salmo salar*). Marsh (1857, p. 9) minced no words when he foretold 'the final extinction of the larger wild quadrupeds and birds, as well as the diminution of fish, and other aquatic animals, is everywhere a condition of advanced civilization and the increase and spread of a rural and industrial population'. Writing that 'human improvements have produced an almost total change in all the external conditions of piscatorial life', Marsh none the less embraced the inevitable trade-offs between a pristine nature and civilized life (*ibid.* p. 11).

Instead of predicting a head-on collison, however, Marsh advised that 'we may still do something to recover a share of the abundance which, in a more primitive state, the watery kingdom afforded' (*ibid.*). He reminded the governor of forgotten fish-breeding practices common to imperial Rome and monastic Europe. The naturalist closed his analysis by imploring that Vermont's lakes and rivers be 'peopled' with salmon and once-abundant species of fish by harnessing the entrepreneurial and scientific talents of fish-breeders. Technological mitigations would be sought to compensate where nature was failing to provide Vermonters with its valuable food fishes. Marsh implored that the state enact legislation protective of commercial fish culturalists.

Some ten years later, following a traumatic civil war, the nation's first significant conservation movement occurred in which fish propagation seized centre stage as a kind of new agricultural science (Bottom, 1995, pp. 3–4).[2] Amid rapidly growing populations and serious postwar threats of food shortages, biologist Dan Bottom (*ibid.* p. 4) writes that

> Fish culture offered a means to restore severely depleted fisheries in the East, to expand the nation's food supply, to provide income for farmers, and to make widely available to all classes of Americans the most desirable food and game fishes of the world. Fish culture transformed the anxiety of resource scarcity into an engineering opportunity of unlimited potential.

Beginning in 1867, the states of Vermont, New Hampshire, Massachusetts, Maine and Connecticut all appointed fish commissions to promote artificial propagation as a form of economic development (Bottom, 1995, p. 7). California geographer Jerry Towle aptly christened the period as 'one of exuberant and haphazard tinkering with the natural order' (Towle, 1987, p. 78). Within ten years, 30 fish commissions existed nationwide, including one housed in California (founded in 1870).

California's original fish commissioners belonged to a gentlemen's club. They were every bit as ignorant as the early scientists about the needs of the fish they were trying to save. However sympathetic they remained to the interests of salmon, commissioners also participated in a gamblers' paradise where, to borrow from novelist Frank Norris, 'gut and get out, was the true California spirit' (Norris, in Brechin, 1995). Consonant with their New England predecessors, California's original fish commissioners abandoned as unworkable any challenges to the root causes of fisheries' habitat decline (e.g. economic forces like mining, extreme deforestation, overgrazing, irrigated agriculture, overharvesting fisheries or dam construction). While they did pass some measures to prevent overfishing, to require fish passage devices over dams and to prohibit sawdust from being dumped into streams, they lacked an enforcement arm to enjoin compliance. Instead, what little funding they possessed went to address the symptoms accompanying fishery collapse by artificially producing more fish, installing fishways around instream obstacles, planting exotic fishes for declining native species and so forth. Early fisheries overseers turned to a succession of productive fixes over environmental protection (Bottom, 1995, p. 7).

By 1900, California's State Board of Fish Commissioners was among the nation's most established and respected agencies in government. In 1907, California's legislature partially caught the progressive-era wave, and approved charging an annual fee for hunting licences. Licence revenues gradually enabled the commission to broaden its focus towards science-based, utilitarian conservation (McEvoy, 1990, p. 157). Fuelled by its newfound wealth the agency became the California Fish and Game Commission (CDFG) in 1912. It boasted game wardens, a full-time staff attorney and legal clout to enforce some laws. It also launched publication of its official journal, *California Fish and Game Quarterly*, soon thereafter. The quarterly promised to build a hoped-for alliance with outdoors enthusiasts (*ibid.*).

Rising tax revenues enabled the CDFG to enlist assistance from scientists at the Scripps Institution and Stanford University for purposes of research. McEvoy observes that departmental and university researchers gathered the world's first comprehensive database for studying marine biology (*ibid.* p. 159). Scientific regulation was wedded to progressive-era theories of maximum sustained yield. Despite its impressive stores of knowledge, within a balkanized political environment, the nation's foremost marine research apparatus was pre-empted from having any effect (*ibid.* p. 184). Commercial interests clearly feared that government science might produce meddlesome regulation.

The US Fish Commission

The US Commission on Fish and Fisheries (later renamed the US Fish Commission), like its state counterparts, was instrumental in formulating federal strategies affecting a conflict-prone commercial fishing industry (Allard, 1978). Director Spencer Fullerton Baird knew his federal agency had no constitutional means of directly confronting those powerful economic forces undermining commercial fisheries. To make matters worse, the Fish Commission was caught in a second institutional bind: 'Indeed, because Congressional appropriations were the lifeblood of USFC research, the agency had little incentive even to try [to control destructive economic growth]. It thus became a promotional agency undertaking research and development so as to expand, not restrict, the [commercial] industry's access to resources' (McEvoy, 1990, p. 102).

Bowing to political and economic expediency, the Smithsonian Institution's US Fish Commission addressed fisheries problems obliquely. In fact, shortly before his death Baird himself concluded 'that the decline of the New England fisheries appeared "to have been the result principally of human agencies," either by way of overfishing or the degradation of inshore habitat' (*ibid.*).

Baird spearheaded a widely embraced strategy of fishery expansion utilizing the substitution of newly discovered fisheries stocks for those that were in a virtual state of collapse. After 1872, Baird's organization sought to expand the nation's food supply through unproven technologies like fish hatcheries. Hatcheries promised to expand the availability of freshwater, anadromous and other coastal fishes. The process of substituting alien stocks for naturally occurring fishes was intertwined with certain commercial interests already paying the price for collapsing fisheries. To secure congressional appropriations the programme was handily billed to provide a wide array of constituents with free food fish. Late in the 1870s, the commission began aiding commercial fisheries by either identifying new fishing grounds or through the introduction of improved harvesting equipment.

The US Fish Commission also sought to bring under one umbrella the scientific and technical experts capable of analysing problems having an impact on commercial fisheries. Baird's utilitarian philosophy required that they 'undertake "a series of thorough inquiries into the general physical and natural history of the seas" in order to "achieve the practical end" with which his commission was charged' (Baird, in Allard, 1990, p. 254).

Between 1871 and 1887, Baird actively engaged in and sponsored marine biological research. The laboratory at Woods Hole, Massachusetts, set the subsequent stage for significant governmental support of utilitarian scientific enterprise. Science began to be recognized as a useful tool to policy-makers who, armed with sufficient ammunition, required information to mediate both domestic and foreign fisheries disputes (McEvoy, 1990, p. 101). In particular 'mandate science' began to emerge – science deemed useful for making public policy (Salter, in Weeks, 1991, p. 14). Baird's scientific vision presaged by three-quarters of a century the prominent role to be played by the nation's national laboratories. In addition to its scientific contributions, it was in the domain of fish propagation that Baird's political, cultural, scientific and technological legacy would have its greatest consequence, for 'although Baird and his colleagues paid homage to the requirements of controlling harvesting and environmental degradation, promising to sustain the economy's supply of fish without interrupting existing patterns of use yielded far greater political rewards' (McEvoy, 1990, p. 106).

Baird's political and cultural premise was quite simple. *Laissez-faire* shibboleths could not be directly challenged. Instead, he believed that 'applied science could keep pace with the inevitable exhaustion of the native fish life . . . incident to the development of the country and the increase in population' (Smith, in McEvoy, 1990, p. 106). In a brilliant disappearing act, public policies would not seek to contain the appetites of entrepreneurs or markets but, rather, would unleash nascent economic development potentials inherent in the nation's yet-to-be-tapped, common resource base. Fish hatcheries would be one among many pure technical solutions. The hatcheries promised a painless, technical solution to this particular aspect of the Gilded Age's environmental problems and were, understandably, enormously popular: '"There are few enterprises undertaken by the United State Government," wrote a USFC official, "that are more popular, meet with more general and generous support, and have contributed more to the prosperity and happiness of a larger number of people than the fish-cultural work"' (*ibid.*).

Baird ingeniously instituted fisheries' policy strategies more protective of business interests than the interests of trout and salmon. Far from being mysterious, institutional behaviour reflected real political and economic constraints. Baird's policies legitimized the further disintegration of nature by promising technical over natural solutions to dismembered river basins. He placated irate commercial interests with the promise of artificial fish propagation and the naming of promising, harvestable substitutes. His researchers identified new fishing grounds (such as fishing for halibut in Alaska) in tandem with new markets for fish products. By fuelling the illusion that salmonids might one day be restored, he also greatly defused an issue of politically explosive content. In keeping with his time, Baird managed to accomplish all this by wedding the ideology of progress with its promise of applied science and technology. Extolling 'change without change' (Wolfe, 1980), Baird's US Fish Commission built the seemingly impossible: a public environmental agency immensely popular with all its various constituencies.

In 1903 the US Fish Commission became the US Bureau of Fisheries (USBF), under the US Department of Commerce. Its commerce role coincided nicely with its primary mission – research in promoting and sustaining the fishing industry (McEvoy, 1990, p. 157). Early in the century their major preoccupation remained that of artificial propagation. However, other serial mitigations for declining fisheries were prevalent including installing fishways around instream obstacles, introduction of exotic species of fish and the barging of fish for downstream release, among others. A postprogressive-era USBF sought rapid economic growth 'over the longest time' to 'the greatest use for the greatest number' (*ibid.* p. 164). When they finally came under the Department of the Interior umbrella in 1940, the US Fish and Wildlife Service (USFWS) also remained wedded to hatchery production.

As a consequence of the Fish and Wildlife Act 1956, the federal agency's commercial and sport-fishing bureaux cleaved and created a separate Bureau of Commercial Fisheries (USBCF) (*ibid.* p. 195). Early in the Nixon administration, the USBCF was itself transformed into the National Marine Fisheries Service (NMFS). Under the US Department of Commerce, the NMFS plotted optimum yield harvests for everything from marine mammals like dolphins to migratory salmon. Despite the bureaucratic innovations, these commercial and sports-fishing agencies still reflected century-old fishery policy assumptions and deep sympathies to commercial interests.

Serialistic policy

From the outset, those entrusted with formulating oversight policies for California's declining anadromous fish carefully tailored their objectives to comply with market attitudes and behaviour. Rather than challenge the profitable destruction of western rivers, state and federal institutional practices begat an oblique holding pattern of compensatory means and ends. By failing to achieve (or even to consider) a 'primary' solution of watershed preservation, successors to both state and national fish commissions instead resorted to a bolder series of 'secondary' objectives.[3] The essence of this strategy was to adapt harvestable fish to a greatly disturbed natural world. Rather than bringing a human behaviour in line with healthy watersheds, California's fish commissioners and their subsequent agency representatives embarked on a much more politically palatable solution to disappearing fisheries by reinventing nature.

As natural resource institutions evolved over the next 100 years, they adopted a set of 'serialistic policies' – a succession of pure technological solutions – to mitigate against collapsing fisheries. Where obstacles such as dams were erected to fish migration, fish ladders appeared. When fish ladders failed to stem the collapse of declining salmonid stocks, hatcheries sprang up. When hatcheries proved inadequate to the task, artificial spawning channels were constructed. When these failed, instream spawning 'racks' were contemplated. When these failed, agencies ordered that suitably sized spawning gravel be dumped into the stream. To succeed at this game of migratory pinball, sometimes even juvenile fish were 'bused' (or barged) past a gauntlet of downstream migratory obstacles. The list of compensatory mitigations was lengthy and ever-expanding.

Serialistic policy describes a deliberately muddled pattern of agency policy goal substitution and decay, followed by the overlay of a fresh batch of technical fixes and their subsequent failure. Excessive destruction of watersheds causes declines in (among others) fish species' populations. It occurs when agencies lack sufficient power (or will) to restrain market-driven overexploitation of 'limiting factor' resources, like water. Rather than reigning in economic actors profiting at ecosystem expense, the ecological instability that results is addressed through technological means.

Ecosystems, like Humpty Dumpty, are vastly easier to preserve than they are to reassemble. Agencies deployed an array of costly, energy-consuming technological fixes to sustain the progressive myth of ecological stability. Initially the entropic costs were borne by a declining fish population, not by those humans profiting at ecosystem expense. Today that relation is reversed. Now agencies like the California Department of Fish and Game, the US Fish and Wildlife Service and the US National Marine Fisheries Service, among others, must throw increasing budgets at diminishing numbers of fish. If we remain trapped in such logic, we will never have enough money – or glue – to reassemble our watersheds.

Serialistic policies themselves rest on four fundamental pillars: one philosophical, one technological, one institutional and one economic. As policy strategies what is most visible is the stepwise failure of technological fixes. Just beneath the surface, however, is a seductively compelling belief in our capacity to manipulate nature. This hubris creates for environmental policy-makers a beguiling technology trap.

What undergirds this practice is the belief that the universe is related, purposeful and understandable (Shay, 1974; Black, 1981, p. 263).[4] Also essential is the axiom that as active agents, human beings, have the pivotal role of intervening in, breaking apart and reassembling a more perfect world (Ehrenfeld, 1978). Such an optimistic doctrine requires science-based knowledge to sever nature at its mechanistic joints, and to recombine its pieces in enlightened, high-yield, utilitarian ways. Humankind's capacity to intervene exhorts us to supersede nature's timescale by accelerating select processes – like that of salmon propagation – towards lasting perfection. Where nature is 'inefficient' we simply need to speed up the time-lapse clock and make it work to our exacting criteria. By imitating nature in the laboratory, *Homo sapiens* are essentially finishing the job of creation left incomplete at the start. Dominion over the earth is sought through an ideology of escalating technological means.

Environmental mitigation practices therefore stem from the axiom that expert-centred, technological systems can eternally improve upon or compensate for devastated ecosystems. In many areas of ecological concern, when things go wrong, public agencies propose technocratic solutions to remedy perceived ills. These ills, however, are part of a vastly more complex picture. Pure technical solutions are frequently sought to avoid making other more controversial political choices. Instead of opening up public debate to invite preventative solutions, political institutions adopt a narrow scientific horizon that justifies equally narrow technological solutions.

By abandoning ecology for engineering, environmental policy becomes self-defeating. While all institutional policies (to a greater or lesser extent) build upon one another in an internally consistent fashion, serialistic policy exhibits certain unique traits that culminate in a negative effect. This is because serialistic strategies are themselves ahistorical. Its practitioners fail to take cognizance of a long-term view of how things evolved to become frozen in current institutional practice (Hilborn, 1992). Under entrenched bureaucratic regimes that are governed by serialistic policy, the means justify the means.

Serialistic policy is anchored in prevailing economic beliefs. Under capitalism, all value in nature becomes subject to exacting quantitative measurement. Each living and non-living element is stripped bare of its context and rendered solely in terms of its exchange value. As 'natural resources', salmon inherit the status of being both object and commodity. If they begin to disappear, in keeping with an agricultural model, the task simply becomes that of producing more. Following an ancient Roman example, fish-culture enthusiasts arose to plug the gap created by disappearing wild salmon. A new breed of entrepreneur became fashionable – those skilled in the artificial propagation of fishes.

From Germany came the magical ideal of managing nature's warehouse for maximum economic utility. By balancing tree-growth rates against periodic harvest, German foresters first articulated the principle of maximum sustained yield. They believed that science could be their guide for weighing optimum harvest rates against an orderly, enduring and equilibrated nature (Worster, 1993, p. 144). Why not apply the same premise to vacillating fisheries? Maximum sustained yield offered a predictive model for managing harvests of renewable crops like fish. Take more fish than you required, so the theory went, and you threatened stability; use fewer and it was outright wasteful (Bottom, 1995, p. 22). Early practitioners believed that economic production functions would guarantee timely delivery of natural commodities ranging from fish to trees. However, as the environmental wreckage of past civilizations exemplifies, nature's economy is neither equilibrated nor predictable. The myth of maximum sustained yield is one of our most enduring – if flawed – environmental policy premises.

Taken together, the combination of philosophical, institutional, economic and technological beliefs constitute a mythic package. By promising earthly salvation through technological means, serialistic policy masked and upheld an unacknowledged pattern of domination. Rather than fight to preserve nature, agencies oversaw the destruction of that which they were mandated to protect. Wild fish were simply replaced by 'designer fish'. Such policy therefore legitimized the further destruction of watersheds by purporting to represent the interests of diminishing salmonids. Hence, such policy strategies provided purveyors the ethical illusion of occupying high moral ground, even as such 'feel good' strategies staved off or indefinitely postponed a true reckoning of those profiting from destroying fisheries and their habitats.

What is more, the longer serialistic policy is practised, the greater the actual cost of perpetuating imaginary, highly unstable solutions persists. Mitigation policies beget additional follow-on policies and 'residue problems' proliferate, giving rise to their own coincident ecological and social backlashes, each of which creates new generations of unresolvable problems.[5] For example, consider the downstream strains accompanying the introduction of hatchery-reared salmon among wild fish stocks. Biologists Ray Hilborn and Stephen Hare catalogue some of their better-known effects: 'competition for space and food; hatchery releases as predators; premature emigration; disease and parasites; stimulation of predator populations; robbing [wild fish] for broodstocks; hatchery structures as barriers; increase in fishing pressure; timing of the water [release] budget; and genetic effects' (Hillborn and Hare, 1992, pp. 9–10).

As westerners abandoned wild rivers in favour of something resembling giant plumbing contrivances, rivers like the Sacramento became what policy analyst Kai Lee calls 'industrialized ecosystems' – an unnatural watershed requiring continuous human manipulation (Lee, 1993, p. 50). Human management, however, often means playing off one set of desirable ends (like power generation, navigability and fish stocks) against another. Driven by relentless water mobilization, the Sacramento basin reflected a biological Ponzi scheme in which, first, we put a price tag on water itself. Second, by selling irrigation water and power at vastly subsidized rates, government frustrated whatever conservation advantages were conferred by market scarcity. Third, citizens often subsidized farmers not to grow water-thirsty crops (like cotton) in a semi-desert (Sweeney, 1991, p. 210). Fourth, we paid in the disappearance of fish and wildlife, as well as for the dizzying string of escalating mitigations intended to reverse their precipitous decline. Finally, we shelled out for the environmental wreckage that coincided with attempts at resurrecting nature, of which we too are a part. Serialistic policy's failure is well illustrated by the plight of Pacific salmon.

In the following section I present a brief case study that illustrates the continuing dominance of technological means to stave off the extinction of Pacific salmon. It illustrates how serialistic policy practices exemplify our transition from know-how to nowhere.

The last mitigation?

During the autumn of 1992, a convoy of trucks swept into the University of California's Bodega Marine Station on the Sonoma County coast.[6] Marked by a sign reading 'Shuttle for Survival', the precious cargo consisted of 740 recently hatched Sacramento River winter-run Chinook salmon (Petit, 1992). The salmon were carefully groomed refugees, the offspring of 20 spawning Chinook salmon, taken near Redding on the Sacramento River. This costly exercise, the brainchild of Nat Bingham, past president of the Pacific Coast Federation of Fisherman's Associations, was part of a desperate, last-ditch effort by the US Fish and Wildlife Service (in tandem with other coalition partners) to 'save' this anadromous fisheries stock from extinction.

Bingham's strategy derived from an article he had once read in *Scientific American* about the distribution of cheetahs (*Acinonxy jubatus*) throughout Africa and India (O'Brien, Wildt and Bush, 1986). To his amazement, he learnt that all surviving cheetahs in the wild descend from a tiny number of breeders. Bingham reasoned that if the world's fastest cat could defy extinction on its own terms, then a human-assisted restoration effort might work for the endangered winter-run Chinook salmon. Model programmes already existed for breeding the peregrine falcon (*Falco peregrinius*), the whooping crane (*Gens americana*) and the California condor (*Gymogyps californianus*) – why not include one for the beleaguered salmon?

At first, Bingham encountered stiff resistance from sceptical scientists whose participation he needed. Eventually, however, the notion of a captive broodstock programme gained currency as a kind of insurance policy against extinction. The meagre handful of returning winter-run Chinook salmon helped Bingham persuade an array of natural-resource agencies (i.e. the Bodega Marine Laboratory of the Univeristy of California, Davis, San Francisco's Steinhart Aquarium, conservation groups and commercial interests) to endorse the restoration effort. Biologists at the US Fish and Wildlife Service's National Coleman Fish Hatchery (on Battle Creek) set aside 1,000 hatchlings to be housed at the Bodega Bay facility in salt and freshwater tanks (Paddock, 1992).[7] The hatchery's winter-run fry were derived solely from three surviving females whose fertilized eggs comprised four family groups. Either these fish serve as seed stock for a permanent breeding colony or it was the end of the line for yet another of California's declining native fishes.

For well over a century, California's salmon have been on their way to becoming true 'domestic' fish, the products of an increasingly 'shorn and crippled' nature (Moyle, 1993). Domestic fish are those that have undergone multiple generations of selective breeding whereas 'domesticated' fish are those of wild parentage (taken from the wild) to be raised in a hatchery and released. The winter-run breeding colony may allow that domestication process to be completed for salmon as it has for trout. As biologist Peter B. Moyle (1993) of the University of California, Davis, remarks, 'Domestic trout are as different from their wild ancestors as a dog is from a wolf or a cow from an auroch'.

Despite the well-meaning efforts of participants, the most remarkable thing about the Bodega Bay experiment was how little the various players in this drama have learnt from history. I maintain that, however well intentioned, the Bodega Bay experiment is yet another false move in a series of failed fisheries mitigations over the past century. Natural resource agencies must take heed of this history because ill-informed action cannot halt fisheries decline which stems from habitat collapse.

Sympathetic as biologists and others (myself included) remain to the winter-run's plight, many sceptical observers caution that efforts to save the stock through technological means are 'too little, too late' (Paddock, 1992). This newfound scepticism signals a challenge to the axiom that technology can eternally compensate for devastated ecosystems. What is visible is an absolute decline in the 'certainty' that once characterized our 'exuberant and haphazard tinkering with the natural order' (Towle, 1987, p. 78). What is new is that many conservationists do not really expect the Bodega Marine Laboratory's breeder colony to provide an enduring supply of winter-run fish.[8] Why go through these costly technical gymnastics to reintroduce domesticated fish into an ever more lethal river, estuary or ocean?

Conclusion

Those scientists tending the winter-run salmon know they are caught in a precarious holding action. Clinging to a threatened DNA gene pool of alleles is only a reprieve from extinction, not a solution. Their heroic efforts will neither reverse damage to collapsing ecosystems nor restore crashing biodiversity. Each participating scientist concedes that that kind of change will require something wholly different.

More and more fish scientists have awakened to find themselves ensnared in a serialistic policy trap where technology may not provide the answer. I view the Bodega Bay experiment as being perfectly congruent with a century of escalating conservation efforts measurable in diminishing numbers of fish. We are caught in a dead heat between running out of money before we run out of wild fish. In fact, because winter-run salmon are cut off by dams from their natal habitats, it may well constitute 'the last mitigation'.

The logic which undergirds the wholesale adaptation of nature to serve utilitarian ends is spent. Just as mitigations don't work, the philosophy of conservationism has run its course. We are stuck with an environmental policy tool-kit of arcane ideals that require fundamental overhaul. We must cease our peripatetic search for an analytical solution to what are political and philosophical problems. This will be no easy task, to be sure, but it is essential to reconceive of a sustainable world.

Fish biologists, like proverbial scoopers following the circus parade, remain stuck at the rear end of a venture that cries for foresight. Instead of gleefully manipulating nature, we must reinvent our own beliefs, behaviours and cultures in keeping with biologically healthy rivers. If westerners pay sufficient heed, wild salmon may just be capable of showing us the way.

Acknowledgements

Frank Fischer, Susan Kitchell and Richard Worthington offered valuable assistance with this chapter.

Notes

1. A stock is a distinct fish subpopulation that does not significantly interbreed with other populations (Nehlsen, Lichatowich and Williams, 1992, p. 20). Anadromous fish are those which are born in freshwater but which spend some significant portion of their lives in saltwater.
2. The early emergence of a commercially driven fisheries science presages later progressive-era environmental reforms by more than 30 years (see Bottom, 1995).
3. As author Alan Lufkin points out, fisheries science in California has probably never pursued the path of ecological adaptation. The first step towards preservation may have occurred when, on 4 June 1892, 27 citizens gathered in a San Francisco lawyer's office officially to incorporate as the Sierra Club (see Smith, 1987, pp. 143–50).
4. By the seventh century AD, the premises which follow comprised the worldview of the alchemists. Cari Shay (1974, p. 264) observes that alchemy was a 'comprehensive system – a religion, a philosophy, an art, a science and a craft.' As such it was dedicated to the transmutation of wild nature into an artfully groomed facsimile. Elsewhere I argue that alchemy's core premises were foundational to the origins of modern utilitarian science (Black, 1981).
5. 'Residue problems' refers to the unpredictable chain of ecological and social effects that accompanies any modification of nature (Schwartz, 1971, pp. 62–8).
6. For a fuller discussion, see 'Tragic remedies: a century of failed fishery policy on California's Sacramento River,' *Pacific Historical Review*, Vol. 64, no. 1, February 1995, from which parts of this section are adapted.
7. In addition to the Bodega Bay facility, a third of the Sacramento River's winter-run captive broodstock programme is housed at San Francisco's Steinhart Aquarium.
8. In a parallel case, it cost $10 million dollars to retrofit the US Fish and Wildlife Service's National Coleman Fish Hatchery on Battle Creek to obtain 100 returning winter-run Chinook salmon (Jennings, 1993).

References

Allard, D.C. (1978) *Spencer Fullerton Baird and the US Fish Commission: A Study in the History of American Science*. Arno Press, New York.
Allard, D.C. (1990) 'The fish commission laboratory and its influence on the founding of the marine biological laboratory,' *Journal of the History of Biology*, Vol. xxiii, no. 2, pp. 251–70.
Black, M. (1981) 'Recalling the homo dei: toward a politics of synecology.' PhD dissertation, University of Oregon, Eugene.
Bottom, D.L. (1995) 'To till the water: a history of ideas in fisheries conservation,' in P.A. Bisson and R.J. Naiman (eds) *Pacific Salmon and their Ecosystems*. Chapman & Hall, New York (forthcoming).
Brechin, G. (1995) *Imperial San Francisco*. University of California Press, Berkeley, Calif. (forthcoming).
Davoren, W.T. (1994) Personal communication.
Ehrenfeld, D. (1978) *The Arrogance of Humanism*. Oxford University Press, New York.

Healey, M.C. (1993) Personal correspondence.

Hedgpeth, J.W. (1941) 'Livingston Stone and fish culture in California,' *California Fish and Game*, Vol. 27, no. 3, pp. 126–48.

Hedgpeth, J.W. (1991) 'The passing of the salmon,' in A. Lufkin (ed.) *California's Salmon and Steelhead*. University of California, Berkeley, Calif.

Hilborn, R. (1992) 'Can fish agencies learn from experience?' *Fisheries*, Vol. 17, no. 4, pp. 6–14.

Hilborn, R. and Hare, S.R. (1992) 'Hatchery and wild fish production of anadromous salmon in the Columbia River basin,' *Fisheries Research Institute*, no. FRI-UW-9107. University of Washington, Seattle, Wash.

Jennings, M.R. (1993) Personal correspondence.

Lee, K.N. (1993) *Compass and Gyroscope: Integrating Science and Politics for the Environment*. Island Press, Covelo, Calif.

Ludwig, D., Hilborn, R. and Walters, C. (1993) 'Uncertainty, resource exploitation, and conservation: lessons from history,' *Science*, Vol. 160, 2 April, pp. 17 and 36.

Martin, G. (1992) 'Fish runs at Red Bluff spell death for salmon,' *San Francisco Chronicle*, 22 June.

McEvoy, A.F. (1990) *The Fisherman's Problem: Ecology and Law in the California Fisheries, 1850–1980*. Cambridge University Press, New York.

Minckley, W.L. and Douglas, M.E. (1991) 'Discovery and extinction of western fishes: a blink of the eye in geologic time,' in W.L. Minckley and J.E. Deacon (eds) *Battle against Extinction: Native Fish Management in the American West*. University of Arizona Press, Tucson, Ariz.

Moyle, P.B. (1993) Personal correspondence.

Nehlsen, W.C., Lichatowich, J.A. and Williams, J.E. (1992) 'Pacific salmon and the search for sustainability,' *Renewable Resources Journal*, Vol. 10, no. 2, pp. 20–6.

O'Brien, S.J., Wildt, D.E. and Bush, M. (1986) 'The cheetah in genetic peril,' *Scientific American*, Vol. 254, no. 5, pp. 84–92.

Paddock, R.C. (1992) 'Test tube salmon in river test,' *Los Angeles Times*, 9 February.

Petit, C. (1992) 'Move to save imperiled salmon,' *San Francisco Chronicle*, 19 September.

Schwartz, E.S. (1971) *Overskill: The Decline of Technology in Modern Civilization*. University of Chicago Press, Chicago, Ill.

Shay, C. (1974) 'The transmutation of alchemy into science and political thought.' PhD dissertation, University of Oregon, Eugene.

Smith, M.L. (1987) *Pacific Visions: California Scientists and the Environment, 1850–1915*. Yale University Press, New Haven, Conn.

Steinberg, T. (1991) *Nature Incorporated: Industrialization and the Waters of New England*. Cambridge University Press, New York.

Sweeney, W.D. (1991) 'The Central Valley project and the public trust doctrine,' in A. Lufkin (ed.) *California's Salmon and Steelhead*. University of California Press, Berkeley, Calif.

Towle, J.C. (1987) 'The great failure: nineteenth-century dispersals of the Pacific salmon,' *Annual Publication of the California Geographical Society*, Vol. xxvii, pp. 75–96.

Webb, W.P. (1957) 'The American west: perpetual mirage,' *Harper's Magazine*, Vol. 214, pp. 25–31.

Weeks, P. (1991) 'Managing the reefs: local and scientific strategies.' Unpublished manuscript presented to the AAAS.

Wolfe, A. (1980) *America's Impasse: The Rise and Fall of the Politics of Growth*. Pantheon, New York.

Worster, D. (1977) *Nature's Economy: A History of Ecological Ideas*. Cambridge University Press, New York.

Worster, D. (1993) *The Wealth of Nature: Environmental History and the Ecological Imagination*. Oxford University Press, New York.

5

Environmental technology and the green car: towards a sustainable transportation policy

LAMONT C. HEMPEL
Claremont Graduate School, USA

Managing the impacts of motor vehicles on the environment has been a major objective of US environmental policy since the early 1960s. Most of the attention has been directed at urban air emissions from tailpipes and at land-use changes resulting from rapid expansion of the motor vehicle fleet. Noise pollution, natural resource depletion, associated oil spills and toxic contamination, and disposal of retired vehicles or parts have also commanded significant attention. During the 1970s, energy-related impacts became highly visible owing to the oil-price shocks orchestrated by OPEC (1973–4) and by the government of Iran (1979–80).

For nearly 25 years, the Clean Air Act 1970 and its amendments have been the dominant instruments for environmental regulation of vehicle manufacturing and operation. Their provisions for ambient air-quality standards and vehicle emissions standards now affect the design and use of approximately 15 million new cars and trucks sold each year in the USA. Second in importance, perhaps, has been the Energy Policy and Conservation Act 1975, which established corporate average fuel economy (CAFE) standards beginning in 1978. The objective of the CAFE law was to double vehicle energy efficiency by 1985, using 1973 as a baseline.

These Acts, and their amendments, have helped determine the type of vehicles now in use, as well as the political economy of their manufacture and distribution. The US auto industry strongly resisted both policy initiatives, declaring that some of the provisions would be impossible to meet in a cost-effective manner and that they would plunge the industry into economic decline. The Japanese introduction of the very clean and efficient Honda CVCC engine, in the midst of efforts by US manufacturers to scuttle or roll back emissions control and fuel economy mandates, had a profound effect in countering protests from Detroit and in opening a new era in trade and development of 'green' cars.[1] When the Honda CVCC was certified as meeting the most demanding of the US emissions standards, domestic manufacturers were forced to alter course, but only after years of footdragging in developing their own models of green vehicles. The result was a shake-up in the auto industry that continues to ripple through the global economy.

Although regulatory burdens, recessions, trade barriers and imbalances have kept world automotive production relatively flat in recent years, improvements in the environmental performance of new vehicles continue to grow. Air quality, energy and safety technologies spurred by environmental legislation have made remarkable advances, as measured by new vehicle performance. These advances included a 96 per cent reduction in tailpipe emissions of carbon monoxide and hydrocarbons, and a 76 per cent reduction in nitrogen oxides from 1960 to 1990. During this period, fuel consumption per mile for new cars dropped nearly 50 per cent and accidental deaths per mile declined 65 per cent (Johnson, 1993, p. 4). In short, emissions abatement, fuel efficiency and auto safety were all major technological success stories. Their achievements were tempered, however, by sheer growth in the number of vehicles, vehicle trips and vehicle miles travelled (VMT). For example, total VMT increased by over 170 per cent between 1960 and 1990. While most of this increase can be attributed to the addition of over 250 million new passenger cars registered during these three decades, per capita increases in travel and VMT also played a significant role. During the 1980s, for example, VMT per vehicle increased by over 16 per cent, contributing to an aggregate increase of more than 40 per cent (Nadis and Mackenzie, 1993, p. 18).

Political driving forces

The politics of green car development is embedded in presidential campaign strategies, state-level initiatives (especially those of California), the actions of influential members of Congress (such as John Dingell and Henry Waxman), bureaucratic struggles within and between the Environmental Protection Agency (EPA) and state regulatory agencies, debates over US technology policy, international competition for environmental leadership, the political economy of trade and job creation, and a myriad of related interest group and advocacy coalition activities, including the influence of UAW and other labour unions (see Jones, 1975; Cohen, 1992; Bryner, 1993). While technology-forcing legislation has been the principal focus of green car politics, growing attention has been devoted in recent years to the use of market instruments for pricing and internalizing the environmental costs of motor travel. Developing green car technologies that are responsive to consumer markets is widely thought by industry insiders to be the only promising avenue for further enhancement of vehicle emissions control and fuel economy. Unfortunately, while R&D advances in green technology have surged in the past five years, consumer demand for them has remained relatively flat. American consumers no longer rate emissions control and fuel economy as major considerations in their motor-vehicle purchasing decisions. Governments, not markets, have driven development of these eco-technologies since 1981, when energy concerns (e.g. gasoline shortages) ceased to be a significant factor in automotive marketing.

Technological breakthroughs that contribute to clean air and efficient fuel consumption are desired by most consumers only to the extent that the marginal costs of these technologies remain low and their application does not result in a loss of vehicle acceleration, comfort, safety and range. Moreover, today's green car technologies are often perceived to have diminished marginal utility, due in large part to successful advertising campaigns by major automotive and oil companies claiming that the emissions and fuel economy improvements of the 1970s and 1980s, along with the reformulated gasoline of the 1990s, have taken care of most of the environmental problems of motor vehicles.

Strongly disputing this view have been various energy efficiency and environmental protection groups, along with policy-makers who championed the Clean Air Act amendments of 1990. Of particular note have been the arguments of groups concerned about greenhouse gas emissions from motor vehicles. Carbon dioxide from highway vehicles, for example, represents approximately one-quarter of all US carbon emissions from fossil fuel combustion. The architects of the Clinton administration's Greenhouse Plan, while making little mention of specific transportation technologies, have attempted to identify alternative vehicles and fuels that could substantially reduce carbon dioxide and other greenhouse gas emissions and be commercially available by the year 2005.

State-level initiatives, led by California's Air Resources Board (CARB), have played an even larger role in sharpening the debate with auto industry leaders. Moving well beyond the requirements of the Clean Air Act, CARB adopted vehicle technology and emissions control measures in 1990 that included requirements for the introduction of zero-emission (i.e. electric) vehicles beginning in 1998. By requiring 2 per cent of new vehicles sold in California to be emission free in the first year, 5 per cent in the year 2001 and 10 per cent in 2003, CARB pushed the emissions control debate beyond measures for cleaning up gasoline-powered vehicles to consideration of alternative fuels and vehicles. When a consortium of northeastern states adopted many of the California measures as part of their own regulatory programmes, auto manufacturers were confronted with a bicoastal movement for non-incremental improvements in clean car performance. Declaring that zero-emission vehicles would be economically unpopular, if not unfeasible, when introduced in such a short timeframe, auto industry leaders began to play up the environmental promise of new emissions control technologies for gasoline-powered vehicles. In this way, the mandate for alternative vehicles helped stimulate industry interest in conventional green car improvements. Advances across the board in green car technology, however, have made it difficult to sort out which combination of ecotechnologies should be adopted as the design standard or be included as standard operating equipment in future vehicles.

The promise of ecotechnology

Technical advances in green vehicle R&D have taken place very rapidly in the past two decades. Another wave of rapid advance is at hand with what are called 'supercar' and 'smart car' technologies. Vehicles with zero or ultra-low emissions, superb fuel efficiency and sophisticated electronics for avoiding congestion and accidents are being touted with growing conviction. However, policy and price incentives for utilizing these technologies are developing more slowly. Part of the reason is that neither auto manufacturers nor environmentalists, with some exceptions, truly welcome these innovations. Their predispositions towards technology and consumer markets work against such acceptance. The manufacturers are reluctant to incorporate new technologies into their vehicles that cannot be justified up front by consumer demand. In the case of environmentalists, there are two major and competing predispositions: 1) that technology 'fixes' have been greatly oversold and will cause more problems than they will solve; and 2) that technological solutions are promising, but problematic because they undermine more basic environmental arguments for changing human lifestyles. For the first group of environmentalists, the conception of a 'green' car is an oxymoron; to the second, it represents a paradoxical improvement – an ecotech solution – and, hence, a *bona fide* threat to the continuing campaign against the automobile as a symbol of environmental destruction. Both environmental approaches favour trip reduction programmes, improved mass transit and greater reliance on bicycling and walking. Having spent more than two decades trying to convince people to break their auto-dependency, the commercial prospect of millions of strong, safe, ultra-light, ultra-clean supercars within a decade or two can only be accepted by such groups with a certain amount of ambivalence.

Adding to the environmental dilemmas produced by automotive innovations are recent advances in intelligent transportation systems (ITS)[2] that may make it possible – through the use of information technology, robotics and electronic guidance systems – to double and perhaps triple the capacity of the current urban transport system, thus reducing much of the traffic congestion and many of the traffic hazards associated with it. For many environmental groups, congestion is a decidedly mixed burden or blessing, due to its inhibiting effects on the use of single-occupancy vehicles and its utility as a procrustean, blunt-edged tool of growth management. Although congestion adds significantly to air pollution and fuel consumption, many environmentalists fear that smoothing traffic flow and automating travel information and route guidance systems will only invite many more drivers (i.e. induced demand) to venture on to previously crowded freeways, thereby offsetting the emissions reductions and fuel economy achieved because of congestion relief. Critics argue that many roadways will quickly fill to capacity, thus making the congestion relief a fleeting achievement. Meanwhile the number of offending tailpipes could increase by as much as two or threefold.

Increasing mobility while reducing emissions has become the leading design challenge for the next generation of transportation technologies, and this explains why the linkage between green cars and intelligent transportation systems has become so important. Development of green cars is becoming a precondition in many urban areas for expansion or improvement of the transportation system. Granted that the cost of innovations may be high, fleet turnover slow and co-operation by auto manufacturers poor, the commercial availability of both green vehicles and enhanced mobility systems would alter energy, environmental and transportation policy agendas in far-reaching ways. Before examining the political implications of these changes, however, it is helpful to examine their basis in technology and in claims about technological progress. These claims relate to a number of specific technological advances in emissions control, fuel economy, vehicle inspection and maintenance, and alternative fuels and vehicles.

Emissions control

As a result of research conducted at the California Institute of Technology in 1950 by Arie Jan Haagen-Smit, scientists have known for at least four decades that automotive emissions were a major source of the ingredients in photo-chemical smog. Since 1961, when California mandated the use of positive crankcase ventilation (PCV) on new cars sold beginning in 1963, emissions control for motor vehicles has devleoped into a major industry. The key advance came in the mid-1970s with the introduction of the catalytic converter, as well as engine gas recirculation and evaporative recovery systems. This was followed shortly by the improved three-way catalytic converter and by electronic fuel injection, which adjusts the air/fuel mixture to meet the exacting specifications of advanced emissions control systems.

As progress has been achieved in overall emissions control and automotive engineering, more and more attention has been devoted to emissions caused by cold engines, vehicle acceleration and deceleration, and fuel evaporation. Emissions from what are called 'cold starts' and 'hot soaks' (tailpipe emissions that occur at the beginning of a trip and evaporative emissions that occur when it ends) account for at least two-thirds of the total emissions from a ten-mile trip under normal driving conditions. Most of these emissions occur in the first minute or two of the trip. Additional emissions are produced by the driver's onroad behaviour. If strong acceleration or deceleration occurs, large emission 'puffs' will usually be produced as a consequence. Given that it has been easier to improve emissions control technology than driving behaviour, potential solutions for cold-start and hot-soak problems look much more promising than public appeals to step lightly on the accelerator and brake pedals. While ITS technology may make its most significant air-quality contribution in this latter problem area by smoothing traffic, or providing automatic speed governors, the biggest payoffs are likely to come in the cold-start category from the installation of new electrically heated catalysts (EHCs).

Because today's catalytic converters must reach temperatures of 250–300°C for optimal performance, the first few minutes of any trip undertaken with a cold engine is a period in which much of the exhaust gas flows through the converter without the catalytic action needed to break down harmful emissions. A cold engine typically requires over 100 seconds to heat the catalyst to its start-up temperature (Farrauto *et al.*, 1992). While heated catalysts have been around for many years, the electricity they consumed from the battery made them impractical. Recent advances in EHCs, however, have sharply reduced the battery drain, making it possible using standard battery and alternator systems to warm up some catalysts in as little as five seconds. The additional cost has been estimated at less than $100 per unit, assuming production volumes of at least 300,000 units (California Air Resources Board, 1994).

Other advances in emissions control technology will add significantly to the air-quality improvements promised by EHCs. They include the use of reformulated gasoline and electronic onboard diagnostics systems (OBDs) that provide real-time information about emissions performance, as well as fault tree-data that can be downloaded for monitoring and repair purposes.

Fuel economy

Given the enormous advances in emissions control technology, it seems reasonable to expect that similar advances have occurred in the fuel efficiency area. The fact is, however, that while major efficiency improvements have been achieved with experimental vehicles, the commercial and near-commercial applications of energy efficiency for automobiles and, especially, trucks, have been disappointing by comparison. Average fuel efficiency of new American cars actually declined by 4 per cent from 1988 to 1992 (Nadis and Mackenzie, 1993, p. 18). Fuel prices, unlike the price of clean air, have not figured prominently in discussions about vehicle design since the early 1980s, although conflicts like the 1992 gulf war served to remind many Americans that a fateful link – oil – still ties US foreign policy and transportation policy together.

In the absence of strong cartel controls on OPEC oil production, the real price of gasoline in the USA has remained very low, especially when compared to European and Japanese markets. Efforts to capture some of the environmental and national security externalities of oil dependency in the price of gasoline have led to repeated federal gasoline tax initiatives, none of which has succeeded in adding an increment of more than 4½ cents per gallon. State gasoline taxes have, likewise, been too low to induce significant changes in travel behaviour and VMT.

While some advocates of supercars (e.g. Lovins, 1993) are touting ultra-light hybrids that they claim will someday travel coast to coast on eight gallons of gasoline, consumer demand for such vehicles is apparently low. Since fuel costs represent less than 13 per cent of the direct costs of driving, there is little incentive for travellers to make fuel economy a major consideration in their modal choices and vehicle purchases. Without higher gasoline taxes, 'feebates' (e.g. taxing gas guzzlers to pay for clean car subsidies), greater political instability in oil-rich regions or the imposition of stronger fuel economy (CAFE) standards, there is little reason to expect that fuel savings of future fleets will approach their emissions savings. While several innovative pricing measures, such as pay-at-the-pump auto insurance, might have a significant salutary effect on both fuel economy and vehicle emissions, the political obstacles to such measures have so far been daunting.

Because congestion contributes heavily to poor fuel economy in urban areas, some energy efficiency advocates have emphasized the potential role of ITS technology in reducing automotive fuel consumption. The role of ITS in helping to achieve energy conservation goals is based largely on the premiss that smoothing traffic flows, finding the most efficient routes and eventually providing automated vehicle control systems will reduce unnecessary VMT and improve actual onroad fuel economy for all classes of vehicles. Initial estimates of US energy impacts of ITS projected 6.5 billion gallons of fuel being conserved by the year 2010; however, these estimates have been reduced substantially as the likelihood of additional induced travel demand resulting from ITS deployment has been considered (Cheslow, 1992).

Vehicle inspection and maintenance

When it comes to air pollution, all cars are not created (or maintained) equal. A small percentage of vehicles accounts for a large percentage of urban smog. The National Research Council (1991) reports that *over 50 per cent of ozone-forming emissions from mobile sources are produced by less than 10 per cent of operating vehicles*. The dirtiest 10 per cent of the vehicles have come to be known as 'super-emitters' or 'gross polluters', and getting them repaired or off the road could make a tremendous difference in air quality. After many years of treating all vehicles equally as part of emissions testing programmes, air-quality managers are now exploring ways to target gross polluters with the aid of new remote-sensing technologies that can measure the exhaust emissions from fast-moving vehicles as they pass a roadside detector. The Clean Air Act 1990 amendments require all US non-attainment areas to develop onroad emissions monitoring capabilities for identifying motor vehicles that fail to meet pollution standards. Although the Act does not specify the ways in which onroad emissions are to be measured, the intent of the author of this provision, Representative Joe Barton (R-Tx), was to advance the use of remote-sensing devices (RSDs).

Perhaps the best known of these devices was developed by chemistry professor Donald Stedman and his colleagues at the University of Denver. Initially designed to monitor fuel economy, the device is now one of the most promising tools for emissions monitoring. Stedman's RSD uses an infrared light beam that is aimed across a traffic lane at a detector or mirror on the other side, which is in turn connected to a computer and to a video camera. The infrared beam is positioned to pass through the tailpipe exhaust streams of passing vehicles (about 10 inches above the roadway surface) and to provide instantaneous measurements of the carbon monoxide, carbon dioxide and hydrocarbon concentrations in the exhaust. The capability to measure nitrogen emissions is currently being tested. The 'snapshot' reading of each vehicle's exhaust concentrations is superimposed on a freeze-frame video picture of the vehicle and its licence plate, allowing pollution control officials to identify the registered owners of suspected gross-polluting vehicles.

Over a thousand vehicles per hour can be monitored using a single RSD unit, at an average cost of about $0.50 per vehicle. The overall technical feasibility of single-lane RSD monitoring is well established. With tens of thousands of vehicles tested by this means during the past few years. Nevertheless, comparisons of remote sensing's accuracy and reliability with that of stationary smog-testing centres have triggered significant controversy within the regulatory community over how much of a role remote sensing should play in future smog control efforts.

Alternative fuels and vehicles

Perhaps the most radical technological solution to both emissions and fuel economy problems is to replace the gasoline-powered vehicle with zero or low-polluting fuel sources and combustion technologies. Recent studies of alternative fuels and vehicles have documented major technical advances in the use of electricity, compressed natural gas, hydrogen and other means of powering transportation, although most commercial applications are still limited to niche markets.

The California mandate The most controversial of the alternatives is probably the battery-powered electric vehicle (EV). The controversy stems in large measure from the California Air Resources Board's mandate that 2–10 per cent of the state's new vehicles sold from 1998 to 2003 be 'zero-emission', which for all practical purposes means electric. While the arguments for and against EV development often hinge on technical performance issues, the most hotly contested issues involve regulatory politics. In particular, they involve the issue of government's role in steering the motor vehicle industry, and the extent to which it can be justified under provisions of the federal and state clean air Acts.

Although all of the major auto manufacturers have EV development programmes – some almost 20 years old – the fact is that little beyond experimental prototypes have been produced until recently. General Motor's introduction in 1990 of an experimental high-performance EV, the 'Impact', buoyed public perceptions of EV feasibility, but company reservations about cost and marketability, along with changes in leadership, soon resulted in a retreat from GM's initial support for rapid commercialization of the vehicle. Subsequent introductions of niche market vehicles (e.g. battery-powered delivery vans) have demonstrated growing popularity of EV technology, but industry representatives caution that ramping up production to meet the California mandate will be very expensive. EV supporters have responded that the actual operating costs of EVs, once production volumes achieve reasonable economies of scale, will be very close to that of conventional automobiles.

The US big-three auto makers have opposed the California mandate from its inception but, after failing to change the state's position and timetable, they have proceeded with preparations to expand their EV sales, while at the same time exploring federal avenues of intervention. In June 1994, Chrysler announced that it would be the first major manufacturer to meet California's 1998 zero-emission vehicle rule. The 2 per cent target for that year amounts to nearly 25,000 vehicles. The numbers will quickly climb to over 100,000 new EVs in 2003, provided that CARB's biennial review of the mandate continues to be favourable. The auto makers, meanwhile, have concentrated much of their lobbying on a group of northeastern states that have adopted many of the measures featured in California's programme. The Ozone Transport Commission, which represents 12 states and the District of Columbia, voted in early February 1994 to implement a low-emissions vehicle programme starting in 1996 and to mandate major emissions improvements in new vehicles beginning in 1999. The role of electric vehicles in this effort has not been finalized, hence the pressure from auto makers and, indirectly, US EPA, which has been urged by the auto industry to discourage air-quality plans that rely heavily on EV development. Given that the populations of these commission states, together with that of California, include over half of the nation's car buyers, the stakes for both industry and for air-quality managers are obviously very high.

Federal initiatives   The major federal programme in this arena has been the Partnership for a New Generation of Motor Vehicles, previously known as the 'Clean Car Initiative'. Proposed by the Clinton White House in February 1992 as part of a new technology policy, the initiative was formalized in September 1993 as an R&D partnership between government and representatives of the auto industry. The long-term goal was to move beyond the internal combustion engine to a vehicle propulsion system that was clean, efficient and commercially feasible. The year 2003 was set as the goal for development of a production prototype that would be three times more fuel efficient than today's average new car and produce almost no harmful emissions. Although the amount of federal money redirected to this effort has been estimated to approach $500 million, the success of the programme will rest primarily on the big-three auto makers, who annually spend over $11 billion on R&D (White House Office of Communications, 1993).

Thus far, the partnership has focused on developing super-efficient, super-clean internal combustion vehicles or hybrids, rather than 100 per cent battery-powered vehicles or other alternatives. A similar partnership for battery R&D – the US Advanced Battery Consortium – was created earlier for EV development, although it represents a much smaller investment of government and industry funds. Because advances in conventional vehicle efficiency and emissions control have arguably developed as fast or faster than performance advances in many alternative vehicles and fuels, the tendency in the automotive research community has been to keep as many options as possible – a strategy that in the short term favours the 'incumbent' gasoline-powered vehicle over a long list of alternative 'challengers'. As long as gasoline prices remain relatively low, and the promise of conventional vehicle technologies (e.g. electrically heated catalysts) remains high, the push for alternative vehicles and fuels will be difficult to accelerate. Although fuel cells and other alternative power sources may be even more promising from an energy and environmental perspective, many researchers fear that government initiatives may prematurely zero in on a particular technology or alternative fuel, thus committing the nation to a path that will later prove to be less effective and less economical than alternatives that would otherwise have climbed to the top of the policy agenda on their own merits.

The preoccupation of many state and federal agencies in the late 1980s with methanol as the 'transportation fuel of the future' illustrates what may have been a premature attempt at green car 'steering' by policy-makers. Methanol, for all its virtues, failed on several criteria to attract broad support from the environmental community. For many green car enthusiasts, methanol was simply too marginal a step. They favoured alternatives that would take them much closer to their ideal of a solar-hydrogen-powered vehicle.[3] Today, they continue to favour quantum-leap strategies over those of the incremental variety. Some of the most enthusiastic supporters of solar-hydrogen schemes argue that a commercially feasible prototype may be ready in time to inaugurate the next millennium. Most, however, appear to believe that a combination of advances in EV battery performance, fuel cell technology and compressed natural gas vehicles will lead the auto industry into the twenty-first century, with hydrogen vehicles perhaps becoming a natural extension of that progress within a few decades.

Technology, politics and markets

Because vehicle-emissions control improvements have been largely the result of technology 'push' rather than market 'pull' strategies, the auto industry has repeatedly complained that the air-quality 'tail' has been wagging the transportation 'dog'. It is customary in industry settings to contrast the promise of new technologies, the dismal impedance of politics and the redeeming pull of the market-place. Only the power of the market, many believe, can pave the way for an affordable green car. Such perspectives lead many executives in the auto industry to view the regulatory demands and constraints placed on Detroit by the Clean Air Act, California's Low Emission Vehicle Program and by CAFE standards as clearly excessive, even counterproductive. According to the conventional wisdom, government intentionally targets auto manufacturers because regulating a few giant firms at the design and production stage is much easier than regulating the travel behaviour and vehicle preferences of over 100 million drivers. Small 'n' regulation at the source of supply avoids direct government intervention in the large 'n' world of consumer demand. Markets, of course, are supposed to provide price signals that internalize the hidden costs of energy and environmental damage stemming from transportation choices, and thereby influence consumer demand for improved fuel economy and cleaner motor vehicles. But as long as auto manufacturers, oil interests and highway users co-operate in preventing significant increases in gasoline taxes and emissions fees, the market 'pull' solution to problems of green car development and deployment will remain illusory.

In the policy arena, tails *often* wag dogs, especially when they are dogs (e.g. transportation) with multiple tails (e.g. air quality, energy conservation, access for the disabled, job creation, etc.). The political challenge of green car development is essentially one of optimizing across competing public policies for the purpose of minimizing the zone of incompatibility between stated or implied policy goals. The transportation community has been preoccupied with the goal of *mobility*, disabled and low-income Americans have emphasized *access* and *equity*, and energy and environmental groups have proposed goals based on *efficiency* and *sustainability*. Efforts to achieve conformity among energy, transportation, air quality, land use and other policy domains have seldom succeeded in pushing or pulling automotive technology in a single direction. Transportation policy remains focused on mobility, often to the detriment of air quality, energy and access objectives. Although some policy convergence has occurred as a result of the Clean Air Act 1990 amendments, the Intermodal Surface Transportation Efficiency Act 1991 (ISTEA), the Energy Policy Act 1992 and the Americans with Disabilities Act 1990, basic incompatibilities remain.

To those untutored in American politics, the idea that official policies often work at cross purposes may seem like an indictment of the policy-making process. But to close observers, a certain amount of incongruity in policy objectives is unavoidable in any political system that depends on compromise and on the strategic use of ambiguity in coalition building. The American system being one that occasionally raises policy incompatibility to absurd heights (e.g. tobacco subsidies and anti-smoking programmes), it should come as no surprise that policy incentives for green car development are frequently undermined by other policies aimed at such objectives as auto safety, highway capacity enhancement, protecting auto workers and improving the US balance of trade with Japan.

Like the challenge of policy congruence, the managerial challenge of green car development and deployment is concerned with the reconciliation of con-flicting goals. It is even more concerned, however, with the reconciliation of different organizational cultures. Green car management and administration has turned out to be more than a linear implementation process pegged to emissions control and efficiency. It is instead a blending process involving multiple goals, objectives and organizational agendas. Given the interjurisdic-tional challenges of federalism, it is a process that requires harmonization of the interests of multiple agencies and levels of government, not to mention harmonization of the different cultures and customs that divide public and private sector actors. The partnership model for green car R&D is only the latest example of an effort to overcome the different organizational styles and incentive structures that divide government and industry.

Measuring costs and benefits

Given that the transportation sector accounts for 17 per cent of US GDP, 15 per cent of the nation's employment force and occupies more land than the entire housing sector, any major change in the use or design of highway vehicles is certain to have repercussions throughout the economy and across virtually every community.

Historically, auto makers have resisted many green car ideas on the grounds that their costs outweighed their benefits. Included in those costs was the claim that green cars would generally be less safe in an accident. Environmental and energy groups openly speculated that the real reason for industry opposition was that the profit margin for green cars would be smaller, largely because the cars themselves would be smaller and less powerful. Air bags and other safety advances have reduced some of the concerns about the crashworthiness of green cars. The related concern about vehicle size has also receded as more and more lightweight materials have been incorporated into conventional vehicle designs, and as improved alternative fuels and full-sized alternative vehicles have been developed. Today, the questions of size and safety continue to be raised, but increasing emphasis is being placed on the equity and international competitiveness implications of green car development. Industry executives argue that the added cost of green technologies will make car buying prohibitively expensive for many low-income drivers. Moreover, some have argued that loading all the clean air and fuel economy improvement costs on to new model vehicles will encourage owners of older, more polluting and less efficient models to hold on to their vehicles longer, thus sustaining higher pollution levels in their effort to save money.

Further complicating the debate over costs and benefits have been a number of research findings on the comparative emissions and fuel economy impacts of three different environmental strategies: 1) emphasizing automotive technology improvements; 2) encouraging behavioural changes among drivers; and 3) improving the cost-effectiveness and availability of mass transit services. Most environmental groups have strongly favoured transportation control measures and expansion of mass transit systems – especially light rail – to discourage unnecessary trips in single occupancy vehicles (SOVs). Energy efficiency advocates, seeing little or no progress on CAFE standards, have likewise sought to target driver behaviour and travel demand management approaches as ways to reduce fuel consumption. Economists and many transportation planners, however, have cast strong doubt on the cost-effectiveness of many transit programmes, especially in dispersed western cities such as Los Angeles, and they have attacked many of the regulatory programmes that are designed to change drivers' travel behaviour, such as 'No drive' days and ridesharing mandates.

While environmental lobbying for improved transit use and trip avoidance strategies has increased in the face of declining transit ridership and increasing trip generation, the expected environmental benefits of such measures, given the need for transportation policies that satisfy near-term conditions of political and economic feasibility, appear to be small in comparison with the effects of cleaning up the private vehicles. For example, removing one vehicle from commuter traffic in 1992 using southern California's rideshare programme (Regulation XV) was estimated to cost nearly $3,000 (Richardson, 1994, p. 17). Investing the same amount of money in remote sensing and related programmes for identifying and fixing, or retiring, gross-polluting vehicles would result in emissions reductions that were many times greater. Similarly, air-quality gains from light rail transit compare very unfavourably on an abatement cost basis with clean car programmes, and offer little justification *by themselves* for the enormous subsidies involved in transit ridership – up to $8,000 per roundtrip passenger per year in southern California (Moore, 1993, p. 27). Congestion relief, of course, may justify large transit expenditures, but analysts need to be clear that the energy and environmental rationales for such investments are, in practice, very limited, especially when compared to measures that repair or retire frequently driven gross-polluting cars and trucks. While many transportation policies and programmes are biased to expand route choices for SOVs without first and foremost increasing modal choices (e.g. enhancing the *ease* of choosing existing transit systems), the strong likelihood remains that the negative energy and environmental consequences of this bias will shrink in the next decade as vehicles become much cleaner and, it is hoped, more efficient. If these improvements fail to materialize, it will largely be for lack of political will, not technological foresight or economic feasibility.

Because of differences in financing, green car policy decisions that involve multibillion dollar price-tags are more likely to attract political controversy than equally costly transit programmes. The former type of policy directly affects the vehicle purchasing decisions of consumers, while the latter is essentially relegated to the mundane category of infrastructure improvements paid for incrementally out of highway trust funds, bond issues and sales taxes. The Urban Mass Transportation Act 1964 eventually created the largest programme of discretionary grant-making in the nation, yet the programme has seldom served as a highly visible 'lightning rod' for critics of government spending. Green car development, by contrast, is held to a higher standard of marginal cost analysis. Moreover, it is constrained by the symbolic politics of an automobile culture that has no real parallel in the transit arena. For those who enjoy the status and excitement of driving 'muscle' cars, the growth of the green car industry may be perceived as nothing short of an assault on their lifestyle. Some auto makers, in attempting to please both sides, have developed high-performance, green sport models (e.g. GM's battery-powered 'Impact') to show that being green doesn't mean being slow or underpowered. Critics, however, worry that the added cost of such high-performance technology will reinforce the notion that only the rich can afford to be green.

Policy tools for development and deployment

In the midst of debate over whether it is better to emphasize changes in vehicle technology, in driver behaviour or in transit alternatives, policy-makers and analysts have become more aware of alternative means for managing transportation-related problems. If there is any discernible common feature of these alternatives, it is the use of incentive structures to affect travel behaviour. The best example of this is an emerging strategy for reducing automotive emissions and fuel consumption through the use of electronic road pricing and similar market-based instruments. With the use of inexpensive transponders installed in vehicles (i.e. automatic vehicle identification or AVI), monthly bills for road use can now be compiled just like those for telephone or electricity use. Related programmes for pricing parking much more extensively (and expensively) have also been advanced. The idea is to treat the public roadways and parking lots as utilities, charging for their use according to demand. Travel during rush hour periods would be priced to discourage unnecessary trips, thus reducing congestion and its associated emissions and wasted fuel. In June 1994, a National Research Council panel proposed a peak period highway toll averaging 10 to 15 cents per mile, arguing that it would reduce congestion, air

Table 5.1 *Policy instruments for green car development*

---

1. Public/private partnerships for research and development:
   e.g. US Partnership for a New Generation of Motor Vehicles; US Advanced Battery Consortium

2. Performance standards:
   e.g. California ZEV standard; tailpipe emissions standards; CAFE standards

3. Technology-forcing standards (sometimes implied by performance standards):
   e.g. catalytic converter mandate

4. Fuel pricing:
   e.g. gasoline tax increase of 1993

5. Road pricing:
   e.g. congestion pricing demonstration project on Oakland Bay Bridge

6. Product labelling:
   e.g. city and highway fuel economy posted on window price-stickers for new cars

7. Vehicle purchase incentives:
   e.g. 'feebates', which tax buyers of relatively inefficient vehicles and rebate the revenue to buyers of relatively efficient vehicles

8. Vehicle buyback programmes:
   e.g. paying owners of pre-1972 model vehicles $700–$800 for the right to retire (scrap) their vehicles, thus accelerating fleet turnover

9. Emissions fees:
   e.g. annual fees based on mileage and emissions level at time of registration renewal

10. Monitoring and enforcement:
    e.g. state I&M testing/rating procedures for tailpipe emissions

11. Government procurement:
    e.g. federal purchase of clean-fuelled cars for agency fleets

12. Mobile emissions offsets/trading:
    e.g. allowing powerplant operators to offset some of their emissions by purchasing green vehicles for fleet use

13. Public education:
    e.g. Public awareness campaigns about the effects of vehicle emissions on health

---

pollution and fuel use. Anticipating strong opposition from motorists, supporters of road pricing argue that the revenue could be used to offset local gasoline taxes, and perhaps other taxes to the extent of being revenue neutral.

Other important policy strategies and options that will affect transportation include the development of telecommuting, emissions trading and government fleet-procurement goals. Telecommuting could be the real 'sleeper' on the options list, but large uncertainties have made transportation and environmental planners cautious in estimating its eventual contribution to cleaner air and energy conservation. Table 5.1 presents a summary of the major policy instruments for achieving green vehicle commercialization, along with examples of each.

Table 5.2 *Target populations and intervention levels associated with green car policy instruments*

		Auto industry	Target population Consumers/drivers	Other sectors
Level of government intervention	High	Technology-forcing standards	'No drive' days Emissions fees	Clean fleet quotas for business
	Medium	Performance standards	I&M Programmes, road pricing, gasoline taxes, feebates, vehicle buybacks	Mobile source offsets for powerplants and refineries
	Low	R&D partnerships	Product labelling, public education	Government procurement

The principal instruments used in green car development can be further characterized according to the type of target population and the level of government intervention required for successful implementation. Top-down mandates targeting auto makers have the administrative advantages of small 'n' regulation, but their application is politically difficult. While most of the costs of such government intervention are passed on to consumers, auto makers complain that the new car market cannot continue to absorb increasing regulatory compliance costs, particularly when so much of the problem lies with older model gross-polluters and when much more flexible approaches (e.g. mobile source emissions trading) would result in more cost-effective environmental results. At the other end of the spectrum are public education programmes that involve low levels of government intervention and large target populations. Because these programmes target human behaviour, instead of technological performance, they suffer from the obvious limitations inherent in human communications, learning curves, knowledge decay rates and resistance to change. At the same time, however, they involve a form of policy learning that is often more enduring and politically significant than that associated with technologically based instruments (Howlett and Ramesh, 1993). Table 5.2 provides an overview in matrix form of targeting and intervention considerations affecting instrument choice. With its emphasis on coercion, target group selection and implementation scale, the matrix suggests a number of potential tradeoffs between effectiveness and political feasibility in green car policy-making.

Policy trends and strategy
The politics of green car development are increasingly driven by three very broad, cross-cutting policy trends that link the goals of clean air, energy security and mobility. The first is the growing preference for demand-side management (DSM) rather than supply-side management of public problems. The second, and related, trend is the growing reliance of governments on

market-based tools for problem-solving (and the concomitant erosion of command-and-control regulation). The third trend, which is much older than the other two, is the expanding application of technology-based solutions to problems that were previously thought to require fundamental changes in human behaviour for their successful management. Green car development is clearly an example of the third trend, but its future pace and scope depend in part on what happens as a result of the other two trends.

While achievements made possible by DSM, market-based tools and technical fixes are often oversold or uncritically accepted (especially in the case of technical fixes), the unmistakable pattern over the past decade has been one of greater reliance on all three approaches. Applications of joint DSM–market incentive programmes have revolutionized some aspects of energy and water resource management, for example, and seem poised, with the help of automatic vehicle identification and road pricing, to offer the same kind of benefits for the management of transportation. Technological innovations, such as ITS, heated catalysts, gas-sipping engines and the information superhighway (e.g. telecommuting), promise large additional benefits that could ease the transition to more sustainable lifestyles and forms of development, despite what are certain to be unforeseen and unintended consequences.

Tying these three policy orientations together in a way that assures broad political support and mutual gains is a matter of some urgency for the transportation community. Without greater attention to the environmental, energy and social consequences of enhanced mobility, designers of our transportation system will almost certainly face growing challenges from environmental groups and other organizations that monitor the air quality, energy and access conformity provisions of recent state and federal legislation. Transportation actors who learnt their trade in the golden eras of interstate highway building and mass transit mega-projects may make the mistake of assuming that growth in the economy will eventually permit a return to large-scale construction. They may even dismiss energy and environmental conformity requirements as a passing fad. However, a long list of failed efforts in this vein – from nuclear power to chlorofluorocarbons – reveal that control of the public agenda is often fleeting (Baumgartner and Jones, 1993). A far more promising strategy may be to develop a common core of tools and objectives that treat environmental, energy, mobility and transportation access issues in an integrated fashion.

One approach worth considering would be to note the consistent patterns in the policy strategies that are developing in each of these issue areas. All reveal the same basic substitution patterns whereby centralized, technology-forcing regulations and supply enhancement programmes are slowly replaced by decentralized, market or performance-based standards and demand reduction programmes. For reasons that will soon become obvious, I have termed this approach the 'wedge strategy' (Hempel, 1994). Figure 5.1 depicts a rudimentary form of the wedge strategy as applied to air quality and energy issues. Each wedge represents a policy instrument that is either growing or declining in use over time. Those showing growing reliance involve demand-side management, market-based tools and green technology innovations. Those

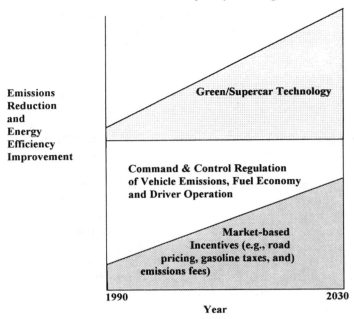

Figure 5.1   *The wedge strategy*

portrayed with a proportional drop in reliance are measures based on supply-side management and command-and-control regulation.

Each wedge is shaped by a combination of constraints and opportunities. Constraints include the steeply rising marginal costs of additional command-and-control regulation and construction of new powerplants and highways. Opportunities include the promise of green technology substitution, market 'carrots' (rather than regulatory 'sticks') and the growing response of consumers to cost-saving demand management measures. The challenge for strategic policy designers is to achieve greater emissions savings, useful energy, mobility and access, in an era of cutbacks in government spending and declining returns to scale for supply-side management. Implicit in the strategy is a process of social learning and value change by which ecological limits to quantitative growth are recognized and accepted, albeit with occasional circumventions by technology.

The wedge strategy is merely a heuristic device for the present; something intended to help in the construction of policy 'packages' that can operate effectively at the intersection of transportation, energy and environmental problems. The point of the strategy is to recognize that good policy design is increasingly an art of blending. In the case at hand, it involves a blending of DSM, market-based pricing and green technologies in order to achieve goal integration and conformity on multiple fronts. Green car development, while probably the most acceptable transportation-related environmental option in the eyes of the general public, is nevertheless only one component of this package.

Sustainable transportation policy

A final consideration in this survey of green car politics and policy is the normative basis for debate and action. Although many different concerns have been expressed as justifications for green car development – public health, conservation of natural resources and national security, to name a few – environmentalists have been pressing for adoption of a unifying theme by which to frame their issues. Most have settled on the theme of 'sustainability' as a comprehensive way to express their values and goals. Although controversial, the theme has emerged as a powerful integrating device for characterizing the goals of the environmental and alternative energy movements. Within the transportation sector, it has been presented as a counterweight to the auto industry's design principle of planned obsolescence and its reliance on market-pull development strategies.

Auto makers have been criticized for conceiving of energy and environmental problems and solutions too narrowly within the confines of benefit-cost analysis, with its contempocentric emphasis on discount rates. From an environmental perspective, many of the benefits of green car development (e.g. effects of greenhouse gas abatement) occur so far in the future that their net present value will be discounted almost to zero. The environmentalist's remedy is found in the emerging insights of sustainable transportation thinking, a variant of the sustainable development approach that was developed in the 1980s and featured at the 1992 Earth Summit in Brazil.

The test of a sustainable transportation technology is whether it is compatible in the long run with the ecological concept of carrying capacity and its application to urban and rural travel corridors. Sustainability in the context of intelligent transportation and vehicle design means that improvements in mobility, accessibility and safety must not result in environmental impacts that exceed the carrying capacity of the region in which they occur. Moreover, since vehicular greenhouse emissions and certain other transportation impacts are global in nature, the notion of corridor-level or regional-level carrying capacity must be expanded to encompass the biosphere as a whole.

In most urban areas, transportation improvements that result in increased levels of service and access must be combined with growth management and environmental protection programmes in order to ensure that they represent perpetual progress, rather than stopgap measures or temporary 'fixes'. Otherwise, the only genuine transportation improvement that can be sustained, ironically, may be the bicycle, due in part to its internalized average speed advantage over motor vehicles. When non-travel hours spent working to purchase, insure, operate and repair a car are included in distance-over-time calculations, the average speed of the typical automobile drops to about 5 mph.[4] Hence the putative advantage for low-cost bicycles.

In 1993 there were 108 million bicycles produced, globally, compared to 34 million automobiles (Brown *et al.*, 1994, pp. 86–9). According to some forecasters, the annual production trends for bicycles and automobiles will be reversed in a few decades, particularly if Asian and eastern European growth in purchasing power begins to approach the latent demand for automobiles. Such a reversal of trends could represent the ultimate challenge of sustainable transportation, requiring not only much cleaner and more fuel efficient vehicles but also enormous advances in intelligent transportation technology and policy to prevent the roadways of major cities from being turned unwittingly into parking lots. In China, for example, the ratio of bicycles to cars is 250 to 1, while the US ratio is 0.7 to 1 (Nadis and Mackenzie, 1993, p. xvi). Over the next decade, however, China plans to increase its auto production fourfold – a total of 600,000 new cars per year (Cogan, 1992, p. 244). Outputs of several million, annually, are anticipated within a few decades.

Green cars and intelligent transportation systems can certainly help in reducing emissions, fuel consumption and congestion in relatively wealthy countries, but these same technologies may not be available and affordable on the scale needed in most developing countries. The technological and financing gaps may be insurmountable for easily transferable vehicle emissions control systems, fuel economy measures and electronic traffic management systems. Hence a major question for researchers interested in sustainability is whether the advances represented by ITS and various 'clean car' initiatives will be adequate to prevent net increases in urban and global pollution (e.g. carbon emissions) as the vehicle fleet of developing countries rapidly expands. It appears that much more attention to issues of technology transfer, information sharing and development assistance will be necessary if humanity is to avoid the mistake of overpopulating the world with both people and 'brown' motor vehicles. Thus the ultimate rationale for green car development is driven by anticipated expansion of the world motor vehicle fleet.

Conclusion

If historic rates of economic growth continue, the world is likely to experience a doubling of the private motor vehicle fleet within the next 40–50 years. The impacts on urban air quality, global climate, oil supplies and congestion may be very large, albeit difficult to forecast. While the last two decades have witnessed tremendous progress in the technical ability of US, Japanese and European manufacturers to control emissions and increase fuel efficiency, incorporating these advances as standard operating equipment into new model vehicles has sometimes increased the purchase price significantly. Consumers in developing countries may not be able or willing to pay for the energy and environmental benefits of the new technology. And even rich countries balk at retrofitting clean air and fuel efficiency technologies of their existing fleets because the retrofit is often prohibitively expensive. Consequently, the fleet turnover rate should be viewed as a critical variable in all vehicular clean air and energy conservation strategies.

California's low emission vehicle mandate and the federal Partnership for a New Generation of Motor Vehicles have positioned the US automotive market for another leap forward in green car design and performance. Ironically, advances in alternative fuels and vehicles – especially electric vehicles – have helped to stimulate major advances in conventional fuels (e.g. reformulated gasoline) and vehicle technology (e.g. heated catalysts), thus intensifying the arguments among government, industry and environmental groups over the future promise of gasoline-powered vehicles. Meanwhile, air-quality regulators and energy-efficiency experts have begun to pay more attention to a small subset of older vehicles – 'gross polluters' – that when driven a great deal account for a wildly disproportionate share of motor vehicle emissions and fuel consumption, due to equipment malfunctions, tampering or design flaws.

If green car technology is to fulfil many of the expectations placed on it by the energy conservation and environmental communities, it will have to be accompanied by ancillary advances in inspection and monitoring programmes, such as the use of remote-sensing devices and advances in intelligent transportation systems. ITS applications, in the form of electronic road pricing and information-based demand management, may ultimately prove to be as important for addressing environmental and energy concerns about land use as green car technology is for addressing air pollution. Even if all the cars in the year 2020 are green, the likelihood that there will be more than one billion of them on the road will necessarily raise questions about threatened open space, habitat, noise and many other environmental matters unrelated to urban air quality or greenhouse gas concentrations. And while energy concerns may largely subside by that time, the fact remains that a difficult transition away from reliance on oil lies ahead, sometime in the next century.

Finally, a word is in order about the economic forces driving automotive politics. Prospects for green car development are often assumed to be solely a function of market and trade conditions. The interdependence of technological innovation, politics, markets and ecological carrying capacity, however, suggests that other key factors will be involved in deciding the future of the green car. As important as markets and trade are in shaping that future, they are nevertheless derivatives of politics, and probably always will be. They cannot operate independently of politics anymore than Wall Street can separate its future from the actions of the Federal Reserve Bank. Based on the premiss that there is no such thing as a free market or free trade, only designed markets and designed trade, the central question becomes how to foster co-operation within and between business and government for the purpose of designing technologies, policies, institutions and markets that will improve our quality of life. Green car development represents a test case for this kind of thinking, and the 'greening' of transportation, if indeed it continues, will reflect a change in values every bit as important as the change it represents in technology.

Notes

1.   The term 'green car' is used in this chapter to refer to both car and light-duty truck technology that significantly reduces the environmental impacts of each mile of onroad travel. It should be noted that light-duty trucks and sport utility vehicles, as a class, are significantly less fuel-efficient than standard automobiles. Since they represent a growing share of new vehicle sales, their fuel consumption and carbon dioxide emissions constitute a growing share of energy and environmental impacts from motor vehicles.

2.   Also known as intelligent vehicle/highway systems (IVHS) or 'smart cars' and 'smart highways', ITS is a bundle of driver and vehicle support technologies that can be used to assist drivers with real-time information about traffic conditions, plan and guide their routes, provide collision avoidance warnings and other safety-related information and eventually control vehicle operation through automated steering and navigation systems.

3. Solar-hydrogen vehicles rely on photovoltaic cells or other forms of solar electricity generation to split water molecules into hydrogen and oxygen (a process of electrolysis). A consortium in southern California led by Clean Air Now and the Xerox Corporation is presently developing a solar hydrogen demonstration programme for a small fleet of vehicles that will take to the road in 1995.

4. Ivan Illich provides a classic reconceptualization of the average speeds of pedestrians, bicycles and motor vehicles in *Toward a History of Needs* (Berkeley, Calif: Heydey Books, 1978). According to Illich, total hours spent acquiring and maintaining a transportation technology should be added to its total travel time in order to determine its adjusted average speed. Given this framework, improvements in bicycle travel appear to be the only truly sustainable transportation achievements of modern history. The adjusted average speed of bicycles has increased relative to the adjusted average speed of automobiles.

References

Frank R. Baumgartner and Brian D. Jones (1993) *Agendas and Instability in American Politics* Chicago: University of Chicago.

Lester Brown *et al.* (1994) *Vital Signs 1994*, Washington DC: Worldwatch Institute.

Gary Bryner (1993) *Blue Skies, Green Politics: The Clean Air Act of 1990*, Washington, DC: CQ Press.

California Air Resources Board (1994) Draft Discussion Paper: Low-Emission Vehicle Program Costs, Sacramento, CA: March 25, 1994 CARB Workshop.

M. Cheslow, Energy Estimates for the Years 2000 and 2010, *Surface Transportation and the Information Age: Proceedings from IVHS America 1992*, Washington DC: IVHS Anerica, Vol. I, pp. 404–12.

Douglas Cogan (1992) *The Greenhouse Gambit: Business and Investment Responses to Climate Change*, Washington, DC: Investor Responsibility Research Center.

Richard E. Cohen (1992) *Washington at Work: Back Rooms and Clean Air*, New York: Macmillan (especially Chapter 5).

Robert J. Farrauto, Ronald Heck and Barry Seronello (1992) Environmental Catalysts, *Chemical and Engineering News*, 7 September, p. 34.

Lamont, C. Hempel (1994) The Greening of Intelligent Vehicle/Highway Systems, paper presented at the National (US) Policy Conference on Intelligent Transportation and the Environment, Washington, DC, June 1994.

Michael Howlett and M. Ramesh (1993) Patterns of Policy Instrument Choice: Policy Styles, Policy Learning and the Privatization Experience, *Policy Studies Review*, Vol. 12, nos. 1/2 (Spring/Summer 1993), pp. 3–24.

Elmer Johnson (1993) *Avoiding the Collision of Cities and Cars: Urban Transportation Policy for the Twenty-first Century*, (Chicago: Academy of Arts and Sciences.

Charles O. Jones (1975) *Clean Air: The Policies and Politics of Pollution Control* Pittsburgh: University of Pittsburgh Press.

Amory B. Lovins *et al.* (1993) Supercars: The Coming Light-Vehicle Revolution, Rocky Mountain Institute, 1739 Snowmass Creek Road, Snowmass, Colorado 81654-9199, Publication T93-10.

J.E. Moore (1993) Ridership and Cost on the Long Beach–Los Angeles Blue Line, *Transportation Research Annual*.

Steve Nadis and James J. Mackenzie (1993) *Car Trouble*, Boston: Beacon Press.

National Research Council (1991) *Rethinking the Ozone Problem in Urban and Regional Air Pollution*, National Academy Press.

Harry W. Richardson with Chang-Hee Christine Bae, Brown Sky Blues: Are Transportation Rx's a Cure?, in *Resource Papers for the 1994 ITE International Conference*, Institute of Transportation Engineers, March 1994.

White House Office of Communications Press Release: (1993) Background Briefing on Clean Car, 29 September.

6

The North American Free Trade Agreement and the environment: economic growth versus democratic politics

DEREK CHURCHILL and RICHARD WORTHINGTON
Pomona College, USA

Introduction

The global industrial system, and the economic paradigm on which it is based, are increasingly considered to be unsustainable, and movements are emerging world wide to explore and advocate alternatives. The concept of sustainable development has gained considerable currency as a label for these efforts, in part because diverse political forces have managed to find space under its broad umbrella.

International trade is one arena where sustainability, and the diverse meanings attached to it, have become increasingly relevant to policy development. The focus of trade policy has traditionally been economic growth, but several profound changes have made it increasingly difficult to isolate trade and growth from ecological integrity and social justice. These include the end of the cold war, which has allowed more issues and actors to secure space on national and international policy agendas; globalization of production and culture, which has undermined the ability of nation-states to guarantee well-being (or the perception of it) to their citizens; and, of course, deteriorating ecosystems and polarizing social structures throughout the world.

Accelerating changes at the global level are thus driving trade towards the centre of the political agenda, at the same time that linkages to issues other than sheer economic growth are becoming more visible. This is the context in which 'sustainability' has become an obligatory allegiance for players in this repoliticized arena.

The North American Free Trade Agreement (NAFTA) which went into effect on 1 January 1994 is the first trade pact to incorporate environmental provisions (the most significant of which were 'side agreements' to NAFTA). Its passage was hotly contested on both environmental and social grounds, reflecting both the signifiance of trade/development issues as well as the clash of political forces that surrounds them. The 17 November 1993 debate in the US House of Representatives over NAFTA crystallized the current conceptions of development in Congress, and provides an excellent opportunity to examine how national and global leaders deal with sustainability. Without meaningful support in the most powerful nation on earth, sustainable development will labour against insurmountable odds, while emerging regional and global institutions, such as the North American free trade bloc that is expected to incorporate other parts of Latin America, will be based on an outdated and lethal model of progress.

We address two issues in this chapter. In the next section we examine the politics of trade and development at the political centre by analysing the growth first paradigm which permeated the NAFTA debate in the US Congress, and the means by which dissent was pre-empted and marginalized by the 'competitiveness' agenda of neoliberals and conservatives. Next we examine participation in NAFTA politics at the grassroots, where sustainability was a more salient concern. Although this mobilization failed substantially to alter the NAFTA agreement or prevent its passage, it was surprisingly effective, and citizen networks which tie North American integration to social justice and sustainability are still active. Such participation in regional integration processes is the key to a sustainable future for North America.

NAFTA and Congress: politics at the centre

The NAFTA debate on 17 November 1993 culminated a stormy two-and-a-half year process. While there was much conflict over the content of the agreement, the means of constructing it was equally controversial. At the outset, for example, the Bush administration persuaded Congress to pass 'fast track' legislation designed to speed negotiations and limit congressional involvement to accepting or rejecting the agreement, in what many considered a bald attempt to limit debate and participation. Advocacy groups also entered the fray. For example, Public Citizen (the Ralph Nader organization), Sierra Club and Friends of the Earth filed a court petition to require NAFTA adherence to a US requirement that all federal projects complete an environmental impact statement prior to final approval. When Federal Judge Charles Richey ruled in June 1993 on behalf of the petitioners, yet another controversy over process erupted in the government, think tanks and op-ed pages (the ruling was soon over-ruled by a higher court). The 17 November debate itself lasted a daunting 13 hours, during which nearly every member spoke. A noteworthy pattern through all these events is 1) substantial conflict from beginning to end over both process and content; and 2) ultimate victory by proponents of NAFTA in every case.

NAFTA proponents in Congress sounded four themes in support of their position. Most placed NAFTA in the context of irreversible and accelerating global economic changes, which left Congress either to embrace these changes or accept a declining status quo. Many quoted President Clinton's sound bite that 'We must make change our friend'. Rejecting NAFTA, they reasoned, would jeopardize the General Agreement on Tariffs and Trade (GATT), relations with the Asian/Pacific countries, a future hemisphere-wide American free trade bloc, and launch a new economic cold war of protectionism. Many raised the spectre of a Japanese 'beachhead' on the North American continent (*Congressional Record*, 1993, H9898, hereinafter *CR*), citing US Ambassador to Mexico Jim Jones, who claimed that the Mexicans were set to turn to Japan for investment and even a possible trade agreement if NAFTA was defeated (Krugman, 1993, p. 13).

Advocates also saw uncontrollable forces affecting employment. While lamenting the loss of jobs to trade-driven restructuring, proponents argued that low-skill manufacturing will continue to shift to low-wage countries with or without NAFTA. Increased exports to a hemispheric market of 700 million consumers were thus presented as the solution that would boost overall employment. Congressmen Franks of New Jersey recounted the following story in support of this argument:

> I stood in the toy department at a brand new Wal Mart Store in Mexico City . . . this store had broken all sales records in its first week of operation. I watched as hundreds of middle-class Mexicans walked away with Fisher Price toys and Scott baby products . . . bars of Dove soap, and cans of Taster's choice coffee.
> (*CR*, 1993, H9986)[1]

After making the case that NAFTA would increase growth and employment, most advocates cited the need to support the economic liberalization plan being carried forward by Mexican President Carlos Salinas de Gortari. 'Keep in mind he [President Salinas] got a Ph.D. in economics here in the States, and that he has Chicago School of Economics in his thinking,' intoned Congressman Crane of Illinois, 'He is our kind of person, and he unilaterally reduced those tariffs' (*ibid.* H9991).

Conceding the authoritarian practices of the ruling Partido Revolucionario Institucional (PRI), advocates portrayed Salinas as an economic *and* political reformer, whose efforts at democratization would be more effective under the civilizing influence of economic interchange with the USA. The side agreements to NAFTA were heralded as the first attempt to include environment and labour rights in a trade agreement. Most emphasized by NAFTA supporters was the argument that growth spurred by increased trade would put upward pressure on wages, thereby increasing the size of the middle class who would demand better working conditions, a cleaner environment and greater democracy. Rejection of NAFTA would humiliate Salinas and undermine political stability. Renegotiation of the treaty, according to the advocates, was not politically feasible.

Most advocates closed with a patriotic flourish. Republican Whip Newt Gingrich of Georgia was typical, speaking of a 'magical historical, and defining moment', and 'the most important decision in U.S./Mexican relations in the 20th century' (*ibid.* H9876). Citing the Louisiana Purchase, the Alaska Territory and the Mexican–American War, NAFTA was presented as an opportunity to expand America through trade instead of territory. As Congressman Gingrich rhapsodized, 'I believe in dreaming heroic dreams. After all, I am an American. I chose to vote to increase American civilization' (*ibid.*).

The 200 representatives who voted against NAFTA were overwhelmingly concerned with the loss of American jobs and downward pressure on wages. The combination of cheap labour, low taxes and lax enforcement of labour and environmental regulations has already led many larger US firms to move production to Mexico (especially to the duty-free zone along the border), taking thousands of jobs with them. As NAFTA goes beyond tariff reduction and aims at economic integration, opponents argued, it will accelerate this process. For example, the treaty would remove barriers that previously prevented many medium and small manufacturing firms from relocating. Citing evidence that companies were ready to shift investment and production to Mexico if the agreement passed,[2] members related many personal histories of manufacturing workers who had lost their jobs and could not find new employment at wages adequate to support a middle-class family. Both on 17 November and through the preceding months, estimates of NAFTA's impact on jobs were widely debated by think tanks and the mass media.

Critics of the agreement framed the changing global economy not as a matter of competition versus protectionism but rather the terms on which the USA would compete. They claimed that NAFTA set up an uneven playing-field in which American communities and workers would have to compete for investment against a low-wage, undemocratic country that repressively kept wages from rising with productivity, with the explicit motive of attracting investment. The pact was depicted as part of a corporate assault on the hard-won achievements of the Ameircan labour, environmental and consumer movements. A commonly used line argued that 'NAFTA protects property and intellectual property rights, but not human rights' (*ibid.* H9898).

Most of the NAFTA opponents agreed that a trade agreement with Mexico was needed and shared the hope for a hemisphere-wide trade area. However, they demanded that any such agreement be fair and embrace wider development goals. In the words of Congressman Dingell from Michigan, 'A properly negotiated NAFTA could give us the tools to help solve the problems of illegal immigration, worker exploitation, and environmental degradation. A well crafted agreement could promote real democratic reforms in Mexico, create jobs, and enrich all three countries' (*ibid.* H9927).

Provisions were proposed to require Mexico to allow independent labour unions, allow outside monitoring of elections, permit right-to-know laws and greater public participation, enforce basic environmental regulation, as well as levy taxes on crossborder trade to fund clean-up and infrastructure development. The European Community's insistence that Portugal, Greece and Spain meet basic levels of democracy for full membership was cited as an example. Opponents insisted that Salinas would renegotiate NAFTA, as Mexico could not survive without access to US markets and would not risk turning to Japan or Europe.

The old-line liberalism at the core of NAFTA opposition was reflected in repeated references to President Kennedy's Alliance for Progress vision of development, in which social and political development was linked with economic growth. The closing portions of anti-NAFTA speeches were shrouded in much of the same patriotism, but emphasizing democracy and fair play. In the words of Congressmen David Bonior of Michigan, 'If we cannot stand up for the working people of America, if we cannot stand up for democracy in Mexico, if we cannot stand up for human rights around the world, what does this country stand for?' (*ibid.* H9859).

The growth paradigm

Beneath the polarized debate over NAFTA lay a remarkable consensus on the primacy of brute GNP growth as the goal of development for North America. The differences which emerged in the debate concerned the means of accomplishing this goal, and were largely driven by the political makeup of the constituencies of individual members.

No less an operative than Bill Daly, scion of Chicago's political machine and head of President Clinton's campaign for NAFTA, captured the gulf between citizens and leaders in observing that passage of the agreement would be a foregone conclusion in a secret ballot. As he put it, 'We have won the intellectual argument on this. The political argument is much tougher' (Blumenthal, 1993, p. 89). Confident in the nobility of their cause, NAFTA's élite constituency in all three countries deployed secrecy, massive public relations and legislative manoeuvring (e.g. fast track) to prevent popular derailment of their growth agenda.

Congressional opponents rarely questioned the human and ecological premises of the current development path. The intellectual reasoning behind the growth paradigm surfaced in the debate in the context of worldwide trade liberalization, which is based on classical free trade theory. This theory presumes that maximizing wealth should be the primary goal of nations. Four free-trade assumptions were affirmed by both sides during the debate:

1. A rising material standard of living translates into an improved human existence by expanding choices in material consumption, education, health care and all other components of welfare.
2. The market will ensure that increases in wealth 'trickle down' to all members of society (as in 'a rising tide lifts all boats' (*CR*, 1993, H9886). The terms 'growth' and 'development' were often used synonymously.
3. Liberal democracy supporting a free market is the ideal political-economic system, as the collapse of the Soviet model and the purported demise of state-driven development in the third world show: 'America was and still is the best idea the world has ever seen' (*ibid.* H10046).
4. Growth is an infinite process without limits. Technological substitution and human ingenuity will overcome any natural barriers to expansion.

If growth is the mainspring of US politics, the limits of the growth paradigm are nowhere more evident than in Mexico. Following revolution and reform earlier in the century, the ruling PRI party from the 1940s onward sustained an 'unrestrained commitment to rapid industrialization' (Mumme *et al.*, 1988, p. 7) and achieved an impressive average of 6 per cent annual GDP growth for some four decades. However, the bubble burst in 1982 as falling oil prices and the debt crisis devastated the Mexican economy. This economic collapse set the political stage for Salinas' efforts to rekindle growth through privatization and liberalization.

This 'religious faith' (Gregory, 1992, p. 159) in the growth paradigm has resulted in a severe environmental crisis that has been widely acknowledged even by its proponents (e.g. World Bank, 1992; Moffet, 1993). Water is everywhere being depleted and polluted, with aquifers being overdrawn at rates up to 20 times natural recharge in Northern areas (Goldrich and Carruthers, 1992, p. 110), and only 15–18 per cent of urban waste water receiving any sort of treatment (Durazo, Kamp and Land, 1993, p. 9). Soil erosion affects 80 per cent of Mexico's land area (as much as 30 per cent irreversibly; Kelly *et al.*, 1991, p. 54); 36 pesticides that are prohibited in other countries are regularly used, causing 13,000 poisonings and 700 deaths in 1989 alone (Durazo, Kamp and Land, 1993, p. 15); and deforestation is proceeding at a rate of 1.3 per cent a year (United Nations Development Program, 1993, p. 182). Mexico City has experienced a 485 per cent population growth since 1950 (World Resources Institute, 1986, p. 252), and the city's lethal air is worsening despite clean-up efforts.

The much-discussed free trade zone along the USA–Mexico border is perhaps the most illuminating example of the disastrous ecological consequences of 'growth first' development. Some 1,500 industrial firms (including more than half of the largest US companies) have set up operations in the zone, and economic growth has averaged 15 per cent annually since the early 1980s (French, 1993, p. 32; Kelly *et al.*, 1991, p. 52). Shanty towns have sprung up everywhere, most with no drainage, electricity, paved roads or running water. A widely quoted report by the American Medical Association called the area 'a virtual cesspool', citing the 206 million litres of raw sewage that are dumped daily into the Tijuana River, the New River and the Rio Grande, and an epidemic of infectious diseases (Farquharson, 1991, p. 34). Workers lack information and protective clothing for hazardous materials and illegal disposal is the norm (*ibid.*).

Mexico's emergency response system remains largely unprepared to prevent or mitigate industrial accidents. Examples include a gas explosion in 1984 at a Pemex factory on the outskirts of Mexico City which killed 452 people and injured thousands; a fire at a pesticide manufacturing plant in Córdoba, Veracruz, which hospitalized 400 people and forced over 1,500 to evacuate; an explosion in sewage ducts near a Pemex plant in Guadalajara in 1992 which killed nearly 200 people; and an accidental release of hydrochloric acid from a 50,000-litre tank at Mexicali's Química Orgánica pesticide plant in 1992. In the Mexicali case, the government ignored its legal responsibility to notify or evacuate the people affected; the incident only became public after being reported by a Mexican environmental group (Durazo, Kamp and Land, 1993, p. 23). In nearby Tijuana, an emergency preparedness official was fired in 1992 after publicizing hazards from an abandoned battery dump (Worthington and Schoijet, 1993, p. B-5), reflecting a broader pattern of repression against environmental investigators and activists (Schoijet and Worthington, 1993).

Table 6.1 *North American development indicators*

	Canada	Mexico	USA
Socioeconomic			
Population 1991 (millions)	27.3	83.3	252.7
Real GDP per capita ($)			
1960	7,758	2,870	9,983
1990	19,232	5,918	21,449
Income distribution (% share)			
Lowest 40%	17.5	11.9	15.7
Middle 40%	42.3	32.2	42.4
Highest 20%	40.2	55.9	41.9
Salaries and wages as % of manufacturing output (1990)	17	9	21
Education (% of age-group enrolled)			
Secondary – 1970	65	22	n.a.
– 1990	100	53	92
Tertiary – 1970	42	14	56
– 1990	70	14	75
Expenditure as % of GNP			
1960	4.6	1.2	5.3
1988	7.2	4.1	5.7
Scientists and engineers in research & development (1988)	61,130	16,679	949,200
Resources			
Energy consumption per capita (kg oil equivalent)			
1965	6,007	605	6,535
1990	10,009	1,300	7,882
Proven oil reserves (millions of barrels) 1987	4,806	54,880	27,280
Proven natural gas reserves (billions of cubic metres) 1990	7,578	2,060	4,930
CO_2 emissions (million metric tonnes)			
1965	68	n.a.	935
1989	444	304	4,826
Average annual marine catch (thousand metric tonnes) 1988	1,521	1,226	5,598
% change 1978–88	18	65	73

Sources: Industry and Development, *Global Report*, 1993/1994; UN Development Program, *Human Development Report*, 1993; World Bank, *World Development Report*, 1993 and *Atlas*, 1993; World Resources Institute, *World Resources*, 1986 and 1993.

Mexico's environmental crisis stems from an interplay of many forces, including an authoritarian and corrupt political system, but the priorities in the political economy which frame them is unambiguous: primacy for economic growth, and secondary, after-the-fact concern for environmental impacts. Environmental quality received only token consideration in the NAFTA, and only appeared at all as a result of grassroots pressure (Thorup, 1991). As in the USA, top leadership focused elsewhere, as President Salinas paid out $8 million to public relations giant Burson-Marsteller to green Mexico's image in the NAFTA campaign and manage the subsequent crisis of the Chiapas rebellion.[3]

While the shortcomings of the growth paradigm are particularly obvious in Mexico, their relevance is by no means limited to third-world countries. In his assessment of global ecosystems, Lester Brown (1992, p. 19) of the highly respected World Watch Institute notes that 'Every major indicator shows a deterioration in natural systems'. The place of North America in these processes is indicated by the data in Table 6.1, which point to the larger sources of global ecological decay. Three issues characterizing the region stand out.

The first is that industrialization itself, rather than the relative effectiveness of environmental policy, is at issue in the ecological crisis. The combined contribution of the USA and Canada to pollution and depletion of resources (as reflected in the energy consumption, CO_2 emissions and fisheries data) are far greater than those of Mexico, even though pollution per unit of output is generally lower. The sustainability of the 'growth first' development strategy hinges on the claim that environmental efficiency gains can sufficiently exceed production increases simultaneously to attain growing material consumption and improved environmental quality. The failures of the developed countries which have made the most concerted efforts to halt environmental degradation (Commoner, 1990) casts grave doubt on the claim that this is possible under growth first regionalization, which weakens regulatory and planning capabilities.

The growth paradigm also abstracts excessively from the social ecology of the North American region. Among the key features of North America are the massive size of the US economy and its unparalleled technological infrastructure, and the availability of primary resources (especially natural gas in Canada, and cheap labour and oil in Mexico) in the other NAFTA partners. The axioms of free trade theory predict that the unconstrained combination of these 'factor endowments' will raise welfare for all trading partners. In the real world, however, the mobilization of US capital and technology with Canadian and Mexican resources in an integrated regional economy will deepen a polluting and unsustainable fossil fuel economy, while the enhanced freedom for USA-based corporations that monopolize finance and technology in many industries will exacerbate economic inequality.

Finally, the growth paradigm ignores the role that politics can play in structuring social welfare. Social democracy and public well-being in North America are greatest in Canada and lowest in Mexico, as the data on educational expenditures and income distribution indicate. The steady southern migration of production facilities along the same axis thus impairs the linkages between social democratic politics and production, while strengthening the linkages between authoritarian politics and production. A Canadian fisheries unionist captured this issue in his comments on the increased export of unprocessed fish generated by the 1989 Canada–USA free trade pact:

> Think about it. The federal government spends $150 million a year to maintain the British Columbia fishing industry, which makes nearly $1 billion a year. If that value starts to move across the border, why should the feds spend the money here on research, habitat protection and salmon enhancement for the American worker's benefit? This country stands to lose a whole resource.
>
> (Pro-Canada Network, 1990, p. 1)

In sum, the ecological consequences of growth first development can be described as the steady accrual of an environmental debt. North Americans are in effect subsidizing growth by deferring the costs of a clean environment and depleting their natural capital. Like any debt accumulation, a growing environmental debt is not sustainable over the long run. It can only be amortized if development is shifted to a sustainable path.

Sustainability in Congress?

The concept of sustainable development has been justifiably criticized as lacking operational content and co-opting or deflecting fundamental challenges to growth first development (see Chapter(s) 2 and 3 in this volume). Yet debate and action around the issue has generated a broad consensus that current development paths cannot be maintained, while framing many issues in terms that challenge the growth paradigm. The World Commission on Environment and Development (World Commission, 1987), for example, observes that rapid growth combined with deteriorating income distribution and ecological conditions may be worse than slower growth that addresses the needs of the poor and sustains the resource base (*ibid*, p. 53). Another mainstream group, the Business Council on Sustainable Development (Schmidheiny, 1992, p. 3), advocates a 'precautionary principle' that acknowledges uncertainty about the irreversibility of degradation by moderating the demands placed on natural systems. The burden of proof must shift on to those wanting to push the limits, and away from those wishing to prevent their violation.

How much has this discourse affected Congress? The concept of sustainable development was mentioned in the preamble of the NAFTA text, but the only direct reference to it in the entire debate on 17 November was made by Congresswoman Unsoeld of Washington. Issues of sustainability none the less undergirded many of the specific items of contention on 17 November. The larger discourse has thus seeped into Congress, but comes nowhere close to defining any significant agendas.

The marginalization of sustainability was most obviously reflected in the exclusive association of environmental problems with Mexico during the NAFTA debate. The environmental and social crisis in Mexico was acknowledged by members on both sides, who called the border region 'an environmental time bomb' (*CR*, 1993, H9888) and cited the social debts arising from structural adjustment policies and 'decades of development with little or no regard for the environment and social needs' (*ibid*. H9897). But these flaws were depicted as shortcomings in a system that could be reformed. By isolating Mexico when critiques of the development process emerged, members uncritically positioned the USA as the source of the solution.

The challenges posed by sustainability concerns to the growth paradigm were contained, deflected or ignored in numerous additional ways. Critics of the side agreements who invoked President Kennedy's Alliance for Progress as a model for equitable development, for example, ignored the fact that the alliance 'lost its way' (Levinson and de Onis, 1970) and never accomplished its objectives, thus citing a failed programme as an alternative to what they saw as a bad NAFTA proposal. There was substantial discussion of the need to deal with Mexico's pollution, but even here advocates of such steps (which in any event were not adopted) called for regulatory changes and pollution control, rather than shifting from after-the-fact clean-up to a policy framework based on resource conservation and pollution prevention. The increased exploitation and unsustainable use of resources such as energy that NAFTA encourages was ignored.[4] And the idea that production should aim for material sufficiency rather than unrestrained consumption was utterly absent from the NAFTA debate. The Wal Mart example cited above went entirely unchallenged, and with it the premise that Mexican emulation of USA consumerism is a sign of progress rather than a threat to sustainability.

The majority, of course, reaffirmed their commitment to the growth paradigm. The treaty need not require even such basic policies as right-to-know laws, because Mexico would inevitably develop such practices as it became richer. Neither side displayed any sense of urgency over Mexico's crisis, and both assumed that Mexico could develop along the same lines as the USA. As Congressmen Inslee of Washington stated, 'Americans believe in progress. Mexico is not yet America but it is making progress' (*CR*, 1993, H9925). Any implication of the precautionary principle was dwarfed by a commitment to rapid expansion that ignored its connection to growing global environmental problems, such as expanding CO_2 emissions and toxic waste build-up. Responsibility towards future generations was invoked, but in terms of material wealth, not a healthy resource base.

On the other hand, supporters axiomatically assumed that growth would democratize politics. Almost all the supporters demonstrated a conception of development as something that is done for people: the government and business establishment ensure employment. The notion of people as full citizens shaping their own development was restricted to entrepreneurial activity, an important but incomplete part of participatory development. The closed decision-making of NAFTA institutions was called 'a commonsense business approach to solving disputes' (*ibid*. H9829), and was not an issue for most NAFTA supporters.

Perhaps the most telling indictment was Congress's failure even to mention North America's indigenous peoples in the 17 November debate. In doing so they ignored a worldwide movement which links the survival of indigenous cultures with a shift from growth first to sustainable development (e.g. World Commission, 1987, p. 114). From northern Canada to southern Mexico, the main effect of 'growth first' progress over five centuries has been to marginalize and eliminate rather than sustain these cultures, which is precisely why they rarely warrant space on the agenda at the political centre: their plight casts doubt on the religion of growth. It thus came as no surprise that an armed uprising occurred in Chiápas, Mexico's southernmost state, a mere 44 days after the NAFTA debate. By allowing US corn (the production of which is subsidized, polluting and energy intensive) into the Mexican market, NAFTA threatens to finish off what remains of the Chiápas subsistence economy of corn and beans. In the stark rendering of a Zapatista leader, 'The free-trade agreement is a death certificate for the Indian peoples of Mexico' (Nelson 19, p. 18).

In sum, three things stand out in the NAFTA debate at the political centre. First, the vast majority in Congress actively subscribes to the growth paradigm. Second, opposition to NAFTA was expressed without seriously questioning growth first development. Finally, sustainability has none the less entered congressional discourse, albeit in a marginal and largely unacknowledged way. These results reflect the reality that Congress responds to organized political forces, not textbooks or commission reports. The corporate agenda which normally dominates policy formation is readily visible in NAFTA, and members were largely subservient to it by formulating the problem as one of maximizing growth to maintain employment in a fiercely competitive global economy.[5] Environmental concerns were thus relegated to the subordinate space which they customarily occupy on the policy agenda, generating ineffective 'side' agreements (Kelly, 1994) that were little more than a sop to pacify critics.

Beyond top-down politics

Greater public participation in development is the most important mechanism to ensure the equity, justice and sustainability of new growth. This priority stems from a recognition that current political institutions are responsible for a large part of the failure of development efforts. The hierarchical, top-down and élite-driven model treats development as something that must be done for people. Instead, sustainable development must be directed from the bottom up; it must be development of people (education, health, etc.), for people (equitably distributed) and by the people (democratic participation). Working people and the poor should be seen as creators of their own development rather than one of its residuals, with employment being a process of empowerment rather than a by-product of production (UN Development Program, 1993, pp. 3, 39). Finally, development must make real strides at eliminating poverty, as a matter of social justice and to break the dependency on unsustainable resource use.

People-driven development clearly requires open and accessible markets. These in turn are based on equitable access to healthcare, education and job training, which require a simultaneous opening and decentralization of political institutions. Right-to-know and freedom-of-information laws that apply to governments as well as private enterprises must guarantee transparency. Moreover, the right to know must be accompanied by the ability to act. Communities must have real power in the consideration, oversight and evaluation of development projects that affect them. As the Business Council put it, 'New development paths must be based on local initiative and supported by international cooperation' (Schmidheiny, 1992, p. 161).

Are there social forces which can promote participatory public discourse and policy deliberation in the arcane realms of trade policy? There is no simple answer to this question, but there are some obvious considerations. Given the deeply embedded character of the growth paradigm, moving beyond it will not take place through existing social and political channels, or modest variations on them. A broader social movement which changes people's visions of the possible and mobilizes them for direct action will be required. We see social movements as forging four types of linkages.

First, social movements have the potential to link issues which are often conceived as separate problems. For example, action against the concentration of hazardous substances in impoverished communities links social justice and environmental quality. Second, social movements link groups that have traditionally been isolated. Consider, for example, the case of Freedom Summer in 1964, which brought together white, northern college youth (disproportionately Jewish) with mostly rural, southern blacks during the US civil rights movement, forging relationships and experiences which animated that movement as well as the student and anti-war mobilizations in the late 1960s (Eyerman and Jamison, 1991, pp. 120–46). Third, social movements can integrate action at different levels of social organization and political authority. This is crucial in transcending a long-standing problem that is exacerbated by globalization: to see only the local is to be reactive; to see only the global can be abstract and irrelevant. Finally, social movements connect alternative visions, political and technological opportunities, and a participatory impulse that is always present (but often latent) in individuals and communities (*ibid.* pp. 70–8).

Democratic openings

The most promising development in environmental politics of the past decade, both in the USA (Gottlieb, 1993) and the third world (Rich, 1994), is the rise of movements for environmental justice which have forged precisely these kinds of ties.[6] While they remain very much on the periphery of most power structures, their accomplishments are noteworthy. These include many successful campaigns against expensive, high-tech development projects such as dams, superhighways and hazardous waste facilities; advocacy of alternatives such as recycling, renewable energy and community-based economic development; and changes in the policies of even the most impenetrable bastions of global capitalism, such as the World Bank (*ibid.*). These movements typically emerge in opposition to state and corporate forces seeking to manage environmental quality by technocratic means which leave their own privileged position intact.

In the NAFTA case, the initial proposal for a trade agreement unintentionally created a forum for critics of neoliberalism. Much of the energy for this came from grassroots activists in all three countries, who forged trinational networks to advocate sustainable approaches to trade liberalization ('fair trade'). These forces successfully expanded the trade policy agenda to include environment, human rights and labour standards (Thorup, 1991; Goldrich, 1994).

The response to this mobilization at the political centre was to co-opt and divide. Major political leaders, including the Clinton administration, effectively split the environmental opposition with the side agreements and other concessions (see Figure 6.1). By September 1993, this approach had succeeded

The two principal outcomes of NAFTA's environmental side agreements are trade-dispute settlement panels and a North American Development Bank to fund infrastructure projects (principally water and sewage treatment) in the USA–Mexico border region. The trade panels will comprise appointed experts operating with no public input in the settlement of disputes. Their weakness as instruments for enforcing environmental standards was best summarized by Mexico's chief NAFTA negotiator, Jaime Serra Puche. Speaking to an audience of Mexican legislators concerned about environmental regulation under NAFTA, Serra Puche observed that the dispute settlement process was sufficiently complex to make it unlikely that trade sanctions would ever be levied (*Mexico and NAFTA Report*, 23 September 1993).

NAD Bank projects will be guided by an appointed, binational Border Environment Cooperation Commission (BECC). A number of concerns about BECC and the NAD Bank have emerged in our interviews and other commentary on BECC: 1) the focus is narrow (water quality in the border environment); 2) environmental expertise is in a small minority on the BECC; and 3) the appointees will represent the political forces which promoted NAFTA. One detailed analysis of proposals to fund border clean-up over the recent past, including those incorporated into the side agreements, notes that past promises have failed to materialize, and that there is little reason to expect even the modest quantities anticipated in the NAD Bank's enabling legislation to appear in this case (Mander, 1993). This outcome is consistent with a pattern of empty promises for environmental funding in other cases, most notably the World Bank (Rich, 1994). As one environmental leader observed nearly a year after NAFTA passed, 'During the debate we kept saying that unless trade is contingent on progress, progress won't occur . . . There has been very little progress' (*The New York Times*, 17 October 1994).

Figure 6.1   *The politics of co-optation: NAFTA's side agreements*

in securing support for NAFTA from most of the national environmental organizations in the USA (Natural Resources Defense Council, Audobon Society, etc.). This reproduced and widened a gulf which had emerged over the previous decade between grassroots advocates of environmental justice and professionalized Washington-based lobbyists (Bleifuss, 1994). With the most visible environmental groups in support of the agreement, however, the political pressures were greater on other fronts. In particular, the Clinton administration was able in the last weeks before the NAFTA vote to focus on cutting deals with various economic interests who were threatened by Mexican imports (such as sugar-beet growers in Florida). The last-minute deals turned a likely defeat into a comfortable victory.

These events invite the cynical observation that the co-opt-and-divide strategy worked, but it should also be noted that the continuing travails of leadership in all three NAFTA countries demonstrate a flagging legitimacy that has left the door open to alternative forces. In the USA, for example, Bush served only one term, and Clinton was elected in a three-way race with only 43 per cent of the vote. In Mexico, Salinas' election in 1988 is widely recognized to have resulted from electoral fraud. His hand-picked successor, Luis Donaldo Colosio, was assassinated in a Tijuana campaign rally in March 1994, and the ultimate PRI candidate (Ernesto Zedillo) won the August 1994 presidential election with 49 per cent of the vote, the least ever for a PRI candidate. So low is the credibility of Mexico's political system that Zedillo's first promise (like Salinas before him) was to reform the system that had just elected him. In Canada, free trade architect Brian Mulroney rushed NAFTA ratification through Parliament, then resigned his leadership position in the hopes that public wrath at his trade agreements would not affect his Progressive Conservative Party in upcoming national elections. The Progressive Conservatives none the less were delivered an astounding defeat in the October 1993 elections, forcing the formation of a coalition leadership headed by the Liberal Party.[7] Combined with broader evidence of growing social and political instability (the election of separatists in Quebec; the Chiápas insurrection, the assassination in September 1994 of the PRI secretary-general and the collapse of the peso in Mexico; and the failure of various Clinton reform initiatives in the USA), it seems unlikely that the passage of NAFTA will successfully tighten the political lid on questions of sustainability and social justice for North America.

Indeed, NAFTA politics generated a remarkable mobilization by those whose backyards and everyday lives are most affected by growth-driven regionalization. In the 'Third Country' (Miller, 1981) along the USA–Mexico border, for example, an entire binational, social movement infrastructure has emerged (Land, 1994).[8] There is a strong environmental component to this movement, which is largely driven by the health impacts of the polluted border environment described earlier in this chapter. However, this environmental concern is increasingly tied to social justice issues and organizations in which ethnic, crossnational, class and gender politics are central themes. Among the issues tied to environment and health are worker rights (e.g. right to know about toxics in the workplace), economic justice (e.g. exploiting low-wage workers in hazardous industries) and gender discrimination (e.g. environmental carcinogens which cause breast cancer). This activism, then, is one concrete example of the growing environmental justice movement mentioned above. The environmentally orientated organizations within this loose network are active at everything from service delivery (tree planting, recycling, cancer prevention and counselling) to policy development and political mobilization.[9]

The staying power and long-range impact of such networks remains an open issue, but the fact that they have served as effective vehicles of popular participation is beyond doubt. Key activists in a US network (the Citizens Trade Campaign) which opposed NAFTA, for example, were overwhelmingly inclined to interpret their involvement in the coalition as a success, even though NAFTA was ultimately enacted. In their minds, the campaign and the broader forces to which it was linked succeeded against overwhelming odds in securing the votes in the House necessary to prevent passage, and were only defeated in the final days before the vote through the extraordinary efforts of President Clinton. Most activists in this network were especially pleased that their own individual organizations (which ranged from environmental groups to labour unions) learnt immensely from the new linkages created by the coalition effort, and felt energized rather than defeated by the experience (Goldrich, 1994).

Another encouraging sign was the integration by the incipient fair-trade movement of local and global issues in ways that gave voice to practical concerns about health and environmental quality, while advancing political empowerment and formulating policy alternatives. For example, we noted earlier that the focus on Mexico (and especially the border region) in congressional debate marginalized the environmental effects of industrialization as a 'third world' issue. Activists were thus put in the position of helping focus attention on environmental destruction along the border, while pointing to the larger forces responsible for this destruction, as well as the North American scope of the ecological degradation for which they are responsible. As one of them put it:

> Perhaps it is ironic that while many national environmental groups put the spotlight on the border environment, Border Ecology Project and other border groups worked hard to expand the NAFTA debate beyond the border region to address issues related to standards and enforcement, natural resource protection, and public participation in all NAFTA member countries. In the process . . . an unprecedented number of new and effective environmental coalitions were developed, linking border groups with organizations in Washington, DC, Mexico City and elsewhere.[10]

It is of course impossible to predict how this activism will develop over time. To summarize our discussion of participatory politics, however, we will note that social movements are not merely a theoretically important component of sustainable development; the makings of a movement focused on North American regionalization are a practical reality.

Conclusion

In an era of globalized production systems, national states which have been the principal form of political organization for four centuries are severely compromised in their ability to promote and protect public well-being. Increased trade, and the institutions which facilitate it, are central to this globalization process. Supranational institutions such as the European Community which include explicit social welfare and environmental standards and agencies have an important, albeit underdeveloped, role to play in sustaining a viable public sphere amid these changes. However, an informed and active citizenry at the local level is the cornerstone of a viable civic realm in a global society. The consequences of globalization are comprehensible and concrete in the locality, and the potential for citizen-driven politics is greatest there. The central requirement for transition to sustainability is therefore widening the scope for meaningful and effective participation in policy and planning which links the locality to global forces.

The corporate agenda remains dominant in the trade environment arena, but grassroots mobilization has been surprisingly rapid, effective and rewarding. The fall of the Berlin Wall shows that political systems can unravel with amazing speed. The participatory impulse is critical to making such crises into opportunities. To quote ecological economist Manfred Max Neef, who ran for the Chilean Presidency in 1993, 'This system is on a collision course with itself, it will collapse. Our job is to be ready with an alternative'.[11]

Acknowledgements

Our thanks to Michael Black, Frank Fischer, Geof Land and Eduardo Silva for their comments on prior drafts of this chapter.

Notes

1. This Wal Mart store is the largest in the world, covering 6 acres with 72 cash registers. Two more planned stores were cancelled due to the peso devaluation and economic crisis of early 1995. Nearly half of the merchandise sold is made in the USA.

2. Of the 455 senior US corporate executives polled, 40 per cent were planning to shift at least some production to Mexico (*The Wall Street Journal*, 21 September 1993).

3. Burson-Marsteller is well known for its image damage control in environmental disasters, most notably Three-Mile Island, Union Carbide's Bhopal disaster killing 4,000 people and the *Exxon Valdez* spill (Nelson, 1994, p. 20).

4. Greenpeace (Alexander and Stump, 1992) stands virtually alone in observing that NAFTA will substantially deepen dependency on fossil fuels and undermine progress towards the development of renewable energy.

5. Congressman Colins of Georgia aptly summarized the pressures that every member of the House is feeling: '"Lack of job creation," that quote alone should be enough to send chills down the spine of every legislator in this Chamber. Job creation is what our economy is all about' (*CR*, 1993, H9946).

6. Europe poses a somewhat different story owing to the greater presence of progressive forces in the state and the relative (compared to North America) success of green parties in electoral politics.

7. The Progressive Conservatives took just two seats in these elections, fewer than the 12 required to maintain recognition as an official party. A quip now making the rounds in Canada goes as follows: 'What's the difference between the PCs and a Honda Civic? The Civic has two more seats.'

8. Of 34 typical organizations in this infrastructure for which we were able to obtain detailed data, 24 were founded since 1985, and most of those since 1990.

9. Examples of such activism include La Red Fronterizo de Salud y Ambiente in the western border region, whose member organizations worked locally, nationally and internationally to shape the content of NAFTA; the Southwest Network for Environmental and Economic Justice in Albuquerque, New Mexico, which organized simultaneous anti-NAFTA demonstrations in cities on both sides of the border; the Environmental Committee of the Tijuana/ San Diego region (California and Baja California), whose membership debated NAFTA and provided input concerning environmental provisions; the Centro de Estudios Fronterizos y Promoción de los Derechos Humanos in Reynosa, Tamaulipas, which kept a database on NAFTA and published materials on human rights concerns in the context of regionalization; and BorderLinks, a faith-based organization in Tucson, Arizona, which arranged sustained visitations of US citizen delegations with Mexican residents in the border region to exchange information and ideas around free trade and related issues.

10. Geof Land of the Border Ecology Project, in correspondence with the authors dated 12 September 1994.

11. Personal interview with Manfred Max Neef, 2 January 1994.

References

Alexander, C. and Stump, K. (1992) *The North American Free Trade Agreement and Energy Trade*. Greenpeace, Washington, DC.

Bleifuss, J. (1994) 'Talk of politics and toxics,' *In These Times*, 21 March–3 April.

Blumenthal, S. (1993) 'The making of a machine: how Bill Daly helped Clinton win NAFTA, Cook County style, *The New Yorker*, 29 November.

Brown, L. (1992) 'Economics versus ecology,' *Eco Decision.* 19.

Commoner, B. (1990) *Making Peace with the Planet.* Knopf, New York.

Congressional Record (1993) Vol. 139, no. 160, Parts 1 and 2, 17 November. United States Government Printing Office, Washington, DC.

Durazo, L., Kamp, D. and Land, G. (1993) 'Environmental and health issues in the interior of Mexico: options for transnational safeguards' (working draft). Border Ecology Project, Bisbee, Ariz.

Eyerman, R. and Jamison, A. (1991) *Social Movements: A Cognitive Approach.* Polity Press, Cambridge.

Farquharson, M. (1991) 'Cleaning up the border,' *Business Mexico,* August.

Goldrich, D. (1994) 'Report to activists of the Citizens Trade Campaign.' Mimeo.

Goldrich, D. and Carruthers, D.V. (1992) 'Sustainable development in Mexico?, *Latin American Perspectives*, Vol. 19, no. 1.

Gottlieb, R. (1993) *Forcing the Spring: The Transformation of the American Environmental Movement.* Island Press, Covelo, Calif.

Gregory, M. (1992) 'Environment, sustainable development, public participation and the NAFTA: a retrospective,' *Journal of Environmental Law and Litigation*, Vol. 7.

Kelly, M. (1994) *NAFTA's Environmental Side Agreement: A Review and Analysis of Key Provisions.* Texas Center for Policy Studies, Austin, Tex.

Kelly, M., Kamp, D., Gregory, M. and Rich, J. (1991) 'US–Mexico free trade negotiations and the environment: exploring the issues,' *Columbia Journal of World Business,* Vol. 26, no. 2.

Krugman, P. (1993) 'The uncomfortable truth about NAFTA; it's foreign policy, stupid!', *Foreign Affairs*, Vol. 5, no. 13.

Land, G. (1994) 'North American free trade and the environment: border environmental groups and the NAFTA.' Border Ecology Project, Bisbee, AZ.

Levinson, J. and de Onis, J. (1970) *The Alliance that Lost its Way.* Quadrangle, Chicago.

Mander, K. (1993) 'Opportunities and promises on the free trade trail.' Institute for Agricultural and Trade Policy, Minneapolis.

Miller, T. (1981) *On the Border: Portraits of America's Southwestern Frontier.* University of Arizona Press, Tucson.

Nelson, J. (1994) 'The Zapatistas versus the spin-doctors.' *The Canadian Forum* (March).

Pro-Canada Network (1990) 'Pro-Canada fleet launched to defend West Coast fishery.' *The Pro-Canada Dossier* (15 August).

Rich, B. (1993) *Mortgaging the Earth: The World Bank, Environmental Impoverishment and the Crisis of Development.* Beacon Press, Boston.

Schmidheiny, S. with the Business Council for Sustainable Development (1992) *Changing Course: A Global Business Perspective on Development and the Environment.* MIT Press, Cambridge, MA.

Schoijet, M. and Worthington, R. (1993) 'Globalization of science and the repression of scientists in Mexico.' *Science, Technology and Human Values.*

Thorup, C. (1991) 'The politics of free trade and the dynamics of cross-border coalitions in US-Mexico relations.' *Columbia Journal of World Business.*

United Nations Development Program (1993) *Human Development Report, 1993.* Oxford University Press, New York.

World Bank (1992) *World Bank Staff Appraisal 10005-ME* (19 March) (cited in Durazo, *et al., op. cit.:* 1).

World Commission on Environment and Development (1987) *Our Common Future.* Oxford University Press, New York.

World Resources Institute (1986) *World Resources 1986.* Basic Books, New York.

World Resources Institute (1993) *World Resources, 1992–1993.* Basic Books, New York.

Worthington, R. and Schoijet, M. (1993) 'The silence of the labs.' *Los Angeles Times*, 1 July.

7

Environmental policy in Chile: the politics of the comprehensive law

EDUARDO SILVA

University of Missouri–St Louis, USA

After decades of neglect environmental issues are rapidly making their way on to the policy agendas of Latin American governments. Much of the change is due to growing concern over the ecological degradation that has accompanied traditional economic development models. Yet developing countries are understandably reluctant to forgo economic growth in the interest of environmental protection. In order to overcome the divisive issue of growth versus environment, the development community formulated the concept of sustainable development: growth with environmental protection and natural resource conservation. Many of the environmental policy prescriptions of developing nation governments spring from this concept. However, because there is no single, technologically correct alternative to traditional developmental paths the environment can become a highly politicized issue area.

This chapter tackles two general questions through the prism of environmental politics during the administration of Patricio Aylwin (1990–4). This was Chile's first democratic government since the military dictatorship of General Augusto Pinochet (1973–89) – a regime that essentially ignored environmental issues. The first question asks, what are the key axes of conflict over environmental policy in developing countries? This chapter argues that differences in two competing views of sustainable development – a market-friendly and a progressive, alternative one – lie at the core of dissension in environmental politics. At issue are relative degrees of continuity and change from established socioeconomic and state-institutional practices. The chapter contends that the principles, norms and institutional structure established by Chile's comprehensive environmental law, enacted in March 1994, facilitate a market-friendly approach to environmental policy and sustainable development. However, this was by no means the only possible outcome when the policy debate began in 1990. Supporters of the alternative approach to sustainable development initially appeared to be in a strong position to have influenced the result more than they actually achieved.

Their failure to translate that advantage into greater influence in the policy-making process leads to the second general question. How and when do ideas, social coalitions, state institutions and international actors influence policy outcomes in the environmental politics of developing nations? In the case of Chile, international actors (principally the US government and the World Bank) played an indirect, or permissive, role in the shaping of policy agendas through 'green' conditionality on aid and trade negotiations. Ideas also shaped the policy agenda. They offered diagnoses of the problem and policy prescriptions. As a result, competing coalitions of state and social actors formed around the market-friendly and alternative interpretations of sustainable development in Aylwin's administration. The final outcome largely depended on the fact that the former controlled a larger measure of state-institutional and economic power.

In order to develop these arguments, the chapter first defines the market-friendly and alternative approaches to sustainable development and fleshes out the general interpretative framework. The next section shows that the debate over Chile's environmental framework law centred on market-friendly versus alternative views of sustainable development. The chapter then turns to an analysis of how and when external factors, ideas, social coalitions and state institutions affected the results of the political conflict over the law. The concluding sections briefly explore the likely policy consequences of the general law for future environmental policy in Chile – including foreign and domestic policy on ozone depletion – and the implications of the Chilean case for other Latin American countries. Here, the role of the World Bank in environmental politics will be examined further.

Two approaches to sustainable development

The main axis of conflict over environmental policy in Latin America is rooted in two competing conceptualizations of sustainable development. They stand at the core of the political struggles over how to deal with environmental and ecological problems. In general terms, the concept of sustainable development attempts to ease the tension between economic development and environmental integrity. The well documented effects of poverty on environmental degradation first gave birth to the concept, as conceived and popularized by the Brundtland Commission (1987). The report stressed the need for an economic development model capable of meeting the basic needs of a developing country's population, while maintaining its stock of natural resources so as not to rob future generations of their use. For policy and programmatic purposes, development economists broke the concept of sustainable development down into three inter-related components: a healthy growing economy (which may necessitate structural adjustment), a commitment to social equity (or meeting basic needs) and protection of the environment (Weaver and O'Keefe, 1991).

From this generally shared conceptual basis, environmental policies tend to cluster around two distinct conceptualizations of the relationship among economic growth, equity and environment. The dominant view, shared by the top government leadership and multilateral lending institutions such as the World Bank, essentially reduces equity and environmental considerations to market-friendly economic growth (World Bank, 1992a). This approach offers the path of least resistance from established economic development models, particularly those of developed countries, but also those of developing nations.

According to the market-friendly view, to achieve rapid growth developing countries must engage in free-market economic restructuring – that is, reduce state intervention, build market economies, integrate them into world markets, pay careful attention to private property rights and increase foreign direct investment. From this perspective the environmental consequences of economic development are considered to be unfortunate side-effects that must be ameliorated. The solution centres on the addition of technologies capable of mitigating the environmental impact of existing industrial processes (end-of-pipe technologies), rather than finding substitutes for them or alternative methods of production (World Bank, 1992a).

By the same token, social equity concerns are also largely reduced to rapid economic growth based on free-market economic restructuring. At its core, the market-friendly view of sustainable development argues that aggregate economic growth brought about by market-orientated structural reforms will improve national income (and therefore housing, education and wealth), and that rising income levels will allow people to become concerned about environmental degradation. Once they become environmentally conscious (and as democracy consolidates) they will be able to organize into interest groups to press for environmental legislation (World Bank, 1991; 1992a; 1992b).

The market-friendly conceptualization of sustainable development advances clear-cut policy prescriptions for dealing with pollution and natural resource use. Because of its strong advocacy of end-of pipe technology, it stresses solutions that emphasize technical expertise to issues framed in a public-goods perspective – water, air, soil, fisheries, forests, etc. In this way its proponents hope to obscure the political nature of the decisions that governments must make. Additional policy recommendations include the promotion of private property rights over co-operative ventures and communal ownership, as well as the elimination of government subsidies that lead to natural resource degradation. Equally important are calls for a drastic reduction in the role of the state to minimize the impact of actual and potential bureaucratic incompetence in the design and implementation of environmental policy; and then to strengthen the institutional capacities in sharply reduced spheres of state action (Hardin, 1968; Repetto, 1988; Mahar, 1989).

The alternative approach to sustainable development takes a different view on most of these dimensions. At its core, it rejects the argument that social equity and environmental quality can be reduced to market-orientated economic growth. It takes each of the central terms of sustainable development – economic growth, social equity and environment – into account in their own right, and then seeks to find reinforcing linkages between them. The alternative approach agrees that healthy economic growth is essential for sustainable development. But it questions whether the orthodox view of free-market economic development is the best path. It is not so much that they do not welcome technological improvements and a more realistic economic accounting of environmental losses as means to reduce environmental degradation (World Resources Institute, 1991) – they fully realize that these techniques can be useful. The concern is more that if policy focuses mainly on those techniques, rapid economic growth on the periphery (and in the centre) will be ultimately self-defeating in terms of environmental and human sustainability (Redclift and Goodman, 1991).

There are a number of reasons for this. First, the emphasis on end-of-pipe technology offers few incentives for firms to attack one of the roots of the world's ecological problems: existing industrial processes. Moreover, these technologies are expensive and therefore less likely to be widely used in developing nations. Second, the history of capitalist development suggests market-based economic growth by itself is a poor tool to reduce either social inequalities, especially in developing nations, or to promote rapid growth. Thus, third, higher levels of state involvement in the promotion of social justice and in industrial policy to guide economic development seem appropriate.

In the alternative approach, more ecologically centred values infuse the diagnosis of the problems and solutions to economic growth, social equity and environmental sustainability. With respect to economic growth, for example, end-of-pipe technology should be supplemented with effective incentives for firms to adopt safer substitutes for toxic industrial processes, and new 'cleaner' products, in short, pollution prevention. Moreover, economic development plans should emphasize smaller-scale over large-scale enterprise, and proactive rather than reactive strategies (Browder, 1989; Commoner, 1990; Hurtubia, 1991; Max-Neef, 1991; Redclift and Goodman, 1991).

The problem of social equity reaches beyond a concern for jobs. It is also about quality of life and measures of human dignity. Thus the struggle over the environment is inextricably linked to larger issues of social, economic and cultural self-determination. Policy prescriptions call for greater sensitivity to urban and rural grassroots development projects that promote local self-reliance and control over a resource in order to achieve a more equitable distribution of wealth. This dovetails with the previously mentioned emphasis on smaller-scale enterprise. In rural areas there is an added emphasis on technologies that mimic natural processes. In urban areas self-help groups for environmental health, clean-up and improvement (green belts) are encouraged (Ghai and Vivian, 1992; Friedmann and Rangan, 1993; Ghai, 1994).

The progressive alternative approach to sustainable development is more holistic than the market-friendly one with respect to the linkages among economic growth, social equity and environment. At the heart of the alternative approach lies the conviction that the ecological impact of human activities cuts across economic, as well as social and political boundaries. Consequently, sector-specific environmental policy must take into account how policies in other sectors affect the proposed project. Each new policy is in essence a reform measure that requires the participation and co-ordinated action of several state institutions.

In conclusion, the market-friendly approach demands the least amount of change from established practices, while the alternative perspective requires more extensive reforms that cut across economic sectors and are more explicitly based in ecological principles. Aside from economic restructuring, the former basically makes few demands on established patterns of capitalist development, either with respect to industrial processes, consumption patterns, the structure of the social order or with respect to placing ecological principles more at the centre of the problem-solving process. The progressive alternative approach, by contrast, makes far more demands on all these dimensions.

Politics and environmental policy outcomes in developing nations

This chapter examines when and how ideas, state institutions, socioeconomic groups and external conditions influenced policy outcomes in the debate over Chile's general environmental law. Essentially, I argue they are all significant (Schamis, 1991; Smith, 1991; Haggard and Kaufman, forthcoming). The relationship between them is basically that of a cascading effect (Haggard, 1990).

International variables usually play a catalytic or permissive role in policy outcomes. The US government and the World Bank – the major external players in the Americas – are increasingly linking trade and aid to market economic restructuring and action on environmental issues (Muñoz and Rosenberg, 1993; Muñoz, 1994). Policy-makers in developing countries are beginning to respond. Given these conditions, there is considerable external pressure to adopt a market-friendly approach to sustainable development. The actual outcomes, however, depend on domestic politics.

In the next step of the cascade, ideas give content to policy – they offer both cognitive frameworks for the diagnosis of problems and a range of policy options to solve them (Hall, 1989). In the environmental issue area, market-friendly and alternative conceptions of sustainable development advance distinctive bases from which to articulate the diagnoses and solutions to environmental problems. Which one 'wins', however, depends on the relative power resources that the supporters of these views can command.

From this perspective, the power of contending coalitions in environmental politics depends on three inter-related factors. The first one is their relative place within the government's political coalition. From an instrumentalist point of view this influences a second element of power – appointments to state agencies (Miliband, 1969). Third, analysis must also consider the economic and organizational power of the social actors that support one or the other view of sustainable development (Ghai and Vivian, 1992; Friedmann and Rangan, 1993). A well organized, economically significant private sector may be an effective advocate for market-friendly environmental policies. Their influence, however, is also conditioned on the relationship of the private sector to the governing coalition. For example, if the government's philosophy and electoral coalition draw heavily from organized lower-class groups in rural and urban areas, sustainable development policies may take on a more alternative cast.

Chile's comprehensive environmental law

The debate over Chile's comprehensive environmental law centred on market-friendly versus alternative views of sustainable development. This was clear with respect to three elements of the bill: 1) its guiding principles; 2) the degree of precision with which the bill outlined a framework for action – from the vague and general to specific instructions; and 3) the attributes of the state institution charged with handling environmental and natural resource affairs, whether it should be a cabinet-level position or a co-ordinating committee within an existing ministry. This section of the chapter summarizes these policy debates and argues that the final bill (and the law itself) conformed more to the market-orientated approach. The next section examines why that outcome prevailed, even though the supporters of the alternative view initially seemed to have been in a strong position to influence policy formulation.

What principles did the supporters of the market-friendly view advance in the debate over Chile's comprehensive law? For one, they attempted to limit the environmental problem to pollution control. This allowed them to focus the debate on end-of-pipe technologies – which business can control – and to avoid the wider debates over sustainable development. A number of additional principles sought to protect the private sector from restrictions on its productive activities and its sociopolitical prerogatives. First, market-friendly proponents privileged private property rights over environmental concerns. Second, they sought to minimize restrictions on natural resource exploitation. Third, market supporters argued that the private sector should be protected from punitive action because their cost impinged on production and economic growth. Fourth, they argued that citizen participation should be minimized; only expert opinion should be considered. Fifth, they advocated a minimum degree of state involvement, and they sought to ensure ample institutionalized access to the policy-making process for business (Geisse, 1987; Renovación Nacional, 1990; Güell, 1991; Infante, 1992; Undurraga, 1991; Agüero, 1992; Sociedad de Fomento Fabril, 1992).

The proponents of the market-friendly approach designed their legislative proposals to maximize the accomplishment of their goals. Chile essentially lacked a state agency to oversee environmental issues. As a result, creating and defining the attributes of such an agency was a key point of contention. Supporters of the market-friendly approach to sustainable development wanted an interministerial co-ordinating agency with little autonomous authority and close contact with the private sector. Environmental policy should be controlled by sectoral ministries, such as mining, economy and agriculture. Business felt comfortable with this arrangement because it already had established channels of access and influence to those ministries. In this schema, piecemeal, economic sector-specific action made it easier to keep the focus on pollution control via end-of-pipe technology. It facilitated shifting the costs of pollution away from the private sector. In short, it decreased the opportunities for more sweeping changes from established socioeconomic arrangements.

In tandem with this institutional arrangement, the supporters of the market-friendly approach sought as toothless a law as possible. They argued that the precise definitions of key clauses should be left to future legislative action and decrees where sectoral ministries would be effectively in charge of environmental policy. For example, the draft law of Renovación Nacional – Chile's principal conservative political party – left environmental-impact reports to future legislation; there was no mention of education, or special funds for research, and the law was very guarded with respect to citizen right-to-know clauses (Renovación Nacional, 1990; Astorga, 1993).

Supporters of the alternative approach to sustainable development differed on virtually all these measures. With respect to general principles, they argued that the bill should open opportunities for change from established practices. They explicitly linked economic development, social equity and environmental sustainability. They contended that the state should have the authority to establish the rules of the game for public and private institutions and persons. They emphasized imbuing economic policy with an environmental sensitivity, which meant intersectoral planning based on interdisciplinary teams of experts. From the alternative perspective, this highlighted the interconnected nature of the problem. In addition to these concerns, they were strong advocates of citizen participation and organization. Within these parameters pollution control was clearly important, but pollution prevention and the preservation of natural renewable resources was of paramount importance (Astorga, 1990; Ministerio de Bienes Nacionales, 1990a; 1990b; 1991; 1992; Girardi and Rodrigo, 1993).

From the perspective of those supporting the alternative approach, the legal framework should specify the direction of future legislation (especially in terms of sectoral policy and natural resources) without closing off options (PPD, 1993). A firm, well defined law would leave fewer loop-holes for private negotiation in the future, thus strengthening the prospects for change. As a result of this posture, their proposals more fully specified policy instruments and guidance. This specificity applied to the treatment of environmental impact reporting for new projects, the principle of the polluter pays, the establishment of environmental research funds (some of which can be dedicated to alternative technologies that will mitigate the need for end-of-pipe technology) and strengthening international co-operation. There was also an emphasis on environmental education to raise the awareness of the public, and detailed avenues for citizen participation. Last, but not least, the legislative proposals of the alternative perspective stressed the role of the state in the national land-use planning (PPD-PS, 1992; Girardi and Rodrigo, 1993; PPD, 1993).

Progressive environmentalists were clearly more interested in change than the market-friendly forces. As a result, they recognized the need for greater state authority to counteract private sector and entrenched state-bureaucratic interests. This was why they consistently supported the creation of a state agency of cabinet rank with an internal structure that recognized the intersectoral, interdisciplinary, holistic character of environmental problems. The actual form of the agency, however, changed over time from advocacy of a ministry of the environment to a ministerial co-ordinating agency whose head would enjoy cabinet rank.

In the end, however, the legislative bill that the government submitted to the Congress in September 1992 – and which became law in March 1994 with virtually no substantive changes – took far more from the market-friendly than from the alternative approach. The principles of both the bill and the law basically reduced environmental problems to pollution control, and omitted references to the problem of social equity and its relationship to economic development. They also emphasized a commitment to minimal change, expressed as gradualism and realism. In keeping with these concerns, the law stressed pollution control through an environmental-impact study requirement. More in accord with positions advocated by the alternative approach, the law also incorporated the principle of the polluter pays, the need for education and sectoral policies. However, these principles were emasculated. Both the scope and the instruments of policy in these areas were either defined in a way that negated the purpose of the measures (as occurred with the principle of the polluter pays) or left undefined, to be fleshed out in future legislation, as occurred with the clauses on citizen participation and the state's oversight capacity. Thus it appears that these issues were addressed mainly as an exercise in lip-service. The bill did not include provisions for a research and development fund nor did it mention the need for national land-use planning (Astogra, 1993; República de Chile, 1994).

In both the bill and the law the attributes of the state agency handling environmental affairs closely mirrored the proposals of the market-friendly approach to sustainable development. The Aylwin administration created an interministerial co-ordinating commission (CONAMA) under the wing of the Secretary General of the Presidency (Segpres), a cabinet-rank agency that was the strategic and tactical nerve-centre of the presidency. CONAMA only had two main functions: to oversee the execution of environmental impact reports and to arbitrate disputes between CONAMA's interpretation of the results and the relevant sectoral ministry. Thus most environmental policy would be left to individual sectoral ministries and private sector consultants. Whatever co-ordination problems arose could be resolved by Segpres according to the political priorities of the presidency (CONAMA, 1992; PPD-PS, 1992).

This arrangement precluded 'capture' of the state's most important environmental agency by progressive, alternative sociopolitical forces. For the co-ordinating commission included supporters of both views, with the expectation that market-friendly/developmentalist advocates would be in the majority. By the same token, should the environmental agency of a sectoral ministry be staffed by experts favourable to the alternative approach, the market-friendly forces would have two lines of defence: allies in the co-ordinating commission itself and pressure on the sectoral ministry that housed the upstart agency.

The politics of environmental policy-making in Chile

What factors influenced the victory of the market-friendly forces in the debate over the comprehensive law? The first section analyses the role of external and internal factors in shaping the Aylwin administration's environmental policy agenda. The second explores how – after an auspicious beginning for the supporters of the alternative approach – domestic factors ultimately favoured the market-friendly backers of the general environmental law.

External pressures, redemocratization and agenda setting

External conditionality played an important role in placing environmental issues on the policy agenda in Chile. In Latin America the most important influences are the efforts of the US government and the World Bank to link trade and aid to sensitivity on environmental issues. On the one hand, World Bank project loans increasingly demand environmental impact statements in order to qualify for funding. On the other hand, US insistence on environmental side-agreements with Mexico as a condition for entry into the North American Free Trade Agreement (NAFTA) sent a clear message to other Latin American nations.

In 1990, Chile was first in line for inclusion in an expanded NAFTA, and the Aylwin administration made the achievement of such a treaty a high priority in its foreign policy agenda (Muñoz, 1994 and Muñoz and Rosenberg, 1993). Chile had experienced a thorough market-oriented restructuring of its economy and society during the military dictatorship, which meant that it had already fulfilled the economic prerequisites for joining a free trade agreement with the USA. Yet the dictatorship had almost completely neglected environmental issues (Grau, 1989). As a result, passing a general environmental law became an inescapable necessity. Economic and social forces that otherwise might have actively opposed any comprehensive environmental law accepted the fact that something would have to be done.

Although external conditionality was key in placing environmental issues on the Aylwin administration's policy agenda, domestic pressures also played an important role. During Chile's redemocratization, the centre-left opposition front pushed environmental problems on to the political agenda from within. Between 1983 and 1989, the Concertación de Partidos por la Democracia (CPD) embraced virtually all socioeconomic and political issues that the dictatorship had ignored or repressed (CPD, 1989a). Given growing pollution and unchecked natural resource extraction during the dictatorship environmental issues clamoured for attention along with social equity and political democracy.

As a result of these pressures, the CPD added an environmental section to its platform during the presidential campaign of 1989. Content analysis, however, shows that the environmental statement was neutral with respect to either market or alternative approaches to sustainable development. It simply recognized the severity of the issue, sketched a list of priorities for action (including a general environmental law) and called for the creation of effective public authority to deal with the problem. Slightly more in keeping with the alternative approach, the final report of the working group that drafted this section of the platform linked social-equity concerns to environmental problems, called for state leadership in environmental research and pushed citizen participation (CPD, 1989b).

Domestic politics and policy formulation: sociopolitical forces and state institutions

Although environment got on the policy agenda, the actual content of the comprehensive environmental law remained undefined. To account for the outcome, this section examines the politics of environmental policy formulation between 1990 and 1994. It analyses how sociopolitical factors and state institutions influenced the relative capabilities of the supporters of the market friendly and alternative views of sustainable development.

Understanding the politics of environmental policy-making in Chile first requires an examination of the power relations among the political parties that formed the Concertación. The CPD was, and is, a centre-left coalition of 16 political parties forged during the transition to democracy between 1983 and 1989 (Oppenheim, 1993). It is dominated by the centrist Christian Democratic Party (PDC). On the left, the most important parties are the Socialist Party (PS) and the Party for Democracy (PPD). Both of these 'renovated' leftist parties have given up revolutionary Marxism and structural reformism. As in Spain, the UK and Germany, the renovated leftist parties are split between sectors that have wholeheartedly embraced market solutions and those that are more traditionally social democratic.

The conservative faction of the Christian Democratic Party – to which president Aylwin belonged – set the tone for the administration that took office in March 1990. But the government consisted of a coalition. This meant that cabinet posts and other choice positions in the executive branch had to be divided among the parties of the CPD. Of course, the most sensitive cabinet posts (such as the ministries of economy, finance, mines and agriculture) went to more conservative or market-orientated Christian Democrats and socialists. Militants of those same political parties – as well as the PPD – who had worked in the environmental technical commissions of their parties, headed and staffed the main environmental agencies in 1990. For those interested in reform, the gulf separating environmentalists from mainstream ministers should have signalled trouble ahead. Nevertheless, as a result of these appointments the supporters of the alternative view of sustainable development in the Aylwin administration believed that they could decisively influence environmental policy formulation in the new government.

To its credit, the Aylwin administration moved quickly in the delegation of responsibilities to draft a comprehensive environmental law. It replaced the military government's ineffectual National Ecology Commission with an interim National Environmental Commission – CONAMA. This was an interministerial co-ordinating commission, without cabinet rank, chaired by the Ministry of National Properties. The minister was a socialist. Both he and his staff – mainly professionals who had worked in either environmental or opposition NGOs during the dictatorship – supported the alternative approach to sustainable development. The ministries of economy, agriculture, mining, planning, public works and transport were also represented in CONAMA.

The actual drafting of the bill, however, was the responsibility of CONAMA's technical secretariat. The Minister of National Properties named a Christian Democrat to head it. He was a prominent professional linked to one of the Chile's foremost environmental NGOs which advocates the alternative approach – the Corporación de Defensa de la Flora y Fauna (Codeff). He had also worked closely with the PS and PPD in drafting of the CPD's environmental policy platform. As a result, the environmentalists in National Properties had reason to believe that he shared their support for the alternative perspective on sustainable development. Given these considerations, the PS and PPD leadership of the ministry were not worried about the fact that Aylwin's political advisers had given the technical secretariat considerable autonomy from CONAMA. As one of them put it: 'We had great confidence in him. We believed he was one of us' (Rodrigo, 1992).

In order to decisively influence policy formulation, the Ministry of National Properties immediately went to work on drafting a version of the new environmental law based on the principles of the alternative approach to sustainable development (Ministerio de Bienes Nacionales, 1990a; 1990b; 1991; 1992). Its staff and consultants were confident of success because their ministry chaired CONAMA, and because a like-minded expert headed the technical secretariat. Their hopes did not materialize.

In the first year of the new administration, the Ministry of National Properties and environmentalists in the PPD and the PS who supported the alternative approach ran into two problems. First, the head of the technical secretariat did not welcome National Properties' attempt to define the policy agenda. Since the secretariat was legally autonomous from CONAMA, he closed himself off from all the political actors who wished to influence him (Grau, 1992; PPD, 1992, p. 54). Work in the secretariat proceeded with frustrating slowness and lack of feedback with respect to its activities. Second, National Properties lost a bruising battle within the Aylwin administration over the function and attributes of the state institution that would take over environmental affairs. According to press reports, in November 1990, the Minister proposed the creation of a Ministry of the Environment. The debate continued until early May 1991. A few weeks later the presidency categorically rejected the possibility.

Serious as these setbacks were, they were merely a prelude to worse difficulties. After more than a year of work, the technical secretariat finally released its first official documents in November 1991. The result disappointed nearly everyone. Instead of a legislative bill the technical secretariat only produced a statement of principles and objectives (CONAMA, 1991). Yet, for all of its deficiencies, the principles and objectives enunciated in the rambling document paralleled many of those of the alternative view. This, no doubt, reflected the thinking of the executive secretary himself who, as previously mentioned, shared many of the basic assumptions of the alternative approach. Not surprisingly, the document said nothing about the state agency charged with overseeing environmental affairs.

The technical secretariat's ineffectualness, the 'incorrectness' of the principles it espoused and the aggressiveness with which the supporters of the alternative approach to sustainable development attempted to influence policy formulation worried the more conservative upper echelons of the Aylwin administration. The presidency's uneasiness sprang from two related sources which posed a dilemma that prompted the administration to take control of the situation.

The presidency's first predicament was that the alternative coalition's policy prescriptions flew in the face of the political bargains struck between authoritarians and the opposition during Chile's recently negotiated transition to democracy. Ironically, although the opposition won the 1988 plebiscite that was supposed to ratify eight more years of rule by Pinochet, the supporters of authoritarianism in Chile – such as business élites and the armed forces as an institution – were not vanquished. This meant that the transition from military to civilian government took place according to the timetable and conditions prescribed by the authoritarian constitution of 1980, which had been designed by Pinochet's advisers. As a result, in order to ease the fears of authoritarians and to ensure the fairness of both the plebiscite and the general election of 1989, the opposition promised essentially to preserve the market-based socio-economic system implanted during the dictatorship (Silva, 1992–3).

As a consequence of this bargain, and in addition to a booming economy and failed heterodox policies in neighbouring countries, three of the Aylwin administration's highest priorities were the retention of the neoliberal socio-economic model, the preservation of the minimalist state and a commitment to continued high economic growth rates. In order to assure investors that a democratic system could provide a good business climate, the Aylwin administration gave capitalists ample access to the policy-making process on most economic, social and labour issues (*ibid.*). In this political context, it is understandable that the emergence of a progressive, alternative challenge to the private sector and market orthodoxy in the environmental issue area caused some alarm within the inner circle of the Aylwin administration. In addition to long-neglected social-equity problems, it no doubt sincerely wanted to address environmental issues. But the presidency wished to approach these problems from a perspective that would introduce the least amount of change so as not to antagonize the private sector.

In addition to this general condition, which colours all issue areas in Chilean politics, the Aylwin administration had to react firmly to a second problem. It had to mollify the supporters of the market-friendly view of sustainable development in the government, the business community, some NGOs and conservative political parties. They felt threatened by the emergence of an alternative to market policy prescriptions. This challenge had snuck up on them. Traditional leftist discourse was essentially vanquished in Chile, yet a new progressive vision was rearing its head from this new and unexpected quarter: the environmental issue area. And it was supported by a budding coalition of environmentalist NGOs, leftist political parties and their representatives in the government. As a result, the market-friendly forces put pressure on the presidency to change this situation. Given the bargain that the opposition leadership had struck with Chilean capitalists during the transition, it felt compelled to oblige.

The Aylwin administration embarked on an aggressive course to bring the bill back to an acceptable market-friendly track – a course that would mollify the private sector and not interfere with continued high investment and economic growth rates. First, the presidency – through Segpres – reined in the head of CONAMA's technical secretariat. In essence, the head of Segpres took control of the policy formulation stage of the environmental legislative bill. Second, Segpres ensured that CONAMA's technical secretariat collaborated fully, and exclusively, with consultants favourable to a market-friendly view of sustainable development. These were drawn from the Centro de Investigación y Planificación del Medio Ambiente (Cipma is a well established environmental NGO), the Ministry of Mines (Solari, 1992) and the private sector (Undurraga, 1991).

Cipma emerged as a nodal point in the development of a well articulated market-friendly response to the challenge of the alternative approach. It quickly established working groups that solidified a market-friendly coalition between prominent government agencies (such as the ministry of mines) and the private sector. That effort culminated in Cipma's Fourth Scientific Congress on the Environment in early May of 1992 (Cipma, 1992). The working groups on 'National Policies for Sustainable Development in Chile' and 'Business Environmental Action' were key. Overall, the list of collaborators on most of the working groups read like a who's who of market enthusiasts among business consultants, private think-tanks and business-peak associations in Chile.

As a result of these efforts, in January and July 1992 most of the already weakly articulated principles of the alternative approach to sustainable development were expunged from successive drafts of the legislative bill. Early attempts to link social equity and poverty to environmental degradation disappeared (with the exception of a vague mention in the presidential message that accompanied the bill). The sections on citizen participation and education were made so general as to offer few guidelines for future legislation on the subject. CONAMA would be an interministerial co-ordinating agency under the direction of Segpres. The burden of proof for infringement of the law would be subjective rather than objective – meaning that the plaintiff had to prove malicious intent on the part of the polluter in order to convict. This gave polluters – the private sector and state enterprises (mainly in mining) – significant protection.

The congressional debate

The bill entered the Chilean Congress in September 1992 and emerged as the law of land in March 1994 without substantial alteration. Nevertheless, it is worth examining the congressional debate over the issue, because it reveals that institution's biases towards conservative, market-orientated sociopolitical forces. Thus, even with very strong support in the congress, advocates of progressive, alternative approaches to national problems face an uphill struggle. With respect to the environmental bill, the main congressional debate turned on the issue of who would bear the burden of proof in cases of violations of the law: the polluter or the plaintiff.

The presidency introduced the bill in the Senate. The authoritarian constitution of 1980 – which gave Chile a 'protected' democracy (Loveman, 1991) – ensures that the Senate is dominated by conservative, promarket forces. Consequently the Aylwin administration expected its bill to pass with relative ease, and it did. The House of Deputies, however, promised to be a greater challenge. Proponents of the alternative approach to sustainable development – principally in the PPD and the PS – were much stronger there. They introduced amendments to lengthen the statute of limitation from a scant five years to twenty. Another measure to strengthen the polluter-pays principle was the shifting of the burden of proof to the polluter (*El Mercurio*, 1994; *La Epoca*, 1994b; Rodrigo, 1994).

The PPD and the PS stitched together a winning coalition in the House of Deputies, and the bill went back to the Senate for approval. But the Senate – as part of the idea of protected democracy – has an absolute veto power over all legislation. As a result, it struck down the objective principle of prosecution set by the lower chamber, and reinserted subjective principles that favoured business (*El Mercurio*, 1994; *La Epoca*, 1994b; Rodrigo, 1994). This suggests that supporters of an alternative approach to sustainable development in Chile face very tough, perhaps almost unsurmountable, challenges in the Congress – the ultimate gatekeeper against the change from the socioeconomic system inherited from the dictatorship.

The policy consequences of the general environmental law

To summarize, this chapter has examined how and when international factors, ideas, social coalitions and state institutions affected the outcome of environmental politics in Chile. In general it has argued that international factors and ideas help to set the policy agenda, but that domestic politics, centred on coalitions of sociopolitical forces with varying resources (rooted in economic and state institutional sources of power) ultimately determined the outcome: that is, whether policy rested on the principles of the market-friendly versus the alternative approach to sustainable development.

A further question remains: what are the likely policy consequences of Chile's comprehensive environmental law? As previously argued it tends to favour market-friendly sustainable development policies over alternative ones. The new law leaves most meaningful action to the sectoral ministries in the future. Effective prosecution against polluters, citizen participation, education, holistic land-use and environmental planning and the creation of bureaucratic counterweights to market-friendly forces, all of these progressive measures will most likely not receive much attention.

This, however, is not to say that all measures will be meaningless or ineffectual. The law will probably be more effective in shaping policy in those areas where the government can secure the co-operation of the private sector and less effective where business actively opposes environmental protection. We can also expect differential effects depending on whether policy affects the control of industrial pollution versus the protection of natural resources. Furthermore, policy outcomes should also be affected according to whether or not Chile is a signatory to international treaties and agreements. To illustrate these points, this section turns to a brief examination of the problem of ozone depletion and the fate of Chile's natural forests. The treatment of each issue area begins with a brief history of the environmental problem. I then argue that one can expect movement on the ozone depletion issue (control of industrial pollution) and stagnation in the area of natural forest use (vital natural resource).

Ozone depletion and native forest policy: Chile's response

Given its geographical location, southern Chile is directly affected by the 'ozone hole' over Antarctica. The hazards of ozone depletion have been well documented. In Chile there have been mounting reports of blind fish, rabbits and sheep, as well as deformed tree buds and an increased incidence of people with allergies, eye irritations and skin complaints. Chileans also worry that higher doses of ultraviolet radiation might disrupt the economy which depends on fish, fruit and timber exports (White, 1993, pp. 60–4). Perhaps because of this direct threat to both health and economy, Chile – even during the military government – was among a relatively small number of developing countries (along with Mexico) to take an active, co-operative part in the Montreal Protocol, signed in September 1987. In fact, both these countries were the first to present a plan to reduce CFC and halogen emissions after 1990.

Many developing nations had looked with suspicion on the developed world's concern with ozone depletion in the middle of the 1980s. They pointed out that developed nations, not developing nations, produced most of the pollutants that harmed the ozone layer. For example, industrialized nations consumed approximately 88 per cent of CFCs with less than 25 per cent of global population. This meant that their per capita consumption was over 20 times more than that of developing nations (Benedick, 1991, pp. 148–9). Moreover, less developed countries also worried that they would not have access to the technology produced to redress the problem. Or if they could get it, they fretted that the substitutes would come at a very high mark-up. Consequently, many third-world leaders railed against yet another effort on the part of developed nations to retard economic growth in the developing nations.

Chile (along with Mexico), however, worked steadily for the success of the Montreal Protocol and follow-up meetings. It was among the first five Latin American nations to sign the protocol, and so keen was its interest that its delegation was elected to the protocol's Executive Secretariat (Brañes, 1991; Rodrigo, 1994). Chile also laboured tirelessly at subsequent encounters, such as the London conference in 1989. These meetings addressed issues such as technology transfers and voting rights for developing nations, as well as the inclusion of substances besides CFCs that are harmful to the ozone layer (Benedick, 1991; Parson, 1993). The World Bank, through the Global Environmental Facility (GEF), has funded six projects under the Montreal Protocol to aid developing nations with its implementation (World Bank, 1992b). So far, Chile has received a soft loan of $1.2 million from the GEF to help medium and small enterprises reconvert their industries (Rodrigo, 1994).

Despite its co-operative stance, Chile has joined other countries in criticizing developed nations for not taking greater responsbility in the financing of solutions to a problem that is largely of their making. At the United Nations

Conference on Environment and Development in Rio de Janeiro in the summer of 1992, Chile joined the developing nations' Group of 77 in demanding that developed nations – which produce the lion's share of CFCs – offer greater facilities for technology transfers. The USA, however, managed to split the G-77 and the effort failed (*ibid.*).

Chile's constructive participation in ozone diplomacy should have a positive effect on future legislation within the framework of the new environmental law. Regarding that law, one of the remaining tasks is to draft the corresponding rules and regulations in three areas: environmental impact studies, land-use ordinances and decontamination. With respect to the decontamination issue, the fact that Chile is a signatory to the Montreal Protocol provides a structure within which to codify CFC use reduction and eventual elimination (*ibid.*). For example, a commitment to atmospheric protection is one of the goals of the second Concertación government of Eduardo Frei, Jr (Concertación, 1993).

But the matter goes deeper than this. As a policy issue, ozone depletion is well suited for market-friendly solutions. It is essentially a problem of point-source pollution control, it can be ameliorated by high technology and it avoids questions of socioeconomic domination. This means that the Chilean government can expect many large-scale Chilean capitalists to support its efforts in this issue area. Business people linked to point-source pollution industries had already begun to articulate a market-friendly environmental discourse – and a policy of corporate responsibility – once it became clear to them that the government was serious about pushing environmental legislation in the early 1990s (Sociedad de Fomento Fabril, 1992). This was a pre-emptive strategy to show that heavy government regulation in the environmental issue area was not appropriate. The business sector loudly proclaimed its willingness to invest in the necessary technology (Guzmán, 1994); one better, entrepreneurs repeatedly pointed out that they were ahead of the state in this game, especially in the light of the state-owned mining sector's lack of environmental planning and investment (Rodrigo, 1994).

Despite these signs of co-operation, one can expect capitalists to disagree with the government on the issue of CFC use-reduction timetables. Most likely, Chilean business will seek to stretch them out in order to ease the burden of adjustment. They will no doubt point to the state enterprises' even greater lack of preparation for reconversion, claiming that it would be discriminatory to require more of the private sector (*ibid.*).

The situation is quite different for issue areas that involve the exploitation of natural renewable resources such as Chile's temperate native forests. With respect to ozone depletion, technological solutions are very appropriate, and supporters of the alternative view of sustainable development can work together with market-friendly backers. They may argue over timetables and targets, but deeper issues of socioeconomic domination can be avoided. The same is not entirely true of the use of native forests. Issues of biodiversity conservation and the livelihoods of peasants and small-holders stand at the heart of the matter. In this instance, one can expect the new environmental law to favour market-friendly forces over progressive ones.

Native forest policy, however, presents different and more serious problems to action. The military dictatorship developed a timber-export industry based on plantations of exotic species – radiata pine and some eucalyptus. The plantations led to pressure to clear cut native forests of little commercial value in order to substitute them for exotic species of high commercial value. The government offered subsidies to the few large corporations – part of Chile's most powerful conglomerates – that could take advantage of them. Exports of timber soared to approximately one billion dollars. Working conditions in the plantations were very bad. Moreover, pressure for clear-cutting of native forest-stands increased as demand for short-fibre woodchips for pulp and paper rose in developed nations (Gwynne, 1993).

Supporters of the progressive, alternative view of sustainable development controlled most of the government agencies involved in forestry and, by presidential request, drafted a native forest law. Its purpose was to create economic incentives for the creation of a sustainable native forest industry that would privilege small-holders and peasants, preserve large tracts of native forest from exploitation and severely limit the substitution of native forest for plantations (Ministerio de Agricultura, 1992).

In a political conflict strikingly similar to the one over the comprehensive environmental law the big timber companies, and the private sector in general, were able to weaken the bill in the policy formulation stage. Then, through their conservative congressional allies in the Senate, they managed to stall it altogether (Silva, forthcoming). Now, conservative market-friendly forces are demanding that the bill be thrown out because it violates constitutional mandates that sanctify private property (Rodrigo, 1994).

The fate of native forest policy suggests that in the face of strong private sector opposition the general environmental law decidedly favours market-friendly over progressive forces. The law does not clarify any of the fundamental constitutional and land-use issues with which large-scale business defends itself. Moreover, it leaves intact the avenues by which they so successfully lobby allied agencies in the government and convince them to come to their aid against 'radical environmentalists'.

Conclusions

What lessons does Chile's experience hold for other Latin American countries? The main implication seems to be that environmental policy in the rest of the region will probably favour the market-friendly over the alternative approach to sustainable development. This is because both external and internal factors increasingly tend to favour market-friendly over alternative social forces. However, this does not necessarily mean that progressive environmentalists should despair. They may well find subordinate niches from which they can influence national, state or department and local policy.

In keeping with the analytical framework previously outlined, this concluding section begins with an examination of the impact of external actors. In a nutshell, they sharply limit the latitude for action of progressive environmentalists.

The most influential international forces in the region – the US government and the World Bank – are committed to a market-friendly approach to sustainable development. Thus one can expect most of their consultants and their trade and aid packages to reinforce market-friendly policies. One can also expect the World Bank to take on an increasing share of the leadership on this issue, as the USA shifts aid from Latin America to the former communist states, and consciously conducts its aid policy through the World Bank. The US government can afford to take this course of action because it dominates the World Bank.

Furthermore, as the financial administrator of the Global Environmental Facility (GEF), the World Bank has become the principal 'manager' of international funds for environmental projects. The United Nations Development Programme and the United Nations Environmental Programme are formally comanagers of the GEF, but are more removed from its programmatic and financial operation. The centrality of the World Bank's role is evident when one considers that it houses the GEF Secretariat, administrates the GEF programme and manages its investment projects. To date, the GEF provides resources in four areas: biological diversity, climate change, international waters and ozone depletion. Land degradation issues – principally desertification and deforestation – are also being addressed (World Resources Institute, 1994, pp. 229–31).

Both the US government and the World Bank incorporate a rhetoric of community participation, livelihoods demands and basic needs issues. Yet given the lack of depth in their treatment one suspects that they will not expend much effort on them. Instead, the emphasis is clearly on urban problems related to end-of-pipe technology, waste disposal and sewage treatment (Nielson and Stern, forthcoming). These, of course, are important issues too, and can help improve the health of a nation's population. But such universal quality-of-life benefits are not axiomatic, and the approach leaves unaddressed a host of additional problems related to basic needs. Furthermore, biodiversity conservation is essentially reduced to a stress on national parks, and additional funds are earmarked for strengthening government institutions that deal with these matters. Again, the programmes skirt the livelihood issue (Ghimire, 1994).

Among developing nations and NGOs, then, there is some concern that World Bank leadership through the GEF, along with trade-driven green conditionality, once again reflects developed country priorities and dominance in north–south relations. Observers point out that for all its recent emphasis on environment, the World Bank's major orientation is still towards traditional models of industrial and agroexport development. These often clash with the new environmental dimension. Since the latter is handled by a much smaller and more subordinate staff, environmental concerns often lose out to more traditional goals of economic growth at any price (Rich, 1993). Moreover, NGOs criticize that the GEF does not focus on key environmental concerns of the south. Solutions still require developing nations to forgo economic growth. They prefer a focus on poverty alleviation and sustainable development (White, 1993, p. 180; World Resources Institute, 1994, p. 231).

Environmental policy, however, is only one aspect of a much larger package of trade and aid conditionality on the part of the USA and the World Bank. Their more extensive agenda also includes market-orientated, neoliberal, economic, social and political restructuring – the so-called 'Washington Consensus' (Williamson, 1990). This affects the relative power of internal actors, for market-orientated political and socioeconomic restructuring has a profound effect on domestic politics. It strengthens the hand of market-friendly environmental forces.

Neoliberal restructuring has this effect for two reasons. First, it shrinks the responsibilities of government, seeking a 'minimalist' state that limits its involvement in the economy and society to the provision and maintenance of rules that facilitate the optimum functioning of markets – basically the price system with a 'safety net' for the extreme poor. Thus, second, domestic and international capitalists acquire great political power because they are the main sources of investment and economic growth. Governments cross them at their peril (Przeworski, 1986). The effects of this arrangement on the power resources of contending actors in the politics of environmental policy were clearly drawn in the Chilean case. Since Chile's economic development strategy has become a model for many other countries in the region, one might expect the same results in cases that take the example to heart.

Whether or not countries emulate Chile's development model, rapid market-based economic growth is the highest priority for almost all the national governments of Latin America. As a result, they should tend to adopt environmental policies that clash the least with that goal. In this context one also has to remember that developing nations depend on developed nations for technology, as well as investment and markets. Consequently, most Latin American political leaders should seek to acquire proven technologies that allow them to supply existing markets and consumer demand. That means an affinity for end-of-pipe rather than alternative technology. By the same token, market-orientated economic restructuring tends to diminish the possibilities for more co-operative forms of economic activity and privileges large-scale capital over small-holders, peasants and poor people in general. At best, the latter will enjoy a minimum social safety net that relies on targeted welfare programmes.

Given this general tendency, what are the prospects for the proponents of the more progressive, alternative view of sustainable development? Contrary to what one might expect given the previous discussion, there are opportunities for them. For the most part, however, they will have to limit their efforts to smaller, more discrete projects and struggle to create the political space necessary to carry them out. In this sense, examples abound in Latin America. To name but a few, there is the fight for extractive reserves in Brazil (Schwartzman, 1991); exciting community-forestry projects in southern Mexico (Silva, 1994); small-holder reforestation, native forest management and household solar-energy pilot projects in Chile (Silva, forthcoming); and biosphere reserve creation and agroforestry in Venezuela (García, 1993).

Establishing these projects depended on the formation of prograssroots development coalitions of both international and domestic actors. The composition of those coalitions hinged on the initial disposition of key government actors to such projects, the involvement of pro–grassroots external actors, the intensity of local conflicts and the extent of community organization. Thus, barring intense government opposition, the adoption and durability of projects that reflect an alternative approach to sustainble development depend on the existence of a coalition of organized communities, domestic non-governmental organizations, some allied governmental actors and support from an international actor. When governments are fundamentally opposed to sustainable development at the grassroots, as was the case in Brazil, much higher levels of community organization, conflict and domestic and international support appear to be necessary (Silva, 1994).

In the final analysis, and paradoxically, the Chilean case also offers a cautionary tale for Latin American countries. A market-friendly approach to environmental policy does not mean *laissez-faire* or toothless legislation. At the very least, it requires effective laws for pollution control. Chile's general law was too weak, it gave too little direction to future environmental policy. As a result, the latest reports are that Chile's eligibility for admission to a free-trade agreement with the USA is no longer a foregone conclusion. The US Congress is demanding that Chile prove that its environmental and labour laws will be compatible with those of the USA. With respect to the environment, the outcome will depend in large part on the content of the rules and regulations of the comprehensive law. These have yet to be written, and will not be ready for another year (Estrategia, 1994). The tug-o'-war between market-friendly and progressive views of sustainable development will no doubt continue, although under general guidelines defined by the former.

References

Agüero, F. (1992) 'Cooperacación Pública-Privado,' in Centro de Investigación y Planificación del Medio Ambiente, *Gestión Ambiental en Chile*. Cipma, Santiago.

Astorga, E. (1990) 'Fundamentos de una política nacional ambiental,' *Ecotribuna*, Vol. 2, pp. 18–21.

Astorga, E. (1993) *Legislación Ambiental: Una Nueva Gestión para Chile*. Friedrich Ebert Stiftung, Santiago.

Benedick, R.E. (1991) *Ozone Diplomacy: New Directions in Safeguarding the Planet*. Harvard University Press, Cambridge, Mass.

Brañes, R. (1991) *Institutional and Legal Aspects of the Environment in Latin America*. Inter-American Development Bank, Washington, DC.

Browder, J. (1989) *Fragile Lands of Latin America: Strategies for Sustainable Development*. Westview Press, Boulder, Colo.

Brundtland Commission (1987) *Our Common Future*. Oxford University Press, New York.

Centro de Investigación y Planificación del Medio Ambiente (Cipma) (1992) *Gestión Ambiental en Chile: Aportes del Cuarto Encuentro Científico Sobre el Medio Ambiente*. Cipma, Santiago.

Comisión Nacional de Medio Ambiente (CONAMA) (1992) *Proyecto de Ley de Bases del Medio Ambiente*, mensaje no. 387–324. CONAMA, Santiago, 14 September.

CONAMA Technical and Administrative Secretariat (1991) *Principios y Objetivos del Proyecto de Ley Base del Medio Ambiente*. Mimeo, Santiago de Chile.

Commoner, B. (1990) *Making Peace with the Planet*. Pantheon, New York.

Concertación de Partidos Por la Democracia (1989a) *Programa de Gobierno*. Mimeo, Santiago.
Concertación de Partidos Por la Democracia (1989b) *Informe Final de la Comisión de Medio Ambiente*. Mimeo, Santiago.
Concertación de Partidos Por la Democracia (1993) *Un Gobierno Para los Nuevos Tiempos: Bases Programáticas del Segundo Gobierno de la Concertación*. n.p. Santiago.
El Mercurio (1994) 'Numerosas divergencias con el Senado: Cámara de Diputados despachó proyecto sobre medio ambiente,' 12 January.
Estrategia (1994) 'Actualidad,' 31 January.
Friedmann, J. and Rangan, H. (eds) (1993) *In Defense of Livelihood: Comparative Studies on Environmental Action*. UNRISD and Kumarian Press, West Hartford, Conn.
García, P. (1993) 'La reserva de la biósfera Alto Orinico-Casiquiare: una opción para el desarrollo sustentable,' *Ambiente*, Vol. 15, no. 47, pp. 19–22.
Geisse, G. (1987) 'El desafío ambiental y la coparticipación pública y privada,' *Ambiente y Desarrollo*, Vol. 3, nos 1 & 2, pp. 169–78.
Ghai, D. (ed.) (1994) 'Development and environment: sustaining people and nature,' *Development and Change*, Vol. 25, no. 1, special issue.
Ghai, D. and Vivian, J.M. (eds) (1992) *Grassroots Environmental Action: People's Participation in Sustainable Development*. Routledge, London.
Ghimire, K.B. (1994) 'Parks and people: livelihood issues in national parks management in Thailand and Madagasgar,' *Development and Change*, Vol. 25, no. 1, pp. 195–229.
Girardi, G. and Rodrigo, P. (1993) 'Medio ambiente y política: una propuesta para un proyecto de país sustentable.' Unpublished.
Grau, J. (1989) *Ecología y Ecologismo* (2nd edn). Ediciones Oikos, Santiago.
Grau, J. (1992) Author interview, Santiago de Chile, 1 July.
Güell, G. (1991) 'Desarrollo y medio ambiente en Chile: la visión empresarial,' *Ambiente y Desarrollo*, Vol. 7, no. 3, pp. 24–8.
Guzmán, J.A. (1994) 'La ley del medio ambiente,' *La Tercera*, 2 January.
Gwynne, R.N. (1993) 'Non-traditional export growth and economic development: the Chilean forestry sector since 1974,' *Bulletin of Latin American Research*, Vol. 12, no. 2, pp. 149–69.
Haggard, S. (1990) *Pathways from the Periphery: The Politics of Growth in Newly Industrializing Countries*. Cornell University Press, Ithaca, NY.
Haggard, S. and Kaufman, R. (forthcoming) *The Political Economy of Democratic Transitions*. Princeton University Press.
Hall, P.A. (1989) *The Political Power of Economic Ideas: Keynesianism across Nations*. Princeton University Press, Princeton, NJ.
Hardin, G. (1968) 'The tragedy of the Commons', *Science*, Vol. 162, pp. 1243–8.
Hurtubia, J. (1991) *Seminario Nacional Sobre Instrumentos y Estrategias de Financiamiento para la Política Ambiental Chilena*, Mimeo. Santiago de Chile.
Infante, P. (1992) 'Roberto de Andraca: los empresarios podemos compatibilizar desarrollo y medio ambiente,' *Revista Industria*, Vol. 1051, pp. 12–15.
La Epoca (1994a) 'Ecologistas piden que Relaciones Exteriores lleve el Tratado de Libre Comercio,' 5 May.
La Epoca (1994b) 'Codeff dijo norma resguarda exclusivamente intereses empresariales,' 3 February.
Loveman, B. (1991) 'Misión Cumplida? Civil–military relations and the Chilean political transition,' *Journal of Interamerican Studies and World Affairs*, Vol. 33, no. 3, pp. 35–74.
Maher, D. (1989) *Government Policies and Deforestation in Brazil's Amazon Region*. World Bank, Washington, DC.
Max-Neef, M. (1991) *A Human Scale of Development: Conception, Application, and Further Reflections*. Apex Press, New York.

Miliband, R. (1969) *The State in Capitalist Society*. Basic Books, New York.

Ministerio de Agricultura (1992) *Proyecto de Ley de Recuperación del Bosque Nativo y Fomento Forestal*. Mimeo, Santiago de Chile.

Ministerio de Bienes Nacionales (1990a) *Propuesta Preliminar de Objetivos y Principios Para la Política Nacional Ambiental*. Document PNA/CHI/4, 28 October. Santiago de Chile.

Ministerio de Bienes Nacionales (1990b) *Hacia la Formulación de la Política Nacional Ambiental*. Document no. PNA/CHI/1, 25 September. Santiago de Chile.

Ministerio de Bienes Nacionales (1991) *Propuesta Para la Formulación de los Objetivos y Principios de la Política Nacional Ambiental*. November, Santiago de Chile.

Ministerio de Bienes Nacionales (1992) *Proyecto de Ley Marco Sobre la Política Nacional del Medio Ambiente*. Draft, mimeo, 28 April. Santiago de Chile.

Muñoz, H. (1994) 'Free trade and the environment: the cases of Chile, Mexico, and Venezuela.' Paper presented at the conference on 'The Politics of Latin American Environmental Policy in International Perspective,' University of California, San Diego, 21–3 January.

Muñoz, H. and Rosenberg, R. (eds) (1993) *Difficult Liaison: Trade and the Environment in the Americas*. University of Miami North-South Center Books, Miami, Fla.

Nielson, D.L. and Stern, M.A. (forthcoming) 'Multilateral lending institutions and the environment: a discussion of the political dynamic between lenders, donors and recipients,' in G.J. MacDonald, D.L. Nielson and M.A. Stern (eds) *The Politics of Latin American Environmental Policy in International Perspective*. Westview Press, Boulder, Colo.

Oppenheim, L.H. (1993) *Politics in Chile: Democracy, Authoritarianism, and the Search for Development*. Westview Press, Boulder, Colo.

Parson, E.A. (1993) 'Protecting the ozone layer,' in P.M. Haas, R.O. Keohane, and M.A. Levy (eds) *Institutions for the Earth: Sources of Effective International Environmental Protection*. MIT Press, Cambridge, Mass.

Partido por la Democracia (PPD) (1992) *Propuestas Para el Período 1992–1993 y Balance de la Gestión de Gobierno Para el Período 1990–1991*. Mimeo, Santiago, April.

Partido por la Democracia (PPD) (1993) 'La dimensión ambiental del desarrallo,' in PPD, *Programa Presidencial Ricardo Lagos: Más Chile para todos*. PPD, Santiago.

Partido Socialista–Partido por la Democracia (PS-PPD) (1992) *Posición Sobre la Ley del Medio Ambiente*. Mimeo, Santiago de Chile.

Przeworski, A. (1986) *Capitalism and Social Democracy*. Cambridge University Press.

Redclift, M. and Goodman, D. (eds) (1991) *Environment and Development in Latin America: The Politics of Sustainability*. Manchester University Press.

Renovación Nacional (1990) *Proyecto de Ley General del Medio Ambiente*. Mimeo, Santiago de Chile.

Repetto, R. (1988) *The Forest for the Trees: Government Policies and the Misuse of Forest Resources*. World Resources Institute, Wasington, DC.

República de Chile (1994) 'Ley sobre bases generales del medio ambiente,' *Diario Oficial de la República de Chile*, no. 34,810, 9 March, pp. 3–10.

Rich, B. (1990) 'Multilateral development banks and tropical deforestation,' in S. Head and R. Heinzman (eds) *Lessons of the Rainforest*. Sierra Club Books, San Francisco, Calif.

Rich, B. (1993) *Mortgaging the Earth*. Beacon, Boston, Mass.

Rodrigo, P. (1992) Author interview, 21 June.

Rodrigo, P. (1994) Author interview, 29 May.

Schamis, H.E. (1991) 'Reconsidering Latin American authoritarianism in the 1970s: from bureaucratic authoritarianism to neoconservatism,' *Comparative Politics*, Vol. 23, no. 2, pp. 201–20.

Schwartzman, S. (1991) 'Deforestation and popular resistance in Acre: from local social movement to global network,' *The Centennial Review*, Vol. 35, no. 2, pp. 397–422.

Silva, E. (1992–3) 'Capitalist regime loyalties and redemocratization in Chile,' *Journal of Interamerican Studies and World Affairs*, Vol. 34, no. 4, pp. 77–117.

Silva, E. (1994) 'Thinking politically about sustainable development in the tropical forests of Latin America,' *Development and Change*, Vol. 25, no. 4, pp. 697–721.

Silva, E. (forthcoming) 'Conservation, sustainable development, and the politics of native forest policy in Chile,' in G.J. MacDonald, D.L. Nielson and M.A. Stern (eds) *The Politics of Latin American Environmental Policy in International Perspective*. Westview Press, Boulder, Colo.

Smith, P.H. (1991) 'Crisis and democracy in Latin America,' *World Politics*, Vol. 43, no. 4, pp. 608–34.

Sociedad de Fomento Fabril (1992) 'Empresarios para un desarrollo sostenible,' *Revista Industria*, Vol. 1049, pp. 26–7.

Solari, J. (1992) Author interview, Santiago de Chile, 21 July.

Undurraga, J. (1991) 'La industria minera frente a la demanda ambiental del país,' *Ambiente y Desarrollo*, Vol. 7, no. 3, pp. 53–6.

Weaver, J. and O'Keefe, K. (1991) *The Evolution of Development Economics*. Mimeo, The American University, Washington, D.C.

White, R.R. (1993) *North, South, and the Environmental Crisis*. University of Toronto Press.

Williamson, J. (1990) *Latin American Adjustment: How much has Happened?* Institute for International Economics, Washington, DC.

World Bank (1991) *World Development Report 1991: The Challenge of Development*. Oxford University Press, New York.

World Bank (1992a) *World Development Report 1992: Development and the Environment*. Oxford University Press, New York.

World Bank (1992b) *The World Bank and the Environment*. World Bank, Washington, DC.

World Resources Institute (1991) *Accounts Overdue: Natural Resource Depreciation in Costa Rica*. World Resources Institute, Washington, DC.

World Resources Institute (1994) *World Resources, 1994–95: A Guide to the Global Environment*. Oxford University Press, New York.

Acknowledgements

This research was funded by the North–South Center of the University of Miami and the University of Missouri – St. Louis. Special thanks to Patricio Rodrigo who made the project possible.

PART III

Towards a sustainable future: environmental values, institutions and participatory practices

The final section examines the kinds of environmental values, institutional processes and participatory practices that are required to put us on a sustainable course. Robert Paehlke's chapter broadly examines the role of environmental values in the pursuit of sustainability. For Paehlke democracy must be the guiding value. Taking issue with those who maintain that ecological limits raise serious questions about the efficacy of political democracy, he asserts that environmental protection will be most effectively achieved through the continuing enhancement of democratic practices. Pluralist democracy advanced as the only system capable of legitimately balancing basic environmental values – ecology, health and sustainability – against other first-order values such as social justice, economic prosperity and national security. Democracy, as Paehlke convincingly argues, is our best hope for mobilizing a transition to environmental sustainability.

Maarten Hajer seeks to take the argument one step further. His work shows that, while necessary, an open and democratic environmental discourse is not necessarily sufficient. Basic to Hajer's analysis are the two major competing policy discourses in the acid-rain controversy in Great Britain, which he dubs the 'traditional pragmatist' discourse (relying mainly on *ad hoc* policy-making strategies) and 'ecological modernization' (which emphasizes sustainable development). After showing how each has struggled to control the discussion, formulation and implementation of acid-rain policy, Hajer elucidates the way in which the hidden politics of institutional practices can be the decisive determinant of policy outcomes. Whereas the discursive practices of the modernization 'discourse coalition' are seen to have triumphed over those of the pragmatist coalition, the discursive victory failed to result in a new policy direction. The reason, Hajer shows, is because the advocates of ecological modernization neglected to supplant the pragmatists' hold on the institutional practices of the environmental ministries. Thus, as he makes clear, an effective green politics cannot stop at the level of political discourse. It must also include the ability to imbed discursive categories in the very structure of the institutional methodologies and practices that shape and guide everyday policy deliberations. Even though the pragmatist policy discourse had begun to lose its

force – if not its credibility – its influence has continued through bureaucratically instrumentalized policy procedures.

Frank Fischer examines the key resource of institutional politics, namely
expertise. In no other policy arena do scientific and technological expertise
play a greater role in the governmental decision processes than in environmental policy-making. Basic to such policy-making has always been the question of
how the ordinary citizen, the cornerstone of a democratic system, can manage
to deal intelligently with the complex technical questions basic to effective
environmental decisions. Many, in fact, have argued that such technical complexities mean we must begin to rethink our understanding of democracy, if
not do away with it altogether. Drawing on two case studies pertaining to
hazardous waste controversies, Fischer challenges the critics of democracy by
showing that citizens movements can and have successfully confronted complex technical issues. Focusing in particular on the uses and abuses of environmental risk assessment in dealing the problem of 'NIMBY' (not in my
backyard), he shows that such movements have not only confronted the risk
assessors on their own terms but they have also in some cases developed
innovative practices of 'popular' epidemiology and 'participatory risk assessment' more generally. Rather than accepting the inevitability of conflict between participatory democracy and risk assessment, Fischer sees this greening
of environmental expertise as offering a new way to revitalize democracy itself.

Paul Shrivastava's chapter takes up the role of green values and corporate
social responsibility in industrial and environmental accidents. Such crises are
rooted in corporate activities, products and production systems. For corporations to respond meaningfully to such crises, argues Shrivastava, they must be
guided by an ethically sound conception of social responsibility. Towards this
end, he critiques the values underlying the existing conception of corporate
social responsibility, characterized as 'anthropocentric, western-centric and
marginal to the actual practices of business'. In place of this conceptualization
he proposes an alternative ethical framework anchored to an 'ecocentric concept' of management, sustainable development and crisis prevention. Using the
example of Union Carbides's responses to the explosion of the Bhopal chemical plant in India, which killed 2,600 people and injured thousands more, he
examines the consequences of the company's failure to accept broad social
responsibilities and speculates as to how such consequences might have been
avoided had the company subscribed to ecocentric management practices.

Finally, Josephine McCloskey and Denis Smith close Part III with an examination of the ways in which environmental values can be integrated into
business policy-making. Focusing specifically on the decision techniques of
strategic management and planning, they employ a 'value-chain analysis' to
show how corporate managers can – and must – introduce environmental
criteria much earlier in the production process. Emphasizing the role of profits,
short-term perspectives and the role of expertise, they conclude with a discussion of the kinds of obstacles and barriers that a greener approach to strategic
management will have to overcome if it is to play a central role in shaping
sustainable economic decisions.

8

Environmental values for a sustainable society: the democratic challenge

ROBERT PAEHLKE

Trent University, Canada

The first Earth Day – 20 April 1970 – was a more seminal political event than was realized at the time. Since that time, environmental issues have gradually, though sometimes haltingly, become first-order political concerns. By the mid-1980s environmental protection was viewed by many as being as import- ant to our collective well-being as national security, economic prosperity, social justice and – for some – even democracy itself. Some, at that time, would even have argued that if and when trade-offs between first-order values must be made, protecting the environment should be 'first among equals', a trans- cendent priority. The real challenge is to know what values must and should be traded off, when and to what extent.

In this spirit this chapter will take a hard look at some of the value, and thereby political, implications of the ascendancy of environmental protection as a societal priority. It will emphasize the new relationship between environ- mental values and the other first-order values: social justice (equity), economic prosperity, national security and democracy. It will argue that while this ascen- dancy is welcome, it is probably dangerous to grant any important value a transcendent status. Indeed, it might well be argued that many of our present- day environmental problems have resulted from our having granted such status to economic prosperity and/or national security. In contrast, it could be argued that Marxist theory granted transcendent status to socioeconomic equity and that when this could not be achieved in Marxist practice, few values other than the pursuit of élite power and wealth prevailed.

Perhaps the most fundamental conclusion in this chapter is that important values must be carefully and democratically balanced. Democracy is the guid- ing value, both as an end and as a means. Environmental protection in particu- lar will be most effectively achieved through the maintenance of, indeed the continuing enhancement of, democratic practice.

The latter assertion flies in the face of the claims and concerns of many environmental and political analysts. Environmentalists frequently asserted in

---

the 1970s that increased scarcity, rooted in resource shortages and ecological limits, would inevitably plague humankind.[1] This scarcity, the result of ecological limits, was viewed by William Ophuls and Robert Heilbroner, for example, as carrying a lamentable threat to political democracy.[2] Some analysts argued that democracy limits society's ability to contend with scarcity and, in effect, redistribute economic decline. Ted Robert Gurr concluded that 'bureaucratic-authoritarian states should be better able than democracies to tolerate the stresses of future ecological crises'.[3]

However, in noting the failings of democratic societies in the face of scarcity, and as pessimistic as he was about the future prospects of democracy, Gurr's analysis also provides an important basis for hope regarding the future. 'The greater the relative increases in scarcity,' he observed, 'and the more rapid its onset, the greater are its negative political consequences.'[4] Therefore, some of these negative political effects could be deflected by early political responses to scarcity. Gurr's view was based, in part, on his pessimism about the ineffectiveness of early responses to environmental problems and resource limitations. The ascendancy of environmental concern in recent years has seen some real gains, real enough at least to buy some time for additional changes, in terms of both technologies and societal value priorities.

Needless to say, all aspects of environmental politics in North America in recent years do not inspire optimism. There were few positive initiatives during the Reagan years, but even then there arose a new momentum for environmental protection, both in terms of public attitudes and in terms of the organizational strength of the environmental movement. Indeed, the Reagan administration provided the movement with more momentum than any 1980s' event save perhaps Chernobyl. In addition, important flaws in the more pessimistic analyses of the relationship between environmental realities and democratic theory have also become more evident in recent years; these will be elaborated on in the conclusion of this chapter. But first let us consider the complex relationships among the first-order political values. The importance of environmental values in the politics of the 1990s and beyond can only be understood through an analysis of the ways in which they intersect with other key societal values such as social justice, economic prosperity and national security. Before turning to that discussion, I will offer a brief summary statement of environmental values themselves.

Environmental values and political decision-making

Historians, philosophers and opinion-survey analysts have observed that the environmental movement involves a considerable transformation of contemporary social values. Hays noted that new values, rooted in postwar advances in prosperity and educational levels, have emerged in virtually all industrial societies.[5] Others have claimed that recent value shifts run deeper than those which sustained the conservation movement. Sessions has concluded that the ecological 'revolution' involves 'a radical critique of the basic assumptions of modern western society'.[6] Inglehart and other social scientists have measured related shifts in popular attitudes, postulating a 'silent revolution' that entails the spread of 'postmaterialist' values.[7]

But what values comprise the essential core of an environmental perspective? In an earlier work, I set out a list of 13 values; others have developed similar lists.[8] This list, I have come to realize, can be distilled to three core environmental values: 1) the minimization of the negative impacts of human activities on ecosystems, wilderness and habitat, as well as the maximization of biodiversity; 2) the minimization of negative impacts on human health; and 3) the determination of resource allocation and use first and foremost in terms of sustainability in the long term. In three words these values are ecology, health and sustainability. Values at this level of generality are not sufficient guides to day-to-day policy-making for many reasons. Some of the principles involved in moving from broad general environmental values to specific policies are noted below.

Essentially, environmental values must compete with other values, but they even – some of the time – conflict with each other. For example, high-yield yet sustainable forests may lack the diversity that would otherwise provide habitats for many animal species. Similarly, even the act of protecting human health, and thereby ensuring that human population will rise, virtually guarantees the diminution of non-human habitat. Such dilemmas do not absolve us of the task of sorting out difficult value questions; indeed, the authoritative allocation of values is the primary function of politics. Political analysts and political practitioners alike should be cautious about leaving such questions unanswered in their rush to pursue narrow, technical solutions.

Day-to-day policy-making must avoid a rush to the technical not only because it may result in bad environmental policy but also because a politically and administratively privileged science can pose a threat to democratic decision-making. There are competent scientists on both sides of almost every contentious environmental issue. Their views are crucial to understanding what ought to be done, but science in and of itself is not sufficient to the task. Environmental policy decisions in almost every case involve a value as well as a scientific component. Scientists can usefully contribute to the value discussion as informed citizens, indeed they should do so, but their views are most decidedly not the only views that must be heard. Technocracy and environmentalism are in many ways opposite poles.

The core environmental values: ecology, health and sustainability

Ecology is at once the most obvious and the most subtle of the three core environmental values. Ecology here is used to represent a complex of related values including non-human habitat, biodiversity and wilderness as well as ecological interconnectedness: the 'web of life'. This value is the only one of the three core environmental values that is not predominantly anthropocentric. It is thereby the value which especially distinguishes environmentalism and which perhaps carries the most radical potential.[9] As well, the emphasis granted to this value and the particular meanings and interpretations attributed to it are the most reliable measure of the variety of 'shades' of green within green politics.

Ecological values embody an appreciation of nature in all its varieties and nuances and acknowledge that human beings do not, and cannot, fully understand the myriad ways in which the natural world, including humans, interconnects. Humans are seen as but one species among many, but also as the one species whose dominance could be so thorough going as to threaten many, if not most, other species and thereby itself. The ecological vision is a radical vision as and when it sees the living world as something other than 'resources' and is repelled by a world wherein all the earth is open to, and indeed experiences, human settlement, exploitation and/or management. At the same time it recognizes that this reality may now be not only inevitable but also upon us.

Thus if anything like the present levels of global biodiversity are to be preserved for future ages, some humans must force other humans to back off, to tread lightly and to keep out. As a species we are even capable of loving nature to death, but it is generally less our love than our greed, fear, stupidity and desperation which are of greatest concern here. In Europe virtually every landscape is a human creation. Even in North America many species, especially large predators, have been reduced to isolated islands of existence and those islands are both inadequate for the long term and threatened in any case. Yet many still imagine, or claim, that replanted forests are ecologically equivalent to the Pacific northwest ancient forests that they replace, while in truth they are much diminished habitat at best. Many species require, for example, standing dead trees – clear-cutting removes such entities from vast segments of land for at least a century and probably for ever. It is common knowledge, of course, that the overexploitation of tropical rain forests threatens thousands of species with extinction or a quasi-existence in zoos and gene banks.[10] From an ecological perspective all the world, save the much-visited 'surviving' islands called parks, will soon become a human farm, an enforced monoculture devoid of variety and complexity and the resilience which only those properties can effectively provide.

Health might be the only environmental value, indeed the only single sociopolitical value, with the potential seriously to rival capitalist economic concerns in the era after the cold war. The focus on health is perhaps especially pronounced within the already wealthy nations. In the USA in particular health care expenditures threaten to create the largest of all national industries, save perhaps the recent, likely temporary, comeback of the North American auto sector. Moreover, the citizens of all western nations have become increasingly health-conscious in recent decades. This health-consciousness manifests itself in a variety of ways including dietary change, increased attention to exercise and fitness and a widespread concern with toxic chemicals in the environment.

The latter of these manifestations is certainly and obviously closely bound up with the rise of the environmental movement, but so too are the other two: diet and fitness. Numerous recent books have combined dietary and environmental concerns focusing variously on food additives and pesticides, on the environmental and health costs of meat-dominated diets (in terms of land, energy and water use among other things) and the links between the beef industry and the overexploitation of tropical rain forests.[11]

The now widespread concern with fitness is linked to a growing demand for outdoor and wilderness recreational spaces and thereby often (though not inevitably) to a demand for more protected quasi-wilderness habitat as well. But it has also, in combination with environmentalist concern regarding climate warming, created greatly increased demands that bicycles and in-line rollerblades be treated as serious urban transportation options.[12] This latter shift dramatically links environmentalism and fitness as do the health research findings which suggest that jogging in some polluted urban settings may do more harm than good as regards health.

In brief, human physical well-being is not easily separated from environmental well-being. None the less, the minimization of environmental impacts on human health has been a most contentious political issue in recent years, most dramatically in workplace settings. But in the broadest of terms Aaron Wildavsky eloquently argued that in almost any clash between health and wealth values, wealth should be favoured by public policy. Wealth, in his view, largely determines health; the wealthier the nation, the healthier the nation.[13] Wildavsky would thus never expend more public funds on health protection than the calculable value of the lives (statistically) saved, or improved, by the expenditures. A contrasting view is put forward by Mark Sagoff who argues that health and environmental protection have distinctive moral value in themselves and must sometimes come first, economic values notwithstanding.[14]

In the USA and elsewhere in recent years the views of those who would balance health costs and benefits in strictly economic terms have prevailed (in, for example, President Ronald Reagan's executive order 12291 and in several recent US Supreme Court occupational and environmental health decisions). In Sagoff's view this administrative and legal trend runs counter to the historic intent of most environmental health legislation. He would prefer that a balance be sought between all economic costs and benefits, on the one hand, and an ethical assertion of a right to health protection on the other. In his view the latter should not be reduced to the former. As well, Wildavsky might have been asked if additional wealth automatically produces increments of health. And how are any increments so obtained to be distributed? His view does not account for the inferior health performance of some wealthy nations, including the USA. Nor for the enormous health costs associated with the single-minded (if ineffective) drive for economic growth within communist eastern Europe and the Soviet Union.

Sustainability is perhaps the core environmental value which addresses most directly the long-term viability of industrial societies rather than their desirability. Concern with sustainability is nothing less than an attempt to shift the attention of contemporary societies to the needs of future generations and to reject the assumption that technology will somehow almost automatically resolve all future resource needs. Sustainability implies a radically reduced dependence on non-renewable resources, a commitment to extract renewable resources no more rapidly than they are restored in nature and a minimization of human impacts on the ecosystems upon which we depend.

Those who address sustainability issues have often come to the conclusion that the long-term viability of industrial society is in doubt. Many analysts in the past have underestimated the capacity for adaptability or erred in other ways. Jeavons did not foresee the then-imminent shift from coal to oil and the *Limits to Growth*, nearly a century later, underestimated future resource reserves, especially as regards metals and non-fuel minerals.[15] But what is clear, nonetheless, is that our future will be radically different from our recent and historic past and that resource availability will play a significant role in the adaptations that will be necessary.

For example, present rates of global population growth suggest that *A Diet for a Small Planet* will be the food future for many and present rates of forest and fish extraction are clearly non-sustainable.[16] As well, there remains no obvious substitute for fossil fuels some two decades after the OPEC-induced energy crises of the 1970s. The transformation associated with a shift away from oil, whenever and however it finally comes, will take many decades and will almost certainly in and of itself involve profound changes for industrial society. Present economic assumptions and economic policies are clearly not up to the many sustainability-related tasks that lie ahead or are already upon us.[17]

Politics and environmental values

What, then, are the overall political implications of these core environmental values? Environmental values can be seen as new issues, recently thrust on to the political stage – a stage already and for ever too full. They signal the rise of ongoing and potential value/political clashes between environmental objectives and other first-order political values. These clashes, together with possibilities for mutuality, compromise and coalition-building, portend the future of environmental politics and policy. Such conflicts notwithstanding, there remain substantial opportunities for advancing several, if not all, these important values concurrently.

Each of the other, non-environmental, first-order political values has an attendant political constituency: investors, corporations and trade unions promote economic growth; defence industries and the military make the case for national security; the poor, urban politicians, organized minorities, trade unions, churches and others advance the cause of social justice and equity. Environmental politics, however, is a politics of a different sort in that it is less dominated by economically self-interested individuals and groups.

This is not to say that economic growth, national security or social justice do not have principled adherents. Many who work hard to advance these values have little or nothing to gain materially from variations in outcome. Nor is it to say that those who promote environmental causes do not have economic stakes in environmental protection. For example, Alaskan fishermen clearly have a stake in avoiding another oil spill, such as the one from the *Exxon Valdez*. In addition, many who are involved in environmental siting decisions are there to defend the value of their property. At the same time many, if not most, environmental advocates oppose pollution because they value health over wealth and understand that environmental objectives may imply real personal economic costs. Environmental politics is thereby refreshing evidence that principles still have a place in politics – and is why many more traditional political figures are so obviously uncomfortable in this realm.

This distinctive political character of environmentalism has several import-ant effects. First, an environmental advocate in one setting may become an environmental opponent under different circumstances (for example, fisher-men may promote overfishing). Second, regardless of economic status, all human beings must eat, breathe and drink. For these reasons and others, it is more difficult for policy-makers to reject claims to environmental protection than to reject, for example, claims to social justice. Having a less focused constituency, however, can have political costs. Indeed, most political scien-tists would argue that without an economically interested attentive public, fewer political and organizational resources are available.

But, as well, this diffusion of interest in environmentalism is not without important political advantages. Because environmentalists are advocates on behalf of future generations and other species, not just themselves, they fre-quently occupy the moral and political high ground. Moreover, many pro-ponents of environmental values have undergone a fundamental revision in worldview; thus they carry a level of conviction that few others can achieve these days. Finally, many environmental objectives may be scientifically under-stood and defended in a way that few other sociopolitical issues can be. (The role of science in environmentalism also has problematic potentials discussed both above and below.) Thus, if there are political disputes with those who place a more exclusive priority on social justice, national security or economic prosperity, it is far from certain that environmental advocates will lose.

Let us briefly, then, examine each of these three points of potential value conflict.

Environmental protection and social justice

As environmental politics has come to comprise a widening portion of the political agenda, there has been some unease that environmental objectives are sometimes achieved at the expense of socioeconomic equity. In the past, en-vironmentalism was seen as predominantly a white, middle-class concern. In this view, money spent on pollution abatement was money *not* spent on inner-city schools; further, environmental protection cost jobs, especially blue-collar jobs. Environmentalists have also been seen by some as placing an unreason-able importance on wilderness – the seemingly legendary places many cannot afford to visit.

What is perhaps surprising, then, is how small the differences are in the acceptance of environmental values by class, race or any other demographic measure.[18] In addition, in terms of economic and social realities (rather than perceptions), the advancement of environmental objectives could, I will argue, improve the everyday lives of ordinary people more than many would expect. This is important not only for its own sake but also for the health of democracy as well. Gurr and other critics ground their fears for democracy by positing that in scarcity situations, 'economically advantaged groups are better able to use market forces and political influence to maintain their positions', and therefore social inequalities will increase.[19] This, in turn, implies fundamental risks for democracy.

Environmental objectives intersect with social justice or equity objectives most significantly in two ways: employment opportunities and relative health impacts. While health objectives are very important politically, they are something of a luxury in some circumstances in recent years – the overwhelming priority is employment opportunities, especially for meaningful work that provides for more than bare survival.

Employment opportunities are affected by environmental decisions in at least three ways. First, environmental protection expenditures affect international competitiveness at the level of the manufacturer and the nation. Second, specific environmental protection decisions can directly result in job losses or gains. For example, not cutting a given stand of timber may eliminate jobs which could exist for some additional years; conversely, new abatement regulations may create jobs in the installation and operation of pollution abatement devices. Third, while quantitative employment effects are important, so too are the character, quality and location of employment gains and losses.

Surprisingly, there are few comprehensive studies of the employment impacts of environmental protection, despite the obvious political significance of the issue. The loss of jobs is frequently raised by industry as an argument against 'too-stringent' environmental protection. Ironically, the opposite may be true: the overall net effect of enhanced environmental protection may be more, rather than fewer, employment opportunities. The threat of environmental job losses may be more bluff and blackmail than reality.[20] Environmental Protection Agency regulations, for example, have probably created more direct jobs than they have cost.[21]

Many types of environmental protection initiatives produce employment. For example, recycling generates large numbers of jobs, whereas the extraction of concentrated virgin (non-recycled) materials is less labour intensive. Bottle bills, which require that containers be refilled, have a net job-creating outcome. The jobs lost in bottle plants are gained in retail stores, trucking, warehouses and bottle-washing facilities. Energy conservation creates more jobs than would have been created in energy production had the conservation effort not been undertaken.[22] Even increased public transportation use may generate net employment gains.[23]

Another dimension of this debate involves the broader question of total economic mix. Non-manufacturing employment, particularly in services such as health care or education, is labour intensive and imposes only low environmental impacts. Thus when these sectors expand proportionally both unemployment and environmental damage decline.

Environmental protection probably fares less well when the quality and location of employment opportunities are considered. Replacing employment on energy megaprojects with jobs in energy conservation or recycling may replace high-paying, skilled, often unionized jobs with lower-skilled, lower-paying jobs, albeit more of them. This employment increase may well be opposed politically because only existing jobs are defended politically. Environmentalists are sometimes thereby pitted against organized labour, while those who might gain employment from the environmental initiatives are left out of the debate.

However, even these generalizations distort the complexity of socio-economic and political realities. Public transportation jobs are frequently unionized and high paying. The manufacture and installation of pollution abatement equipment requires highly skilled workers. Employment in teaching and health care is not without appeal. As well, from the perspective of the poor, the low-skill and high-skill *urban-centred* jobs that environmental protection generates are urgently needed. Also, full employment, even if achieved through reduced work time at constant hourly wages, would carry social savings partially to offset costs. There would be reduced costs for unemployment insurance and welfare, a broadened income tax base and, possibly, reduced costs for police protection and health care.

What of the distribution of environmental health impacts: are they felt evenly by rich and poor? Everyone eats, breathes and drinks but, for example, some infants now consume 'organic' baby food – at double the cost of ordinary brands. It is well known that hazardous waste sites, incinerators and landfills are disproportionately found in poor and/or black neighbourhoods.[24] Air quality varies by location, often to the disadvantage of the less well-off and health risks vary by occupation though there is evidence that the lowest-paying occupations do not always carry the highest risks. (Nor do the highest-paying professional, sales and managerial jobs). All and all, the better-off are likely at least marginally to be advantaged by lower environmental exposures. The poor, then, would gain disproportionately in any across-the-board environmental clean-up.

There are recently strong indications that environmental advocacy is no longer the exclusive preserve of the white middle class. There are now many organizations that have an active interest in the environmental concerns of the urban and rural poor.[25] There have been several recent environmental issues that have mobilized the poor and helped to build small bridges across racial barriers. None the less, in membership and leadership, the major environmental organizations remain predominantly white.

While environmental protection *can* be implemented at the expense of the poor, it can also be achieved either neutrally or to the relative advantage of the less well-off. The distributional effects of environmental protection depend on which socioeconomic groups are mobilized in defence of the environment. The 1980s saw ground lost on the environmental front, or at least a slowed rate of gain. They also saw an overall decline in political involvement, especially among the less advantaged sectors of society. Apathy and cynicism carry with them real risks for the quality of democracy. Hence an environmental politics of expanding scope should not exclude the concerns of the less advantaged for many good reasons. There are clear limits to the political capabilities of an environmental movement that does not activate and serve all segments of society.

Environmental values and economic growth

Gurr, Ophuls and Heilbroner all envisioned a linkage between environmental
damage and economic scarcity, and between economic scarcity and declining
democratic prospects. Ophuls and Heilbroner each carefully reviewed a wide
range of sustainability issues and concluded with a lament for democracy. They
considered energy availability, agricultural capabilities, resource availability, pollution, population growth and other environmental impacts. 'Once relative abundance and wealth of opportunity are no longer available to mitigate the harsh
political dynamics of scarcity,' Ophuls wrote, 'the pressures favoring greater inequality, oppression, and conflict will build up so that the return of scarcity por-
tends the revival of age-old political evils, for our descendants if not for ourselves.
In short, the golden age of individualism, liberty, and democracy is all but over.'[26]
Heilbroner went further in imagining what would follow: 'a social order that will
blend a "religious" orientation and a "military" discipline.'[27]

But there are many possible alternative futures. *Our Common Future* concluded that economic growth must and can continue and that it all but requires
enhanced environmental protection.[28] Much earlier, in 1966, economist Ken-
neth Boulding contrasted economic output with what he called energy and
material throughputs.[29] In the perspective this concept opens up, economic
activity can increase while the total amount of energy and materials used
declines. Both environmental damage and resource shortfalls are a function of
energy and materials use, not of economic activity *per se*.

In other words, it may well be the case that there is not a one-to-one
relationship between resource use and economic activity. Most materials in an
economy can be used and reused: metals, paper, glass, plastic, wood, chemicals
and agricultural wastes are recyclable. Moreover, many high-technology products including computer chips, fibre optics, biotechnologies, calculators and
portable compact-disc players require very little material and energy. The same
is true of human services, including education, the arts and entertainment – all
high-growth sectors. In fact, energy and materials used per unit of GNP have
been in almost continuous decline for a century or more. As well, the oil-price
hikes of the 1970s slowed economic growth, but also induced a further increase in the efficiency of energy and materials use within the total economy.

Why is this important? It means that a widespread sense of extreme strin-
gency can be avoided even if energy and materials use must be curtailed though
the changes involved will be neither automatic nor easy. Thus, while our
economies will change radically over the coming century, the total value of
goods and services will not necessarily shrink. This would be particularly true
if societies were deliberately to accelerate the necessary changes by altering
production and consumption habits and preferences. These habits are not fixed
and immutable. On the contrary, market-based change is always rapid, even if
induced by changes in taxation or subsidy policies. As well, the large share
of GNP now devoted to military procurement could be scaled down even
further, freeing existing economic capacity for other, less environmentally
problematic uses.

Environmental protection, national security and world peace

Our Common Future placed the links between environmental protection and world peace front and centre. This report, descended from the *World Conservation Strategy* (1980), Olaf Palme's *Common Security: A Blueprint for Survival* (1982) and Willy Brandt's *World Armament and World Hunger* (1985) has had a quite wide impact for a document drafted within international diplomatic circles. *Our Common Future* is also, as regards some questions, surprisingly candid. Regarding peace and security, for example, it notes: 'The arms race – in all parts of the world – preempts resources that might be used more productively to diminish the security threats created by environmental conflict and the resentments that are fueled by widespread poverty.'[30]

Our Common Future emphasizes the three-way linkage among peace, development and environmental damage. 'Environmental stress,' it states, 'is both a cause and an effect of political tension and military conflict. Nations have often fought to assert or resist control over raw materials, energy supplies . . . and other key environmental resources. Such conflicts are likely to increase as these resources become scarcer and competition for them increases.'[31]

Real security, in the view of *Our Common Future* and in the view of many environmentalists who reject this report's view that economic growth is necessary to the achievement of environmental protection, requires a massive transfer of funds from military expenditure to sustainable development. Global military expenditures are equivalent to more than $1,000 per year for each of the world's poorest one billion humans – an amount well beyond their present average income. Simply returning military spending to the proportion of global GNP it represented prior to 1960 could provide $225 annually to each of those persons. Alternatively, investing this amount ($225 billion annually) in sustainable agriculture, reforestation, wetlands restoration, habitat protection and renewable energy could rectify environmental damage *and* transform economic prospects throughout Asia, Africa and Latin America.

Less grandly, using *Our Common Future*'s figures, a 0.1 per cent tax on global military expenditures could provide family planning globally. A 0.3 per cent tax could achieve global literacy and a 0.6 per cent tax would fully fund current proposals to alleviate global desertification and deforestation. What is missing are the political and institutional mechanisms to achieve such historic shifts. What is necessary is the widespread actual achievement of environmentalist Amory Lovins' 1980 phrase 'the demilitarization of the security concept'.[32]

Environmental protection and democracy

While democracy may (or may not) be vulnerable to greater scarcity within poorer economies, it may be the most effective means of handling such limitations within wealthier societies. John Passmore, writing around the same time as Ophuls and Heilbroner, noted that 'the view that ecological problems are more likely to be solved in an authoritarian than in a liberal democratic society rests on the implausible assumption that the authoritarian state would be ruled by ecologist-kings. In practice there is more hope of action in democratic societies'.[33] Environmentalists must be ever wary that the real links between science and environmentalism are not overinterpreted. Environmental protection is in the end a value preference, not privileged information rooted in science.

Passmore's perspective is valid for at least three reasons: 1) authoritarian rulers are unlikely to be sensitive to or informed about ecological matters; 2) authoritarian regimes are not necessarily good at inducing positive behaviour, especially in the long term; and 3) democracy provides a good climate for social and economic mobilization and even, if necessary, for developing an acceptance of shared hardship. The changes in the Soviet Union and eastern Europe in the late 1980s lend contemporary support to these conclusions – pollution is widespread in those regions and it has become increasingly clear that neither environmental protection nor economic growth were maximized in the old authoritarian regimes.

There is also something amiss in Passmore's observation in terms of the contemporary situation. Not all who fear for democracy in a world of scarcity and ecological destruction envision benign (or not so benign) ecologist-kings. Authoritarianism, or quasi-authoritarianism, could be imposed with precisely the opposite intentions. Such regimes might impose environmentally undesirable economic activities on unwilling localities. They might distort or suppress scientific findings (or simply commission 'alternative' findings), or protect the economic or ecological well-being of one locality at the expense of another. Such regimes might well not even intend to solve ecological problems – a frightening vision, but indeed a vision made more plausible the longer global environmental change is delayed.

There are at least five reasons to be more optimistic regarding democracy and the environment than were Gurr, Ophuls and Heilbroner. First, the environmental movement has consistently helped to strengthen democratic practice in important ways. Second, as previously discussed, enhanced domestic economic equity is in many ways compatible with environmental protection, where population levels have not yet outstripped ecological underpinnings. Third, at higher levels of economic development 'sustainable' becomes as important as 'development'; a reasonable balance between the two may be more easily attained politically. Fourth, as noted earlier, many 'postindustrial' forms of economic activity are probably less damaging to the environment than are basic industrial forms. Fifth, greater technological sophistication results in improved environmental monitoring and in 'decoupling' economic activity and environmental damage by means of 'technical fixes'. I will conclude with a brief elaboration of the first two items in this list.

Conclusion

Most North American environmental legislation in the 1970s and 1980s contained a significant mechanism for public participation. These institutional innovations have strengthened democracy and helped it adapt to new issues. More than that, environmental organizations have consistently worked to open administrative processes and industrial society itself to expanded public scrutiny.[34] Such scrutiny is the essence of democratic practice. In the early days of environmentalism (the 1960s), openness was seen as a means of avoiding the administrative 'capture' to which earlier conservation bureaucracies were prone.[35] More recent legislative initiatives, including workplace and community right-to-know legislation, have gone further.

Rather than merely opening up governmental decision-making, these newer initiatives have taken matters that were once private and opened them to public observation. The movement, use and storage of hazardous materials are now subject to both democratic and market decision-making processes. For example, Title III of the Superfund Amendments and Reauthorization Act 1986 requires that industrial toxic emissions be made a matter of public record. Workplace right-to-know legislation mandates that industrial workers be informed regarding the exposures they encounter. Some Canadian industrial workers have also attained administrative protection of their right to refuse unsafe work. Community right-to-know laws in many US jurisdictions have provided information regarding the use, storage and transport of hazardous substances.[36] Firemen and other emergency workers, residents and environmentalists alike have learnt from this. The state of California has gone the furthest in requiring notification regarding all carcinogens, be they gasoline additives or supermarket product ingredients. Most such right-to-know measures can help mobilize public opinion and activate people both as consumers and as democratic citizens.

It may well be that in the future environmental decisions will increasingly test the mobilizing capacities of democratic systems. It would appear that several new environmental issues will require solutions that are less 'regulatory' in character, requiring broad behavioural shifts, rather than the regulatory coercion of a small number of economic actors. For example, both recycling and the wider use of public transportation involve such behavioural changes. Behavioural changes involving whole communities are less effectively monitored and enforced than promoted and encouraged. The regulatory mode is inappropriate in altering individual consumer and workplace behaviour (as distinct from workplace equipment).

These newer forms of change require a citizen majority willing to accept and/or participate in such changes. Democracies and democratically managed markets in combination can mobilize educated citizens. So too can authoritarian-bureaucratic systems under some circumstances. But the demise of the Soviet Union suggests that there are limits to the mobilizational capacities of such systems at advanced levels of economic development. Those who are pessimistic about democracy on ecological grounds have not seen this, nor do they allow the possibility that educated populations simply will not be mobilized by regimes they have not chosen.

Just as industry willingness and co-operation is necessary for effective regulatory compliance, citizen willingness is necessary for non-regulatory compliance. But citizens will not change their behaviour unless they perceive that industry and government are also doing what they can. Educated citizens will not participate effectively in collective efforts unless they have been party to decisions regarding priorities. Industry will feel less singled out only if it is not alone in bearing costs.

Thus an effective pluralist democratic system is the best source of balanced, participatory initiatives. Active involvement by individual citizens and private organizations require a sense of mutual effort. Political science research shows that a sense of political efficacy is necessary. It is here that democracy, at its most effective, may prove absolutely essential to the achievement of environmental protection. Cynicism and indifference will undermine any collective ability to protect environmental life-support systems.

Democracy itself must be enhanced effectively to deal with environmental problems. One means of doing this is to expand the environmental powers and roles of municipal and regional governments. A second is to introduce an environmental role within all governmental subdivisions, at all levels. The environmental mandate should not necessarily be concentrated within a single agency. Agencies not traditionally involved with environmental matters, including procurement offices, could be ordering ceramic dishes and organic food for the cafeteria, reducing chemical spray programmes in parks, downsizing the fleet of vehicles and ordering recycled paper. Other divisions should be taking other appropriate initiatives. All should have citizen-based environmental advisory committees. Third, environmentalists must realize that a political democracy will not likely run very far ahead of a nation's commitment to economic equity and social justice. Gurr saw a threat to democracy from the potential inequity of environmental scarcity. While Gurr is accurate in his assessment of the relationship between equity and democracy, this dangerous outcome can be avoided.

In an effective democracy the economic security of the less advantaged cannot be perceived as the price for environmental protection. Environmental activists must be more sensitive to the widespread fear of job loss and displacement. Citizens active in environmental politics must be sensitive to the difference between locally unwanted facilities that are environmentally necessary and carefully sited and those that are not. The fate of environmental protection and the quality of democracy will be very much intertwined in the future.

There is little doubt that human activities pose multiple threats to the habitat of most species on the planet. Doubts remain whether future human numbers are sustainable at present or higher amenity levels in the long term. This is not, however, the same thing as saying that the human species is in grave and immediate danger. None the less environmental dangers have reached such complexity and magnitude that they now intersect with questions of social justice, world peace and global economic development. The simultaneous handling of all these challenges will require both intelligence and enhanced democratic institutions.

Notes

1. See the work of Thomas R. Malthus, W. Stanley Jeavons and others discussed in R.C. Paehlke, *Environmentalism and the Future of Progressive Politics* (New Haven,

Conn.: Yale University Press, 1989), Ch. 3. See also D.H. Meadows *et al.*, *The Limits to Growth* (New York: Universe Books, 1972); W.R. Catton, jr, *Overshoot: The Ecological Basis of Revolutionary Change* (Urbana, Ill: University of Illinois Press, 1980).

2.   See, in particular, W. Ophuls, *Ecology and the Politics of Scarcity* (San Francisco, Calif.: W.H. Freeman, 1977); R.L. Heilbroner, *An Inquiry into the Human Prospect* (New York: Norton, 1974); T.R. Gurr, 'On the political consequences of scarcity and economic decline,' *International Studies Quarterly*, Vol. 29, 1985, pp. 51–75.

3.   Gurr, 'On the political consequences of scarcity,' p. 70.

4.   *Ibid.*, p. 54.

5.   S.P. Hayes, 'From conservation to environment: environmental politics in the United States since world war two,' *Environmental Review*, Vol. 6, Fall, 1982, p. 20.

6.   G. Sessions, 'The deep ecology movement: a review,' *Environmental Review*, Vol. 11, Summer, 1987, p. 107.

7.   R. Inglehart, *The Silent Revolution: Changing Values and Political Styles among Western Publics* (Princeton, NJ: Princeton University Press, 1977).

8.   See Paehlke, *Environmentalism*, Ch. 6.

9.   R. Eckersley, *Environmentalism and Political Theory: Toward an Ecocentric Approach* (Albany, NY: SUNY Press, 1992).

10.   See N. Myers, 'Biodepletion,' in R. Paehlke (ed) *Encyclopedia of Conservation and Environmentalism* (New York: Garland, 1995); J.A. Livingston, *Rogue Primate* (Toronto: Key Porter Books, 1994); C. Tudge, *Last Animals at the Zoo* (Washington, DC: Island Press, 1992).

11.   F. Moore Lappé, *Diet for a Small Planet* (New York: Ballantine Books, 1975); L. Pim, *The Invisible Additive: Environmental Contaminants in Our Food* (Garden City, NY: Doubleday, 1982); J. Robbins, *Diet for a New America* (Walpole, NH: Stillpoint Publishing, 1987).

12.   M. Lowe, *The Bicycle: Vehicle for a Small Planet* (Washington, DC: World-watch, 1989).

13.   A. Wildavsky, *Searching for Safety* (New Brunswick, NJ: Transaction, 1988).

14.   M. Sagoff, *The Economy of the Earth* (New York: Cambridge University Press, 1988), 195–6.

15.   See the discussion of Jeavons and *Limits to Growth* in Paehlke, *Environmentalism*.

16.   This is not to say that *Diet for a Small Planet* is a world that should provoke fear or even concern, though obviously overfishing and forest depletion rates are alarming.

17.   See, for example, P. Ekins (ed.) *The Living Economy: A New Economics in the Making* (London: Routledge, 1986); D. Pearce, *Economic Values and the Natural World* (London: Earthscan, 1993); as well as the journal *Ecological Economics*.

18.   Milbrath, L.W. (1984) *Environmentalists: Vanguard for a New Society*, Albany: State University of New York Press.

19.   Gurr, 'On the political consequences of scarcity,' p. 58.

20.   R. Kazis and R.L. Grossman, *Fear at Work* (New York: Pilgrim Press, 1982).

21.   Several relevant studies are cited in F.H. Buttel, C.C. Geisler and I.W. Wiswall (eds) *Labor and the Environment* (Westport, Conn.: Greenwood Press, 1984); see, in particular, their annotations 016, 017, 040, 050, 064, 105 and 159.

22.   Regarding recycling and refillable containers and employment, see W.U. Chandler, *Materials Recycling: The Virtue of Necessity* (Washington, DC: Worldwatch Institute, 1984); C.M. Gudger and J.C. Bailes, *The Economic Impact of Oregon's Bottle Bill* (Corvallis, Oreg.: Oregon State University Press, 1974). Regarding energy conservation and employment see, for example, sources annotated in Buttel, Geisler and Wiswall (eds) *Labor and the Environment*.

23.   B. Hannon and F. Puleo, *Transferring from Urban Cars to Buses: The Energy and Employment Impacts*, (Urbana, Ill.: University of Illinois, Center for Advanced Computation, 1974).

24. See, for example, R.D. Bullard, *Dumpling in Dixie: Race, Class, and Environmental Quality* (Boulder, Colo.: Westview Press, 1991); C. Lee, *Toxic Waste and Race in the United States* (New York: United Church of Christ Commission for Racial Justice, 1987); L. Blumberg and R. Gottlieb, 'The new environmentalists: saying no to mass burn,' *Environmental Action*, Vol. 20, January/February, 1989, pp. 28–30.

25. See R.D. Bullard, *Unequal Protection: Environmental Justice and Communities of Color* (San Francisco, Calif.: Sierra Club Books, 1994).

26. Ophuls, *Ecology and the Politics of Scarcity*, p. 145.

27. Heilbroner, *An Inquiry into the Human Prospect*, p. 161.

28. World Commission on Environment and Development, *Our Common Future* (New York: Oxford University Press, 1987).

29. See K. Boulding, 'The encounters of the coming spaceship earth,' in H.E. Daly (ed.) *Economics, Ecology, Ethics* (San Francisco, Calif.: W.H. Freeman, 1980), pp. 253–63.

30. World Commission, *Our Common Future*, pp. 6–7. See also International Union for Conservation of Nature and Natural Resources (IUCN), *World Conservation Strategy* (Gland, Switzerland: IUCN, 1980); Independent Commission on Disarmament and Security Issues (Olaf Palme, Chairman), *Common Security: A Blueprint for Survival* (New York: Simon & Schuster, 1982); W. Brandt, *World Armament and World Hunger* (London: Victor Gollancz, 1986).

31. World Commission, *Our Common Future*, p. 290.

32. A.B. Lovins and L. Hunter Lovins, *Energy/War: Breaking the Nuclear Link* (New York: Harper & Row, 1980), p. 153.

33. J. Passmore, *Man's Responsibility for Nature* (London: Duckworth, 1974), p. 183.

34. For a broad consideration of environmentalism and administration, including the issue of openness, see R. Paehlke and D. Torgerson (eds) *Managing Leviathan: Environmental Politics and the Administrative State* (Peterborough, Ontario: Broadview Press, 1990).

35. See, for example, G. McConnell, 'The conservation movement – past and present,' *Western Political Quarterly*, Vol. 7, 1954, pp. 470–1.

36. The broad issue of participation and the right to know is discussed in S.G. Hadden, *A Citizen's Right to Know: Risk Communication and Public Policy* (Boulder, Colo.: Westview Press, 1989).

9

Acid rain in Great Britain: environmental discourse and the hidden politics of institutional practice

MAARTEN A. HAJER

University of Munich, Germany

Introduction

The attitude of the UK government in the 'acid rain' controversy has earned Britain the label of 'the dirty man of Europe'. In the face of an international moral outcry, the UK has been notoriously stubborn in denying accusations that the sulphur dioxide and nitrogen oxide emissions of its coal-fired power stations caused environmental damage abroad. Analysts trying to pinpoint the reasons for the UK's failure to deal with the problem point to inherent conflicts of interest. Its unwillingness to act is interpreted as governmental delaying tactics, while the government's reference to scientific uncertainty is described as using science as a 'figleaf' for policy. The inaction is explained in terms of the conscious exercise of power by key actors.[1]

It seems obvious that powerful vested interests such as the electricity industry have tried to delay preventive action, but acid rain in fact signifies a more fundamental conflict in environmental politics. In this chapter the acid-rain controversy is interpreted as a linchpin in a controversy over the legitimacy of the concepts and practices within which environmental problems were conceptualized. According to the prevailing 'traditional pragmatist' policy discourse, acid rain was an incidental problem for which a pragmatic solution should be found. The alternative policy discourse of 'ecological modernization', on the other hand, interpreted acid rain as a typical example of a new generation of pollution issues. According to the ecomodernist view, new issues such as acid rain, global warming, the depletion of the ozone layer or the nitrification of water mark a new era in the politics of pollution. Above all, they signify the structural nature of the new environmental issues. The non-incidental nature of the new environmental issues has rendered the prevailing *ad hoc* policy-making strategies obsolete. What is called for is a policy of 'sustainable development'. The acid-rain controversy was one of the first sites where this conflict over the interpretation of environmental problems became manifest. It thus was not a regular conflict of interest, and transcended the debate over scientific and technical facts alone. What was at issue was not merely whether or not to install scrubbers but the future criteria of what counted as legitimate arguments in environmental policy-making.

This chapter seeks to illuminate this deeper meaning of the acid-rain controversy and aims to show how the various interests involved positioned themselves in the broader debate. It examines the argumentative structure in documents and other written or spoken statements and the practices within which specific positions were generated. To facilitate this it introduces two concepts: discourse and discourse coalitions. Discourse should be understood as a specific ensemble of ideas, concepts and categorizations that is produced, reproduced and transformed in a particular set of practices and through which meaning is given to physical and social realities. 'Discourse coalitions' refers to the way in which a particular discourse gets its social power. Here the term 'coalition' is meant to underline that this is not necessarily a matter of concerted and strategically negotiated action but might be the result of far more pragmatic, incidental alliances that shape up around specific 'story-lines'.[2] 'Sustainable development' is an ecomodernist example of such a story-line. Despite the fact that the new ecomodernist interpretation of the phenomenon of acid rain could count on substantial support within the environmental domain, this discourse nevertheless failed to put its mark on the actual process of regulation. It is argued that this was to a large extent the consequence of the degree to which a traditional pragmatist bias was structured in a set of routinized organizational practices that resisted the application of anticipatory thinking on the case of acid rain.

A brief history of the British acid-rain controversy

The acid-rain controversy really started in 1972, but concern about acid rain has a much longer history.[3] The current concern originates from the 1968 publications of Svante Odén, a Swedish soil scientist who related the acidification of Swedish freshwaters to the sulphur dioxide emissions from continental Europe and Britain. The Swedish government first raised the issue to the Organization for Economic Co-operation and Development (OECD) in 1969 and subsequently to the 1972 United Nations conference on the human environment, held in Stockholm. Here Sweden formally launched its international campaign against transboundary air pollution. During the 1970s acid rain was almost exclusively discussed by a limited circle of scientific experts.

In June 1982, the tenth anniversary of the 1972 UN conference, the Swedish government organized a conference to evaluate progress. This conference heralded a new period in the history of the acid-rain controversy. First of all, prior to the conference the Swedes assembled an international forum of experts, who agreed that enough was known about the nature and impact of acid rain to warrant the definition and implementation of an effective abatement policy.[4] What is more, at the actual Ministerial Conference on Acidification of the

Environment, the Swedish government received unexpected support for its push for international action from the West German government which, in response to the discovery of the scale of forest dieback in the southern part of the Federal Republic, announced a comprehensive programme to retrofit their coal-fired power plants with SO_2 scrubbers, so-called flue-gas desulphurization equipment (FGD). With the exception of Scandinavia, the German FGD programme was the first clear-cut policy commitment to combat acid rain in western Europe. It was, at the same time, a clear case of the poacher turning game keeper, since until then Germany had not only been a major pollution culprit but had also been a fierce opponent of international agreements on sulphur emission control.

The UK's contribution at Stockholm was limited to the announcement that it was willing to reverse its earlier decision to cut research funding on acid rain. The UK government emphasized that there was no firm evidence that its SO_2 emissions were responsible for the fish death and acidification of the Swedish lakes and therefore argued that it could not justify the high costs of SO_2 scrubbers. It also argued that since the UK was responsible for just 10 per cent of the Swedish SO_2 imports, it was unlikely that emission reduction would result in substantial environmental improvements.[5]

Finally, the UK government questioned whether emission reduction through the use of FGD was the most cost-effective way of improving the environmental situation; it argued that tall stacks (to 'dilute and disperse' pollution) and the liming of lakes (to counterbalance the acidifcation) were much cheaper and more effective means.

Yet, from the 1982 Stockholm conference onwards, the legitimacy of the UK argumentation quickly eroded and the government found itself under increasing pressure to act. The FRG, eager to shake off the competitive disadvantage that resulted from having FGD equipment installed unilaterally, made sure that the European Community became active on the issue. In 1988, after five years of laborious negotiations, during which the UK refused many a compromise, the member countries agreed on a large combustion plant directive,[6] which required that new plants should be fitted with FGD equipment and low NO_x burners. Furthermore, all EC countries agreed to reductions of SO_2 emissions. The UK, however, managed to secure a more lenient percentage in the negotiations.[7]

On the domestic front protests built up more slowly. To be sure, acid rain was never likely to become a popular public issue, being an invisible, cumulative pollutant that damaged (foreign) natural environment more than it harmed people and that also asked for expensive solutions that would have to be paid for by consumers. Moreover, in the early 1980s the environmental debate was preoccupied with the lead issue. It was not until the debate about lead was resolved in April 1983 that campaigners, politicians and government officials really became sensitive to the issue of acid rain.

The fact that acid rain became so central an issue reflected its metaphorical meaning: acid rain was an issue that, according to many, signified the institutional incapacity to deal with the structural nature of environmental degradation.

One of the high points in the UK controversy was the 1984 inquiry into acid rain undertaken by the House of Commons Select Committee for the Environment, whose hearings clearly indicated the polarized nature of the debate. A majority of the experts who gave evidence argued that enough was known about acid rain to warrant taking action. A small but influential group argued that 'policy was in danger of running ahead of science', as the Minister of the Environment, Patrick Jenkin, put it. The select committee report, however, in the end argued that enough was known and urged the government to join the '30 per cent club' (30 per cent reduction of SO_2 emissions by 1993). In December 1984 the government responded with a proposal for a reduction in SO_2 emissions of 30 per cent by the end of the 1990s but did not accept the necessity of installing expensive FGD scrubbers.[8] Then, in September 1986, on the basis of 'new scientific evidence', the government suddenly proposed to install FGD equipment in all new coal-fired power stations. The government also announced plans to retrofit three of its 12 existing large coal-fired power stations with FGD equipment at a total cost of approximately £600 million.

Two discourse coalitions in UK pollution politics

The acid-rain controversy reflected as much a conceptual challenge as a straightforward conflict of interest. Until the early 1980s pollution problems were predominantly conceptualized in terms of what I call a traditional pragmatist policy discourse with historical roots in the nineteenth century. In 1863 the British Alkali Inspectorate, the world's first air-pollution inspectorate, was created. At that time pollution control was a marginal state interest. Pollution was perceived as a problem only if it posed a direct and acute threat to human health. The organization of pollution control was reactive in nature; it aimed at minimizing organizational disturbances and searched for pragmatic, piecemeal solutions.[9] The discourse was widely shared; the critics of the government that initiated the Alkali Acts of of 1863 saw as their goal to ascertain 'whether legislative measures could be introduced . . . not only without injury, but with profit to our manufacturers'.[10]

Since the Alkali Act 1863, pollution has been defined as an apolitical matter best left to the discretion of scientific and technical experts. Over the years both Conservative and Labour governments have reinforced this practice. In 1969, for instance, Prime Minister Harold Wilson (Labour) initiated both the Central Scientific Unit on Pollution and the Royal Commission on Environmental Pollution (finally sworn in 1971). This increased co-ordination between government and science, and *de facto* reinforced the existing traditional pragmatist discourse coalition.

The wave of environmentalism that rolled over the UK during the late 1960s and early 1970s was the first seriously to put the traditional pragmatist style of policy-making on trial. Whereas the prevailing sentiment among the grassroots movement was a moral critique on the instrumentalist attitude to nature, some of the movement's leaders in fact added another line. In the much celebrated study *Small is Beautiful*, for instance, E.F. Schumacher emphasized that the negligence of nature is not only morally wrong but is in fact also grossly inefficient.[11] In the end this realist element in the environmentalist critique led to the formulation of a workable alternative to the traditional pragmatist policy discourse in the early 1980s, which we will call 'ecological modernization'. This newly formulated approach to the politics of pollution[12] was well expressed in the World Conservation Strategy (1980) which became a constitutive document for the discourse coalition of ecological modernization. The ecomodernist approach was further disseminated in such documents as the UK response to the World Conservation Strategy, the tenth report of the Royal Commission on Environmental Pollution and, in 1987, the Brundtland report *Our Common Future*.[13] The principal point of ecological modernization was that in the face of what was known about environmental degradation it no longer made sense to see pollution as incidental. Instead, pollution control had to be integrated into the overall process of societal modernization and in industrial production in particular. As the royal commission put it, 'Control of environmental pollution is not an optional extra: it is a fundamental component of national economic and social policy'.[14]

This new discourse obviously shed a different light on the institutions of pollution control. Rather than reacting to pollution incidents and aiming at remedial strategies after the occurrence of pollution problems, ecomodernist discourse was disorientated towards pollution prevention and innovation. The rationale was simple: pollution prevention pays or, as the Confederation of British Industry argued in 1983, 'Environmental protection makes sense – as many companies have found to their gain'.[15]

In the early 1980s actors within the government also became aware that the old a postiori traditional pragmatist approach was rapidly losing its legitimacy. In 1984 the Department of the Environment (DoE) started to contemplate the introduction of a policy discourse based on ecomodernist principles. In November 1985 the Central Policy Planning Unit at the DoE produced the *Environmental Policy Review*, a restricted internal-review document. It came out strongly in favour of ecological modernization.

This rethinking of the basis of policy-making at the DoE had been strongly promoted by both the chief scientist at the DoE, Martin Holdgate, and the junior minister for the environment, William Waldegrave, who had joined the DoE in June 1983. Until that time the department had been primarily reactive in its approach to environmental problems. The new leaders argued pollution control had to be integrated into the economic system. One of the key features of the new approach would be that the government would encourage industry 'to adopt a new positive philosophy – to build environmental impact, with its cleanliness, energy efficiency and public acceptability – into the first sketch of its new ideas'.[16]

The discourse of ecological modernization that emerged in the 1980s can be captured in five points:

1. Nature should no longer be regarded as a 'sink'. In economic terms this calls for a recognition of nature as a resource. Damage was now regarded as usage of natural resources which has to be paid for.

2. Pollution prevention was put forward as a more rational approach than piecemeal reactive response.
3. It recognized the intricate nature of environmental problems and the inherent complexity of ecosystems. Rigorous and unambiguous scientific proof should therefore no longer be regarded as a *sine qua non* for political intervention.
4. The discourse recognized the importance of the social perception of risk. The public's perception of risk should no longer be simply refuted as irrational.
5. In the light of points 2 and 3, the new discourse argued for the reversal of the burden of proof: a substance should no longer automatically be regarded as innocent until proven guilty, but more often as guilty until proven innocent.[17]

In the face of the moral outcry over the state of the environment during the 1980s, the policy discourse of ecological modernization, with sustainable development as the central story-line, came to be the most legitimate way to speak about environmental problems.[18] However, if ecological modernization was indeed to be executed, a fundamental shift from remedial to preventive action was necessary in the actual institutional practices. The key word, implicit in all five points, in the ecomodernist vocabulary was 'precaution': on the basis of the perceived seriousness of the environmental crisis one anticipated the worst and aimed to prevent extra 'stress'. Between 1979 and 1988 this discourse of precaution had become well structured into the environmental domain. In 1979 the environment ministers of the European Community agreed on a declaration that recognized precaution as the cornerstone of future environmental policy; in 1988 the UK government fully endorsed the UN report *Our Common Future* and announced that it would reconsider its policies in this light. Yet the translation of this discourse into institutional practices was quite a different matter.

It is interesting to note that during the early 1980s the debate on the conceptual basis of environmental policy drew heavily on the experiences of concrete problems such as lead in the environment or acid rain. These issues functioned, as it were, as metaphor for the much larger problematic of environmental decline. In ecomodernist policy discourse acid rain in particular was constantly put forward as a case in point to show that the new environmental problems were of a different order and called for conceptual and institutional renewal. But what was the impact of the new discourse on the debate on acid rain?

The meaning of acid rain

Above we gave a brief account of the historical developments in the British acid-rain controversy. Here we want to show that the acid-rain controversy, although seemingly about technical and scientific facts, is best understood in the context of a struggle for hegemony between two competing discourse coalitions. The discursive space in which the acid-rain controversy was played out, i.e. the arguments that were used to argue for or against remedial action, was dominated by the challenge of the traditional pragmatist discourse by the discourse of ecological modernization. Each discourse coalition had its own story-line on acid rain, yet what was essential for the relative influence of the two policy discourses on the regulation of acid rain was the degree to which they were institutionalized. Whereas the new discourse of ecological moderniz-ation relatively quickly became hegemonic in practices concerned with long-term policy strategy, the traditional pragmatist discourse was institutionally well entrenched in the practices concerned with the regulation of concrete environmental problems.

The traditional pragmatist story-line

The most eloquent and outspoken protagonist within the traditional pragma-tist story-line was the Central Electricity Generating Board (CEGB). Even the government more or less echoed the detailed arguments presented by the CEGB, adding its own political dimension. The traditional pragmatist story-line on acid rain evolved around a scientific argument: it doubted whether any genuine environmental damage was attributable to power-plant sulphur emis-sions. If this cold be proven, however, and if FGD equipment could be shown to be both environmentally effective as well as the most cost-effective solution, FGD scrubbers should be installed. However, the CEGB argued that the avail-able evidence was anecdotal and intuitive and that 'proper' research was needed.[19] It argued that there was no real scientific understanding, let alone a consensus, of the mechanisms involved in lake acidification. In 1984 the Chair-man of the CEGB, Lord Marshall (then Sir Walter), maintained: 'I do not accept any of the scientific arguments I have yet seen.'[20] This position implied that until SO_2 emissions were proved to be harmful to the environment, CEGB emissions should be allowed to continue.

The CEGB presented its own argument to the view of the Scandinavian and German governments. In the early 1980s these governments argued that no further research was needed and claimed that the state of knowledge at that time justified immediate action. The CEGB, on the other hand, pointed at the lack of scientific understanding. In so doing the CEGB portrayed the politi-cians of foreign governments as emotional and irresponsible and itself as level headed, rational and scientific. A key element to substantiate this scientific commitment was the SWAP research project. The SWAP project (Surface Wa-ters Acidification Programme), launched by the CEGB in September 1983, was a major £5 million research study into the acidification of freshwaters funded by the CEGB and the British Coal Board. In the political process the actors within the traditional pragmatist discourse coalition frequently referred to SWAP and to the involvement of the Royal Society of London and the Swedish Royal Academy of Sciences, which were put forward by the CEGB as the 'most prestigious scientific academies in the entire world'.[21]

The traditional pragmatist discourse drew heavily on the scientific core of the argument to enhance its own credibility. This exemplified the utilitarian basis of this approach to the regulation of acid rain. The UK government always insisted that it would be willing to act if action would be 'environmentally effective and economically feasible',[22] arguing that it did 'not believe that the very substantial expenditure (running into hundreds of millions of pounds) which would be required to install flue gas desulphurisation plant at existing power stations can be justified while scientific knowledge is developing and the environmental benefit remains uncertain'.[23] Here the governmental emphasis on the need for a better chemical understanding was positioned against 'giving in' and making 'heroic efforts' because politicians rush (EC) or are in danger of rushing (UK) to conclusions on the basis of fallacious data and argument. Like the CEGB the government thus positioned itself as more rational than its foreign counterparts. The target of the 30 per cent club, for instance, was perceived to be an irrational and arbitrary basis for action which would place the UK at an unfair disadvantage.

Traditional pragmatism as a political practice

The traditional pragmatist discourse coalition had been dominating the field of pollution politics for more than a century. It is hardly surprising, therefore, that this discourse was well institutionalized. In the context of the acid-rain controversy three sets of institutional practices stood out: 1) the urban and health-orientated definition of air pollution reflected in the system of air pollution monitoring; 2) the science-based policy approach; and 3) the politics of consultation and best practicable means. Each practice encompassed a bias that worked against swift action on the acid-rain issue.

The urban-health bias and the urban monitoring system   UK air-pollution control was originally a response to the notorious smogs that haunted the Victorian city. Even as late as 1952 a period of smog caused thousands of deaths. British air pollution was always primarily perceived as an urban problem, and policies were aimed at clearing up the urban skies and reducing health risks. What was important was reducing the concentrations of particles, smoke and heavy metals such as lead. If SO_2 was perceived as a problem, it was always as ground-level concentration (where it was a direct threat to human health) and not its emission as such. For that reason the official SO_2 policy remained 'dilute and disperse': until 1986 high stacks were seen as the appropriate strategy towards SO_2 emissions.

This urban and health-orientated definition of the air pollution problem solidified in institutional arrangements and became a distinct institutional bias: institutions of pollution control were simply not perceptive of other forms of air pollution. One particularly important practice in this respect was the monitoring system. Most monitoring stations set up under the Clean Air Act 1956 were confined to cities: only 150 out of 1,200 were located in rural areas. This urban bias in monitoring helps to explain the prevalence of the myth that acid rain did not affect the British countryside: for a long time there simply were no data to show the contrary. However, SO_2 was at least recognized as a problem. This was certainly not true for two other acid rain-related pollutants: ozone and NO_x. In 1984 the lack of monitoring stations prevented a clear picture of the effects and distribution of these pollutants in the UK.

This urban and SO_2-related definition of air pollution proved to be a particularly persistent and powerful element in the traditional pragmatist storyline on acid rain. It kept reappearing, although as early as 1976 a government spokesman had already officially admitted that British acid rain fell on Scandinavia and thereby acknowledged that the air pollution problem was far from being confined to the urban realm.[24].

The urban definition was reinforced by new confirmations; for example, by Secretary of State for the Environment Michael Heseltine in 1979:

> Sulphur dioxide emissions . . . fell [after 1970] by about 16 percent and recently seem to have been roughly stable at a new low level, while average urban concentrations have fallen about 50 percent since the early 1960s; the difference between the patterns in emissions and concentrations is the result of more effective means of dispersal, e.g., higher chimneys.[25]

The paper fails to mention the then well-known fact that the unintended negative consequence of the tall-stack policy was the aggravation of the acid-rain problem abroad. The CEGB also used the lack of data to reinforce its case. In evidence presented to the select committee, the CEGB argued that 'recently there were 104 occasions when a particular value [for ozone pollution] was exceeded in Germany and only once in the United Kingdom'.[26] Considering the lack of measurement, this was hardly surprising.

An additional reason for the persistence of the urban-health bias is explained by the fact that rural conservation in the UK, as with so many issues, has always been defined in terms of land-use planning. Countryside conservation in the UK is interpreted as protection against urban sprawl, not pollution. This is reflected in the institutional practices of the environmental movement, for instance in its expertise and in the direction of its lobbying activity.[27]

The science-based policy approach Decisions on pollution issues rely on a scientific assessment of the seriousness of the situation. This dominant role of science in UK pollution control originally was meant to keep decision-making insulated from pressure groups and to keep pollution control policy out of the sphere of corporatism and interest groups. It was meant to make sure that abatement measures will be introduced only when there is firm scientific understanding of the phenomenon. It is essential to appreciate the fundamental part played by this science-based policy approach in the acid-rain controversy. As William Waldegrave, then minister at the DoE, said in 1984: 'We see no point in making heroic efforts, at great cost, to control one out of many factors unless there is a reasonable expectation that such control will lead to real improvement in the environment.'[28]

The science-based policy approach to environmental politics is clarified in *Pollution Paper no. 11*, in which the government describes UK environmental policy:

> People are naturally very much concerned about the effects of pollution on health . . . It is inherent in our society that such pressures should arise, but to accede to them unquestioningly could often involve a waste of resources as well as the possible loss of activities and benefits on which society places value . . . It is

important to ensure that the standards being imposed do not rest on an unsound scientific justification or require disporportionate economic costs, since this would make it difficult later to introduce further measures, however well founded. In explaining standards, however, the risk of gross misinterpretation of data and the need to avoid disclosure of truly confidential information need to be borne in mind.[29]

Here the government imposed a distinction between real, objective risks and perceived risk based on misinformation. At the same time the government suggests that decision-making cannot be based on social concern; it has to be legitimized through scientific discourse.

This science-based policy approach can be shown to have a hidden institutional dimension. It would be quite wrong to suggest that the government's reading of the scientific evidence reflected the opinion of the British scientific community at large. The 1984 House of Commons inquiry indicated that a majority of experts actually were of the opinion that enough was known. The government, however, legitimized its stubborn refusal to act by reference to the opinion of the Royal Society of London. Although primarily concerned with pure research, this prestigious scientific institution's influence on the regulation of acid rain can hardly be overestimated. The traditional pragmatist story-line on acid rain held that to be recognized as firm evidence, research should meet the strong epistemological criteria characteristic of fundamental scientific disciplines, such as physics and chemistry. Other scientists, however, argued that pollution-related research should be seen as something fundamentally different from experimental science and that knowledge was a product of gradually accumulating evidence from many different corners. So, in March 1984, Patrick Jenkin, Secretary of State at the DoE, could argue that it was 'necessary to establish a clear idea of the cause and effect before spending millions of pounds which might turn out to be useless',[30] whereas scientists working in the field maintained that 'the complexity of acidification processes is such that absolute proof of causality in terms of acid deposition affecting biota, is never likely to be obtained'.[31]

In retrospect, two moments appear crucial. First, in September 1983 the Royal Society organized a major conference on acid rain to discuss the state of knowledge on the effects of sulphur and nitrogen compounds on the environment. Although the initiators had hoped the conference could provide a basis for action, it ended up criticizing the partial and imprecise data available. This served the cause of the electricity industry. Lord Marshall (then Sir Walter), the Chairman of the CEGB and himself a fellow of the Royal Society, announced the launch of the SWAP project, which was to be conducted jointly with the Royal Swedish Academy and the Norwegian Academy of Science and Letters.

Second, in June 1984 (i.e. during the select committee inquiry), the Prime Minister invited leading scientists from the major research institutions working on the topic to the Prime Minister's retreat at Chequers to get an update on the state of knowledge on acid rain. The CEGB represesntatives, having done by far the most research, dominated the debate. They emphasized the lack of knowledge and referred to the SWAP project, which would soon provide answers to the many questions. In so doing they not only postulated the supremacy of Royal Society science but also ridiculed those who argued for immediate action. Other specialists failed to convey to the Prime Minister, indeed failed to argue, that in environmental affairs conclusive evidence of biochemical mechanisms is rarely found and that less rigid epistemological requirements are usually applied to environmental phenomena.

As a result, the SWAP project came to be the linchpin in the acid-rain controversy. The government's decision to retrofit three power stations with FGD scrubbers in September 1986 can be shown to be linked to developments in the SWAP project. In June that year two CEGB directors had accepted the results of certain SWAP experiments as being decisive: they accepted the evidence that sulphur emissions contributed to fish death, albeit in a more complicated way than environmentalists had maintained. The great political commitment to SWAP and the involvement of the Royal Society meant that these projects could not easily be dismissed; certainly the 1986 decision would not have occurred without SWAP.

However, although the SWAP results played a key role, they do not suffice for a full explanation of the 1986 decision. As a matter of fact, the emergence of this scientific evidence coincided with the internal publication of new forecasts of energy demand, which predicted an important increase. This implied that SO_2 emissions would increase rather dramatically. The new knowledge acquired through SWAP made it clear that this would cause a dramatic increase in acidification levels. What is more, it would go against all existing UK commitments to contain SO_2 emissions. Apart from this, the scientific basis fitted the managerial concerns nicely. The research indicated that the CEGB would not need to initiate a crash programme as the Germans had done; it could wait until new plants came on line around the turn of the century, thus avoiding the costs of extra retrofits. The 1986 decision was, in other words, not evidence of a reversal of policy, but much more of the fact that one had found the scientifically defined critical limit.

To summarize, the symbolic order of the Royal Society, the co-operation of the Norwegian and Swedish academies and commitment to a socially constructed practice of 'good science' tied up the participants and precluded any discussion. The science-based policy approach was not just a rhetorical device but a complicated policy practice that structured the argumentative process through which power was exercised and interests were mediated.

The politics of consultation and the 'best practicable means'   UK air-pollution control has always relied on close consultation between the inspectorate and the polluting industries.[32] In the UK, pollution control is not a matter of setting uniform standards and forcing the industry to comply. The idea is more to help individual industries find practicable solutions to avoid pollution. In this respect the Alkali Inspectorate requires industries to use the 'best practicable means' (BPM) to avoid pollution. BPM has been used in air pollution control since 1874 but was first properly defined by statute in the Clean Air Act 1956: '"Practicable" means reasonably practicable having regard, amongst other things, to local conditions and circumstances, to the financial implications and to the current state of technical knowledge.'[33] Like the science-based policy approach, BPM allocated a central role to the expert. The inspectorate regularly publishes *Notes on BPM* to determine which pollution abatement strategy is considered the best practicable means. This practice thus eliminates both politics and the public: BPM works on the basis of a relationship of mutual trust and respect between experts from the inspectorate and industry.

BPM is a practice that can, in principle, work surprisingly well in initiating new abatement strategies, but in the acid-rain controversy it did not speed up action. Here the discursive creation of the inspectorate as a strong and autonomous institution played a key role. In fact both the government and the inspectorate kept up this image. For instance, in 1984 the government argued that

> flue gas desulphurisation is a proven technology for removing sulphur dioxide from power station plumes but the . . . Inspectorate have not required its installation, because at a capital cost of some 150 million pounds for each major power station, they have regarded it as too expensive an imposition to constitute 'best practicable means'.[34]

This suggests that the inspectorate is indeed an autonomous institution that will take the initiative to set the standards if necessary. Consequently, if the inspectorate does not require FGD equipment, politicians can use this as an expert argument against popular pressure. Here the costs of preventing acid rain, i.e. the price of electricity, which is essentially a political issue, is made into a quasi-nonpolitical technical decision.

Had the inspectorate been an autonomous institution it might have argued for the installation of FGD equipment to combat acid rain. Yet for political reasons it never did. The inspectorate was a lame duck that in the end did not consider FGD equipment to be the best practicable means until after both the government and the industry had agreed to install scrubbers. Yet again it shows how the reference to the Alkali Inspectorate as an autonomous institution with a 'proud record' in fact had a hidden political meaning.

The ecomodernist interpretation of acid rain

Over the years the traditional pragmatist story-line on acid rain was fiercely attacked by actors both within Parliament and outside. Three key actors can be distinguished: the House of Commons Select Committee on Environmental Pollution, the Royal Commission on Environmental Pollution and the NGO Friends of the Earth UK (FOE). All three employed ecomodernist reasoning.

The ecomodernist story-line on acid rain inevitably started from the perception that acid rain was not just another incidental issue: the select committee saw acid rain as 'one of the major environmental hazards faced by the industrial world today'; the royal commission argued that 'acid deposition is one of the most important pollution issues of the present time', while FOE contended that 'acid rain is already widespread in Britain'.[35]

The ecomodernists acknowledged that knowledge about acid rain was imperfect, but held that time was running out. 'Enough is now known', ecomodernists argued from 1982 onwards, to justify the spending on curative measures. They also knew what had to be done: like the Swedish government they saw the CEGB power stations as the main culprit, and so retrofitting power stations with FGD scrubbers was put forward as the proven technology to cure the problem. In reply to the figure showing the overall decline in SO_2 emissions presented by the traditional pragmatists, the ecomodernists illustrated their argument with a graph that indicated the relative increase of the role of power stations therein. Furthermore, the ecomodernists emphasized that the UK was still the largest producer of SO_2 in western Europe.[36]

The most influential statement of the ecomodernists on acid rain was undoubtedly the fourth report of the House of Commons Environment Select Committee, published in 1984, which was entirely devoted to the problem of acid rain. It pulled together various elements of knowledge and assessed the consequences of the strategies available.

Like the traditional pragmatist story-line, the ecomodernist argument evolved around a scientific core, yet with the opposite outcome: it argued that science showed that enough was known. It referred to alternative yet much respected expert bodies such as the National Environmental Research Council and the Nature Conservancy Council that were invoked to legitimize the claim that decisions could and should be taken. The select committee also argued for direct symbolic action: the UK should join the 30 per cent club immediately.

Interestingly, the ecomodernists presented only part of the acid-rain problem. For strategic reasons the select committee especially emphasized the fact that acid rain is responsible for damage to historic buildings: acid rain is 'slowly but surely dissolving away our architectural heritage and modern buildings', it argued.[37] Later, emphasis was put on the effects of acid rain on British broadleaf trees. This reflected a conscious strategy to make the issue more appealing for the British public. The select committee thus also gave a certain emphasis in apportioning the blame. It argued that non-nuclear power stations were responsible for most of the SO_2 and NO_x emissions, and that action should therefore focus on that single source.[38] In its recommendation to install FGD equipment, the select committee thus carefully left small industrial plants and private traffic (cars) out of the issue.[39]

More insight into the ecomodernist discourse coalition can be derived from the contributions of a second key actor: the Royal Commission on Environmental Pollution. Its tenth report (1984) was a celebrated *tour de horizon* evaluating the main environmental issues of its day. The report argued that the government should exercise a responsible stewardship to the environment, and echoed key ecomodernist convictions such as pollution prevention pays. However, the commission's recommendations on acid rain did not, in fact, really match the ecomodernist tone of the tenth report. Although the commission asserted that enough was known about the damage due to acid rain and argued that FGD retrofits are the only short-term solution available, it failed to make the recommendations that would match its analysis. Its recommendations boiled down to statement that 'high priority should be given to research on acid deposition, in particular on the causes and effects, on the interaction with other pollutants, and on remedial action'. In addition it recommended that the CEGB should introduce, on a pilot basis, certain abatement options thus falling a long way short of the ecomodernist idea that pollution was to be prevented in principle. For strategic reasons it also refrained from recommending that the UK should join the 30 per cent club.[40]

The third key actor operating within the ecomodernist frame was the NGO Friends of the Earth. FOE emphasized the extent to which acid rain threatened the British flora and fauna. Twice the FOE had organized a survey of tree health in Britain to prove that acid rain is not just a problem for far-away Scandinavia. The FOE argued strongly for an electricity conservation programme that would reduce demand by 5 per cent as an additional measure to the FGD retrofits. This should be based on the usage of more efficient appliances of various sorts. Later, this sort of prevention should replace scrubbing as a policy strategy. The FOE promoted this preventive strategy on the basis that 'it is likely to be more expensive to act later than sooner'.[41] Like the royal commission, the FOE referred to the conservation and development programme for the UK as a useful way of looking at environment problems. The FOE was strongly in favour of joining the international initiative of the 30 per cent club.

Ecological modernization as political practice

Political entrepreneurs who tried to make a case for a preventive acid-rain policy found themselves not only arguing an intricate technical case but also challenging the key institutional practice of UK pollution politics at the same time. First, the build-up of support for action was hampered by the lack of available data on the effects of acid rain on the British countryside (as opposed to effects on far-away Scandinavia). Breaking the urban bias in the air pollution monitoring network was essential. The first reliable evidence of rainfall acidity in Britain was established by the Institute for Terrestrial Ecology (ITE), which had created its own monitoring network in 1977. The ITE was, perhaps not surprisingly, among the first scientific bodies to claim that the levels of acid deposition warranted action.[42] Another important activity in this respect was the three health surveys the Friends of the Earth conducted in 1985. The significance of both initiatives was not restricted to the realization that acid rain might affect the beloved British countryside. It also brought to light the intimation that the picture of the UK's 'proud record' in air pollution control might be false.

Second, ecomodernist actors had difficulty finding the right approach to the mobilization of bias contained in the science-based policy approach. The fact that the tenth report of the royal commission failed to argue for immediate action on acid rain despite its endorsement of ecological modernization was due to the fact that it realized that it would be pointless to speak out for action before at least some results of the SWAP project were known.[43] The appraisal does not seem inaccurate: many other recommendations of respected quasi-governmental agencies were over-ruled because the Royal Society had not yet given its opinion. Furthermore, the science-based policy approach prevented the royal commission from arguing in favour of joining the 30 per cent club. The 30 per cent figure had been identified by many UK institutions as purely arbitrary (which it was, of course), and the royal commission wanted to be seen as committed to the science-based policy approach. Speaking out in favour of something symbolic and political in nature might harm its reputation.

Third, the role of the inspectorate in operating the BPM practice also hampered the application of ecomodernist principles. In the first place, BPM was to be understood as best practicable *available* means. The industry was under no obligation to develop new technologies. BPM thus failed to stimulate the invention and implementation of new pollution-abatement equipment. Second, 'economic incapacity' was a legitimate reason for inaction which made BPM both vulnerable to conjunctural economic change and to biased presentations of costs and economic capacity of firms. Moreover, even though the inspectorate has to judge the economic possibilities of firms, it employs neither economists nor accountants.[44]

Conclusion: the paradox of ecological modernization

The UK acid-rain controversy was a prime site of trying to put the new ecomodernist rhetoric to work. The intricate nature of the issue (that experts understood only in part), the possibility of extensive environmental damage and the widespread concern among the public made acid rain an ideal issue to show that the old traditional pragmatist policy discourse was not fit to deal with the new environmental problems and was therefore in need of replacement. Acid rain appeared to be, to use the words of philosopher of science Jerome Ravetz, a typical case that called for hard decisions made by politicians having at their disposal merely 'soft' or potentially controversial scientific evidence.[45]

In the general debate on environmental politics ecomodernist thinking can be shown to have made headway during the 1980s. Politicians and policymakers at the highest level could be seen paying lip-service to ecological modernization. However, the case study on acid rain illuminates the fact that the actual process of regulation was still conducted according to the format of the traditional pragmatist discourse.

Earlier I distinguished five key elements of the challenge of ecological modernization in the UK: nature should no longer be regarded as a 'sink', pollution prevention pays, unambiguous scientific proof should no longer be regarded as a *sine qua non*, public perceptions of risk should no longer be refuted as irrational, and substances should more often be regarded as guilty until proven innocent. Official government publications recognized the credibility of these claims. Good reasons might be given for this apparent success: the concepts formed a suitable reply to the spreading public concern over the environment, the ecomodernist concepts constituted a coherent and reasonable perspective which did not threaten the basic social order and, last but not least, prevention of pollution appeared to make economic sense.

However, the analysis of the content of the controversy 1) focused on the *damage* caused by acid rain, which suggests that emissions as such were still regarded as legitimate; 2) emphasized the costs involved in avoiding pollution; 3) showed that only unambiguous scientific proof could persuade the UK government to install FGD equipment; 4) showed that the public perceptions of the problem were not allowed to have an immediate impact; and 5) indicated that until SO_2 was proven guilty it was regarded as innocent. So, when put to the test, the ecomodernist discourse coalition failed to impose its discursive logic on the actual regulation. What is more, it failed to use acid rain as a case in point to expose the anachronistic nature of the existing institutional arrangements. In the end the ecomodernists and the traditional pragmatists in fact argued the same case: both were committed to FGD equipment as 'proven' solution, with the only differences regarding the timing and intensity of the remedial programme. How is this paradox to be explained?

The first element of the explanation concerns strategic action. The *de facto* agreement between ecomodernist and traditional pragmatists regarding the social construction of the problem – acid rain being an SO_2–FGD–CEGB-related problem – was based on the strategic consideration of ecomodernist actors to opt for a symbolically appealing, immediately understandable and politically straightforward construction of the problem. In fact the ideas of ecological modernization would have called for much more emphasis on the need for energy conservation and for the analysis of the way in which many central social practices (including car-based mobility) were implicated.

Moreover, ecomodernists could have taken a more offensive approach by arguing that unambiguous scientific proof should not be seen as an essential precondition for policy-making, and that, in the face of the implied risks, prudence was just as valid a basis for decision-making as 'proper' scientific knowledge. The realization that air pollutants acted in combination gave extra weight to this claim. Instead, ecomodernists try to beat the traditional pragmatists in their own game by employing utilitarian and scientific arguments. In the end all the actors tried to show they were the 'right kind of people': FOE did not want to be portrayed as dreamers, the royal commission did not want to lose its image of respectability and thoughtfulness in a direct confrontation with the highly regarded Royal Society, and the select committee wished to prove that it kept its distance from interest-based politics and was much afraid of 'getting its science wrong'. However, in respecting all these positionings, the ecomodernists effectively conformed to the old institutionalized standards of credibility and failed to challenge the routinized mode of thinking. This despite the fact that ecomodernist arguments such as precaution had already been employed by government officials in the parallel debate on the principles of environmental policy-making and had also already been accepted in international forums, such as for instance the EC Environmental Action Programmes.

The second element that explains the convergence of the ecomodernists and the traditional pragmatists is the institutional context of the three sets of practices described above. These practices – related to the monitoring system, the science-based policy approach and the politics of consultation and best practicable means – reflected the institutionalized patterns of domination of the past. In the acid-rain controversy these practices routinely reproduced the traditional pragmatist discourse: actors who chose to play by the rules of the game had this inherent discursive logic imposed upon them. Both the science-based policy discourse and the best practicable means were explicitly designed to depoliticize pollution control, while the urban-health bias in the system of air pollution monitoring reflected long-standing political priorities. Although each set of practices had a discursive logic of its own, they together routinely produced the traditional pragmatist way of regulating acid rain. This engendered a discursive bias that militated against anticipatory response to the acid-rain problem, which would have been characteristic of an ideal-typical ecomodernist approach.

A third element can be derived from the strength of the symbolic order that was reproduced by the traditional pragmatist discourse coalition. In the argumentative game the normative appeal of the long-standing policy practices, with their alleged 'proud record' in combating air pollution problems, hampered the argument for institutional change. In many cases the traditional pragmatists legitimized inaction by reifying their institutionalized way of regulating pollution: the traditional pragmatist practices were presented as a permanent, natural state of affairs. The references to past success suggested that the traditional pragmatist way of dealing with pollution was not a historically specific, transitory state of affairs that, if circumstances changed, might have to make way for another approach. Furthermore, the discussion of the science-based policy approach illuminated the ideological strength of 'pure science' epistemology and the symbolic significance of the Royal Society. This was so well embedded that actors such as the royal commission refrained from calling for immediate action, in anticipation of a certain rebuff.

Moreover, the fact that FGD equipment was finally installed also illustrates the symbolic nature of politics. Placing scrubbers on a chimney was a clear act which could be interpreted as a sign of success by actors operating in both coalitions. The critics could point to change,[46] and the traditional pragmatists could claim that the legitimacy of their policy discourse held.[47] What is more, it accorded with the popular perception of the problem and avoided a direct conflict with the larger part of the community.

A fourth element in the explanation comes from a reflection on the position of environmental politics in the overall order of governmental activity. First, ecological modernization would, if put into practice, affect the institutional practices of more than just the Department of the Environment. It would affect the Departments of Industry, Transport, Agriculture and, above all, Energy. All the actors knew from the very beginning that the introduction of a new discourse would succeed only if it was supported at the highest level, that is, by the Prime Minister. Although government ministers might have appreciated the value of the *idea* of ecological modernization, they would certainly resist the institutional repercussions; that is, the repositioning of their departments according to the principles of this discourse. In this respect acid rain was merely the first test case for ecomodernist policy discourse. Clearly, the Prime Minister's support was not available at the time. Second, the acceptance of ecological modernization would not only jeopardize the institutional autonomy of many departments, it would also imply a major reorientation in the overall ordering of government priorities. Environmental politics in the UK, as, indeed, in most other countries, has always been subordinate to general industrial and economic politics.

In the period after the second world war, the traditional pragmatist discourse in environmental politics worked in the context of Keynesian welfare-state politics. The Keynesian hard-core values concerned the management of a 'positive sum' growth-orientated economy, based on a social contract between capital and labour with all kinds of welfare policies in a supportive role. With the coming of the neoliberalist era under Prime Minister Margaret Thatcher in 1979, environmental politics was even more unlikely to shake off its peripheral status. Thatcher's priority was the restructuring of UK industry and the restoration of British competitiveness. Ecological modernization assumed that the environmental dimension would be taken into consideration in this restructuring, but the Thatcher government preferred a policy of non-interference regarding goal-setting as opposed to imposing ecologically sound innovations on industry. Subsidies, if given at all, came with no strings attached; and neither large public expenditure on FGD equipment nor the higher prices in electricity that would result from it were in accordance with the core polices of Thatcherism.

The net effect of this course of affairs was the reproduction of the predominant 'single problem – single answer' construction of the challenge of environmental politics. The acid-rain controversy was resolved by implementing another end-of-pipe solution. The most important insight to be derived from the case study of acid rain is the degree to which routinized institutional practices can obstruct or uphold the change towards a more sustainable policy discourse. Yet ecological modernization is not the sort of policy discourse that will whither away. It is much more likely to change slowly the prevailing policy practices. Concepts like the precautionary principle, that are now widely endorsed, might be far more powerful than they initially seemed and generate a social dynamic of their own. As of yet, ecological modernization is a story with an open end.

Acknowledgement

This is an abbreviated and edited version of the contribution 'Discourse coalitions and the institutionalization of practice: the case of acid rain in Britain' that appeared in J. Forester and F. Fischer (eds) (1993) *The Argumentative Turn in Policy and Planning*, Duke University Press, Durham, NC, pp. 43–76.

Notes

1. See S. Boehmer-Christiansen, 'Black mist and the acid rain: science as a figleaf of policy,' *The Political Quarterly*, Vol. 59, no. 2, 1988, pp. 145–60; S. Boehmer-Christiansen and J. Skea, *Acid Politics: Environmental and Energy Politics in Britain and Germany* (London: Belhaven, 1991); C.C. Park, *Acid Rain: Rhetoric and Reality* (London: Methuen, 1987).

2. For an elaborate presentation on the principles of discourse analysis, see M. Hajer, *The Politics of Environmental Discourse: Ecological Modernization and the Policy Process*, Oxford University Press, 1995).

3. The best accounts of the history of acid rain are E.B. Cowling, 'Acid precipitation in historical perspective,' *Environmental Science and Technology*, Vol. 16, no. 2, 1982, pp. 110A–23A; G.S. Wedstone, 'A history of the acid rain issue', in H. Brooks and C.L. Cooper (eds) *Science for Public Policy* (Oxford: Pergamon Press, 1987).

4. As it happened, this immediately followed the publication of a paper on rainfall acidity in northern Britain in *Nature* which revealed that the acidity of rain was comparable with the areas of Scandinavia and North America where fish populations had been depleted. See D. Fowler *et al.*, 'Rainfall acidity in northern Britain,' *Nature*, Vol. 297, 1982, pp. 383–6.

5. Later evidence suggested that the UK is in fact responsible for 43 per cent of the acid deposition on southern Norway (*Nature*, Vol. 327, p. 648).

6. L. Kramme, 'National and international pressures in environmental policy override neo-classical prescriptions: the case of the EC's large combustion plant directive. Paper presented at the ECPR Joint Sessions, Paris, 1989.

7. Because of differing geographical, economic and fuel-supply circumstances some countries were allowed different percentages. The UK, as a large coal-burning country, would only have to reduce its emissions by 20, 40 and 60 per cent (by 1993, 1998 and 2003, respectively) as opposed to the FRG and The Netherlands, for instance, that were committed to a 30, 60 and 70 per cent reduction by the same dates.

8. The discrepancy was bigger than immediately meets the eye since at that time it was believed that this percentage would be achieved by the then-apparent tendency of SO_2 emission to fall.

9. For the history of air pollution politics in the UK, see E. Ashby and M. Anderson, *The Politics of Clean Air* (Oxford: Clarendon Press, 1981).

10. Lord Derby, in *ibid*. p. 21.

11. E.F. Schumacher, *Small is Beautiful* (London: Abacus, 1974). Another early protagonist of this modernization element in the environmental movement was Amory Lovins with his concept of 'soft energy paths'. For a detailed discussion, see R. Paehlke, *Environmentalism and the Future of Progressive Politics* (New Haven, Conn.: Yale University Press, 1989).

12. For a good introduction, see A. Weale, *The New Politics of Pollution* (Manchester University Press, 1992).

13. Anon., *The World Conservation Strategy – Living Resource Conservation for Sustainable Development* (Geneva: International Union for the Conservation of Nature and Natural Resources, 1980); Anon., *The Conservation and Development Programme for the UK: A Response to the World Conservation Strategy* (London: Kogan Page, 1983); Royal Commission on environmental Environmental Pollution, *Tenth Report: Tackling Pollution – Experience and Prospects* (London: HMSO, 1984); World Commission on Environment and Development, *Our Common Future* Oxford University Press, 1987).

14. Royal Commission, *Tenth Report*, p. 179.

15. In *ibid*. p. 178.

16. W. Waldegrave, 'Economic development and environmental care – the role of government,' in *Environmentalism Today – The Challenge for Business* (proceedings of a conference organized by the UK Centre for Economic and Environmental Development and by National Economic Research Associates, April 1986).

17. For a much more elaborate discussion, see Hajer, *Politics of Environmental Discourse*, Ch. 1.

18. Department of the Environment (DoE), *Our Common Future – A Perspective by the United Kingdom on the Report of the World Commission on Environment and Development* (London: DoE, 1986).

19. Lord Marshall, in *New Scientist*, 25 September 1986, p. 23.

20. Lord Marshall, in House of Commons Select Committee on the Environment, *Fourth Report: Acid Rain, Vol. 2: Minutes of Evidence* (London: HMSO, 1984), p. 20.

21. *Ibid*. p. 36.

22. Statement of the DoE at the ministerial conference on acid rain held in Munich, June 1984.

23. DoE, *The Government Reply to the Fourth Report of the Environment Select Committee* (London: HMSO, 1984), p. 3.

24. This was first acknowledged in a statement by L.E. Reed at the presentation of the DoE report *Effects of Airborne Sulphur Compounds on Forests and Freshwaters* (*Pollution Paper no. 7*) (London: HMSO, 1976), before the 1976 Telemark conference (Norway).

25. DoE, *The United Kingdom Environment 1979: Progress of Pollution Control* (*Pollution Paper no. 16*) (London: HMSO, 1979), p. 3.

26. CEGB in Select Committee, *Fourth Report, Minutes of Evidence*, p. 18.

27. See, for instance, T. O'Riordan, 'Culture and the environment in Britain,' *Environmental Management*, Vol. 9, no. 2, 1985, pp. 113–20.

28. Speech to the closing session of the Munich conference on acid rain, 27 June 1984.

29. DoE, *Environmental Standards: A Description of United Kingdom Practice* (*Pollution Paper no. 11*) (London: HMSO, 1977), pp. 7–8.

30. In Park, *Acid Rain*, p. 222.

31. National Environmental Research Council, in Select Committee, *Fourth Report, Minutes of Evidence*, p. 228.

32. The best account of the fascinating early years of the Alkali Inspectorate is undoubtedly R.M. MacLeod, 'The alkali Acts administration, 1863–84: the emergence of the civil scientist,' *Victorian Studies*, Vol. 9, no. 2, 1965, pp. 85–112; for a good case study on the more recent abatement practice, see K. Hawkins, *Environment and Enforcement* (Oxford University Press, 1984).

33. In Royal Commission, *Tenth Report*, p. 45.

34. DoE, *Controlling Pollution: Principles and Prospects – The Government's Reply to the Tenth Report of the Royal Commission on Environmental Pollution (Pollution Paper no. 22)* (London: HMSO, 1984), p. 2.

35. Select Committee, *Fourth Report, Minutes of Evidence*, p. 1; Royal Commission, *Tenth Report*, p. 147; FOE in Select Committee, *Fourth Report, Minutes of Evidence*, p. 39.

36. Royal Commission, *Tenth Report*, 144; FOE, in Select Committee, *Fourth Report, Minutes of Evidence*, pp. 37, 40; Select Committee, *Fourth Report, Minutes of Evidence*, pp. xi, xiii.

37. Select Committee, *Fourth Report, Minutes of Evidence*, p. xx.

38. *Ibid.* p. lii.

39. *Ibid.* p. lxxi.

40. Royal Commission, *Tenth Report*, p. 147.

41. FOE, in Select Committee, *Fourth Report, Minutes of Evidence*, pp. 8, 42, 51.

42. See Fowler *et al.*, 'Rainfall acidity.'

43. It did not help that the Chairman of the royal commission at that time, Professor Sir Richard Southwood, was also chairing the SWAP project.

44. See D. Vogel, *National Styles of Regulation* (Ithaca, NY: Cornell University Press, 1986, pp. 80, 83.

45. J.R. Ravetz, 'Usable knowledge, usable ignorance: incomplete science with policy implications,' in W. Clark and R. Munn (eds) *Sustainable Development of the Biosphere* (Cambridge University Press, 1986).

46. As indeed they did; see House of Commons Select Committee on the European Communities; *First Report: Air Pollution*, 2 vols (London, HMSO, 1988).

47. As indeed they did; see evidence to Select Committee, 1988.

10

Hazardous waste policy, community movements and the politics of Nimby: participatory risk assessment in the USA and Canada

FRANK FISCHER
Rutgers University, USA

During the late 1970s and 1980s news reports of oil spills, nuclear disaster at Chernobyl, near-disasters at Three-Mile Island, pesticides in the food chain and DDT damage to wildlife have frightened people around the world (Piller, 1991). The result has been a widespread distrust of industry and a collective fear of all chemical-processing facilities. As the public has become increasingly aware of the extent to which chemicals now pollute the environment, the result has been a new anxiety often described as 'chemophobia'. Polls show that citizens are more concerned about the presence of toxic wastes than any other environmental problem, even though the Environmental Protection Agency maintains that it is not the most severe health threat. Problems such as the ozone hole and the greenhouse effect are said to be much riskier. Such public fear is seen by many experts and commentators to be irrational.

One of the clearest manifestations of this anxiety has come to be called the 'Nimby syndrome'. Much discussed in both the academic and popular presses, Nimby (not in my backyard) is now blamed as a major stumbling block for solving a growing number of environmental problems. As numerous commentators have pointed out, the public formerly accepted everything, but now it seems to oppose just about everything.

Nimby covers a wide range of activities: 'Whether the matter is health, peace of mind, or protection of property values, few Americans (activists or not) care to live beside chemical-waste dumps, airports, petrochemical refineries, nuclear power plants, or other standard features of a modern industrial society' (*ibid*. p. 12). But Nimby is not a term designed to reflect just any opposition. As a theoretical construct, Nimby is a phenomenon based on a specific type of opposition. It is a reflection of a public attitude that seems to be almost self-contradictory – that people feel it is desirable to site a potentially hazardous type of facility somewhere as long as it is not where they personally live.[1] Nimby, moreover, seems to be spreading to one policy area after another: landfills, prisons, power plants (nuclear or otherwise), industrial parks, housing for the homeless, treatment facilities for drug addicts and hazardous waste facilities (Dear, 1992). Portney (1991, p. 11) gives the following example:

> Nearly everyone seems to agree that more prison space is needed if the criminal justice system is to be able to treat convicted criminals as harshly as the public mood warrants. Yet no one wants a prison in his or her city or town . . . Most people seem to agree that such facilities are a necessary and acceptable result of living in an industrial society.

Community resistance to the siting of risky facilities can now only be described as a 'full-scale public malady', a kind of dysfunctional social 'syndrome' (Portney, 1991, pp. 10–11). Writers speak of 'policy gridlock' and 'policy stalemate'. In the case of hazardous-waste treatment facilities, for example, sitings have virtually ground to a halt during the past decade.

Nimby and hazardous waste

Nowhere has concern about this public 'irrationality' been more prominent than in the political conflicts associated with the siting of hazardous-waste treatment facilities. Such facilities are required to process the large number of industrial and commercial chemical waste products that possess such characteristics as toxicity, reactivity, corrosivity or ignitability. Since the 1970s, Americans have become more aware of and concerned about the growing amounts and types of such hazardous wastes generated by industry and government, especially the military. A study conducted by the Congressional Budget Office, for example, concluded 'that approximately 266 million metric tons of hazardous waste are generated in the United States annually, which amounts to more than one ton per person residing in the country' (Davis, 1993, p. 4).

The production of hazardous industrial by-products is not a new phenomenon. Rather the problem is found in the dramatic increase of such by-products since the end of the second world war, 50 per cent of which are directly attributable to the chemical products industry. The largest share of this increase has resulted from petroleum-based chemical products such as pesticides, plastics, synthetic fabrics, new paints, solvents and wood preservatives. Other important sources of hazardous waste include the paper, fabricated metals and food industries.

A statistical profile of such wastes can inform policy-makers about the 'who', 'where' and 'how much' of such waste production, but conveys little about the actual risks to public health or environmental quality associated with such materials. And it is just this question that has been the source of the problem. Despite concerted attempts to assure the public of the safety of sophisticated treatment facilities, community groups have, by and large, been unwilling to accept the assurances offered by their managers. Especially acute has been the issue of incinerating hazardous materials. Although many argue that incineration offers the safest – i.e. least risky long-term alternative for disposing of such wastes – it has encountered fierce community opposition. No one wants their community to be the site of the incinerator or a landfill. Activists opposed to hazardous-waste treatment facilities are quite varied in their strategies and objectives. Basic to their efforts, however, are a number of common characteristics: 'Nearly all begin with the frustrated rage and fear of people who perceive themselves as victims and who see their quality of life threatened' (Piller, 1991, p. 12). Highly focused on protecting their home environments, Nimby activists have wasted little time at becoming skilled at petition drives, political lobbying, street confrontations and legal proceedings. If their frustrated rage and anxiety is the most general characteristic that unites these groups, the most specific is their rejection of experts and technocrats as the ultimate arbiters of technological risk and change. Often, in this regard, the zeal of Nimby groups is proselytic and self-righteousness. In fact, some have likened Nimby activists to other moral and religious movements that have gained large followings by advancing what can be described as 'a spiritual critique of medical or scientific teachings and practices'. Piller (*ibid.*) puts it this way: 'Although the link between Nimby groups and right-wing religious movements are otherwise tenuous, they share irreverence for official versions of reality offered by scientists and technocrats.' Indeed, it can be ironically argued that Nimbyism 'is partly a reaction to the effects of the quasi-religious faith in science that emerged in this country following the Second World War'. It represents the contemporary burial of the technological optimism that has long defined the 'American Century'.

Nimby and environmental risk assessment

Nimby is an 'intractable' or 'wicked problem' (Fischer, 1994). All accounts of the phenomenon use such terms as 'recalcitrant', 'undisciplined', 'uncontrollable' and 'unmanageable'. Not only do Nimby groups renounce the government's policy objectives for the use of their own local land but they also fundamentally reject the analyses of the policy analysts who seek to define the problem for them. In this latter respect, the conflict has most often centred around government and industry's use of risk assessment, a major policy analysis technique which has come to dominate environmental policy decision-making (Figure 10.1).

The official response of government and industry to fears accompanying toxic risks has been to submit the dangers to a risk assessment (Wynne, 1987; Fischer, 1990). Formal policy analysis has been used in an attempt 'rationally' to decide the issue by focusing the risk debate on technical factors. Specifically, the purpose has been to shift the political discourse to a search for 'acceptable risk'. The supporters of the modern technoindustrial complex argue that risk must be seen as a mixed phenomenon, always producing both danger and opportunity. Too often, they argue, the debate revolves purely around potential dangers (frequently centring on high-impact accidents with low probability – e.g. nuclear meltdowns or runaway genetic mutations). The approach is

Risk assessment has developed in response to the special decision-making problems associated with technoindustrial society, in particular the array of technological and environmental hazards that have accompanied it. The methodology has not only emerged as a widely approved decision methodology but has also been formally adopted by the Environmental Protection Agency as the basic decision test governing the development and evaluation of all regulations pertinent to the environment.

Risk assessment is specifically employed to evaluate risk resulting from both hazardous technologies and toxic health threats (Covello, 1989). The goal is accurately to predict the health implications of a hazard before or after it exists, and to establish valid safety standards to protect the exposed population. The methodology typically involves four inter-related steps: 1) a process of hazardous identification, e.g. does a waste incinerator emit dioxins or heavy metals?; 2) an assessment of human exposure, e.g. can the various routes of the toxin to the effected population be traced and how much of it enters the human body?; 3) the modelling of the dose-responses, e.g. what is the empirical relationship of the exposures to the chemical under investigation and the frequency of adverse impacts?; and 4) a characterization of the overall risk, e.g. how does the data as a whole provide an overall evaluation of the toxic's implications for human health, most commonly defined in terms of cancer? In an effort to err on the conservative side of safety, risk assessors most often use 'worse-case scenarios'. The overall risk is generally expressed as the probable number of cancers per million people exposed over the course of a standard life expectancy.

Figure 10.1 *Risk assessment*

grounded in the view that technological dangers have been grossly exaggerated, especially by environmentalists with a vested interest in exploiting the public's fears. The result, it is argued, is a high degree of ignorance among the general public about technological risks (Wildavsky, 1988). The classic illustration is the layperson who tends to worry a great deal about the safety of air travel but thinks nothing of driving his or her car to the airport, which statistics demonstrate to be much more dangerous.

The point, then, is to supply the public with more objective (technical) information about the levels of risks themselves. That is, the 'irrationality' of contemporary political arguments is to be countered with rationally demonstrable scientific data. The solution is to provide more information – standardized scientific information – to offset the emotionality plaguing uninformed thinkers, i.e. the proverbial 'man in the street'. Towards this end, risk assessment has been bolstered with a new subspecialty of risk management known as 'risk communication'.

But these risk methodologies have tended not only to heighten the conflict but they have also often become the very sources of contention. The typical conflict involves a government study that shows a very low level of risk and a public – or at least the community groups most directly involved – that is adamantly opposed to accepting the findings. In short, people have remained unswayed by risk assessments and the result has been a near halt in the siting of hazardous waste facilities over the past 15 years. This reluctance to accept such risks – at least after having been shown the outcomes of the analyses – has compelled environmental officials to label them 'irrational'. Oppositional groups have either rejected the experts altogether, or sought to commission their own analyses. The result has become an impending crisis: in the face of growing mounds of dangerous waste, there is no place to treat or store it.

The critique of risk assessment

Those opposing risk assessment contend that the process – wittingly or unwittingly – biases risk decision processes in favour of the dominant techno-industrial system and its values (Gutin, 1991). Through tacit assumptions that support the industrial status quo, the methodology pre-empts or undercuts the very kinds of discourse about environmental problems that the environmentalists and others seek to interject. Some, in fact, see risk assessment to be a strategy designed to do just that, namely to deflect the environmental movement's ability to rally political support against mounting hazardous risks.

Consider, for example, the argument advanced by Langdon Winner, a leading critic of the methodology. Winner argues that the methodology's analytical emphasis on risk functions to shift inquiry away from traditional concepts such as 'dangers' and 'hazards' to a more subtle and sophisticated exploration of statistical probabilities (Winner, 1986). What otherwise appears to be a fairly obvious link between technological causes and dangerous effects – for instance, the relationship between hazardous chemicals and cancer – tends to be transformed into a question fraught with scientific uncertainties. Whereas a hazard is easily recognized as a danger to health and safety – and thus reasonable people readily agree that something should be done about it – the conceptual transformation of a hazard into a question of risk works to soften and defuse the threat.

Equally problematic is risk assessment's emphasis on expert decision-making. When parties to an environmental decision about technological hazards agree to risk assessment, they commit to the studying, weighing and comparing of the costs and benefits associated with different levels of risk. In doing so they enter into a realm of enormous uncertainties over which there is little chance of a relatively simple, straightforward consensus. Not only are the commonsense assumptions upon which the concern for hazards and dangers normally rely abruptly suspended but any confidence people might have had in their own ability to deal with such hazards also vanishes in favour of excruciatingly detailed inquiries. Furthermore, because the exact nature of this (technological) cause–(environmental) effect relationship is very difficult to 'prove' in the scientific sense of the term, the question of risk always remains open to interpretation. That is to say, the interpretation remains open to the judgements of those who purport to have expertise in the matter.

This over-reliance on experts thus becomes an intellectual barrier to popular participation. Beyond merely underplaying certain kinds of interests and values, the methodology functions to impede the very participatory processes that make the advancement of community interests and values possible. In place of public discourse about what ought to be done, the decision process is *de facto* increasingly dominated by the opinions of experts. Experts, rather than the citizens themselves, decide whether or not people will live next to a hazardous waste site. This too has been described as a deliberate technocratic strategy to limit structurally the public's role in issues basic to the advance of technoindustrial society.

The participatory alternative

Essentially, the strategy of risk assessment has been employed to get around what is widely seen to be the ordinary citizen's inability to deal rationally with complex technical problems. As a technocratic strategy, the approach has explicitly sought to circumvent democratic political processes in an effort to avoid citizen participation. But is there an alternative? Many environmentalists argue that the answer is democracy itself; they call for 'environmental democracy' (Kann, 1986; Paehlke, 1990; Thornton, 1991).

Environmental democracy has become a basic component of what has come to be called the 'environmental justice' movement. Activists committed to environmental justice have emerged to challenge the social injustices associated with mainstream environmental policy, particularly as they have pertained to class, race and gender. Opposed to centralized, hierarchical decision-making, whether in government, industry or within the environmental movement itself, the movement has emphasized local participation. Catalysed by the toxic waste problem in particular, it has sought to define and organize environmental struggles in terms of ordinary life – it assumes that *people* are an integral part of what should be understood as the 'environment' (Di Chiro, 1992, p. 96). Basic to the movement has been the forging of new forms of grassroots political organization based on environmental democracy, understood in the words of one writer as 'the right of the public to participate in – even collectively determine – decisions about technology'. The goal is to render obsolete the 'expert' status of government and industry's scientists in order 'to make every citizen conversant at all levels of environmental debate' (Thornton, 1991, p. 15).

For most mainstream economic and political leaders such language is merely ideology. Recent experience, however, has begun to suggest that there is more to the argument than first appears to meet the eye. Two types of evidence now seem to validate – at least provisionally – the environmentalists' emphasis on democracy. One concerns the nature of the siting decision process; the other concerns the emergence of new siting experiences that illustrate the importance of democracy. The first has to do with the failure of risk assessment's attempt to circumvent the political process. Further research into the question of why communities have so adamantly rejected the advice of the experts now offers quite a different perspective. Whereas risk experts have dismissively portrayed the public as incapable of digesting complex technical findings, and thus is left to fall back on irrational fears, writers such as Plough and Krimsky (1987) make clear that such a conclusion misses the nature of the community decision-making process. In their work, they distinguish between two different types of rationality that guide risk assessment, 'technical' and 'cultural' rationality.

'Technical rationality', according to Krimsky and Plough, is a mind-set that puts its faith in empirical evidence and the scientific method, appeals to experts for justifying policy decisions, values logical consistency and universality of findings, and judges non-quantifiable impacts to be irrelevant to political decision-making. 'Cultural rationality', in contrast, tends to emphasize (or at least give equal weight to) the opinions of traditional and peer groups over those of experts, focuses on personal and familiar experiences rather than depersonalized calculations, holds unanticipated consequences to be fully relevant to near-term decision-making, and trusts process over evidence. That is, decisions are judged as much by the social processes through which they are reached as by the outcomes. Beyond probability and risk-benefit ratios, then, public risk perception is shaped by the circumstances under which the risk is identified and publicized, the place of the individual in his or her community and the social values of the community as a whole.

While laypersons tend to be culturally rational in their decision-making processes, few people think or act exclusively in one mode or the other. Such modes typically change with circumstances. Sandman (1986; Chess and Sandman, 1989, p. 20) has demonstrated this with a simple test. He asked experts to imagine themselves in situations in which they were not in control of the circumstances and to think of themselves as fathers rather than as engineers and businessmen. In such situations, the experts were themselves found to abandon the technical rational model of decision-making for the culturally rational mode of the citizen. The conclusion from this work is clear: cultural rationality is only a different kind of knowledge and has to be built into the decision-making process.

From this work we learn that the public decision 'process' is as important as scientific 'evidence', sometimes more so. Citizens react as much to who is talking as they do to what is being said. In this respect they are responding to the possibilities of deception and manipulation often associated with hierarchical decision structures and other asymmetrical communicative relations. Citizens want to know that the decision is reached fairly without bias or deceit. Does the process reflect hidden interests? The answer to such mistrust requires a more open set of communicative relationships.

This brings us to the second type of argument for environmental democracy. If the foregoing discussion suggests that citizens are not so hostile to technical data *per se* – i.e. that they might well be inclined to accept data that is the product of an open and democratic process – such a conclusion appears to be just what new experiences in Canada are demonstrating. In particular, the siting of a hazardous-waste treatment facility in the Canadian province of Alberta has begun to cast a new ray of hope on the Nimby problem. Contrary to the traditional technocratic approaches, this case provides convincing evidence that solutions require more, rather than less, democracy. The most impressive example comes from Alberta. Faced with the Nimby syndrome, the regional government of Alberta sought to address the opposition openly and squarely (Paehlke and Torgerson, 1991; Rabe, 1991; 1992). By establishing an open and democratic participatory process, the government has managed successfully to site, build and operate the single major new incineration facility in North America in over a decade. Working together, government, industry and local groups in Alberta devised a participatory process in which the conflictual issues of siting were transformed in such a way that all the major stakeholders preferred negotiation to conflict and, through the process, came to believe that they could all reap the benefits of co-operation. Gone were the winners and losers that have typically framed the 'zero-sum' politics of Nimby.

Participation in the project was built into the decision process from the beginning, commencing with a local plebiscite about the acceptability of the siting decision. The regional government then supplied the local community with funds to hire its own experts and consultants and it organized extensive public meetings to discuss with community members and their consultants the nature of the plant and its consequences. Once the site was accepted, the government provided the community with monies to offset the extra burdens incurred by the local infrastructure and for the hiring of its own expert advice.

The community group in Alberta has used the money to establish a local committee to organize seminars and meetings for the community residents regarding hazardous waste treatment. Meeting on a monthly basis, particularly to provide facility managers a source of information regarding community attitudes and ideas, the local committee now also reviews environmental monitoring reports. The reports are translated from technical language into an easily understood format. The government also provides the means for the community to hire a permanent consultant to assist them in monitoring the facility's operations.

Though the Canadian experience might not work everywhere, it has shown that a positive, democratically inspired discourse can help bring about a positive end for the most complex and fear-invoking type of facility. It has lead numerous writers to argue that the Canadian experience shows that long-term oversight arrangements based on greater community involvement, power and risk sharing enhance the likelihood of effectively siting facilities in acceptable locations (Mazmanian and Morell, 1993, p. 28). Contrary to technocratic assumptions, citizen participation can thus prove to be anything but irrational.

Finally, if the local community is to monitor plant operations, the need for some adjustments to the standard hierarchial model of expert advice giving might be anticipated. As already noted in the Canadian example, consultants translate the operational reports from a technical language into a format easily understood by the ordinary citizen and further help grapple with the key issues in the reports. If, however, the community is to become truly involved in such deliberatory processes, one might expect to see this process evolve as something more than an oversight function. And that in fact is what has begun to happen.

Since the beginning of Nimby and the community movement against the siting of toxic wastes, a number of environmentally concerned scientists have begun to experiment with new forms of participatory advice giving, including the possibility of a form of community risk assessment (Chess and Sandman, 1989, p. 20). Such experts emerge to help the community 'understand the significance of new developments, plot strategies, and even take on adversaries directly' (*ibid.*).

Accounts of the Love Canal Homeowners Association's struggles with state and local officials emphasize the work of a cancer researcher who helped the community associations 'to reinterpret government data, develop the capacity to collect additional information, and interpret this information credibly inside and outside the neighborhood' (Edelstein, 1988).

A direct outcome of this Love Canal experience was the formation of a national organization designed to provide just such alternative expertise to other Nimby groups (or 'Niamby', i.e. not in anybody's backyard) across the country. The Citizens Clearinghouse for Hazardous Wastes was started by Lois Gibbs, the Love Canal housewife who had organized the community and extracted major concessions from the State of New York and the federal government (Gibbs, 1982). With only a high-school education and no former experience in such matters, she went on to establish a major Washington-based organization to assist other communities across the country in struggles against toxic wastes. The Citizens Clearinghouse has become a major organization in the environmental social justice movement. Among its various activities, the clearinghouse offers instruction and advice on how to deal with the technical dimensions of the hazardous waste problem, in particular the problem of incineration (Collette, 1987).

Participatory expertise

Underlying such alternative forms of advice giving is the emerging practice of 'participatory research'. Evolving in the context of struggles against environmental hazards in both the community and workplace, participatory research is founded on the efforts of citizens both to broaden their access to the information produced by scientists and to systematize their own 'local knowledge'. It has involved attempts 'to develop cooperative relationships between scientists and citizens, with a view to research that meets people's needs' (Merrifield, 1989, p. 20).

Participatory research is put forward as an effort to gear expert practices to the requirements of democratic empowerment.[2] Rather than providing technical answers designed to bring political discussions to an end, the task is to assist citizens in their efforts to examine their own interersts and to make their own decisions (Hirschhorn, 1979). Beyond merely providing analytical research and empirical data, the expert is conceptualized as a 'facilitator' of public learning and empowerment. As a facilitator, he or she becomes an expert in how people learn, clarify and decide for themselves (Fischer, 1990). This includes coming to grips with the basic languages of public normative argumentation, as well as knowledge about the kinds of environmental and intellectual conditions under which citizens can formulate their own ideas. It involves the creation of institutional and intellectual contexts that help people pose questions and examine technical analyses in their own ordinary (or everyday) languages and decide which issues are important to them.

The practitioners of participatory research point to two important payoffs. First, it identifies very real and important dangers that hide behind the assumptions and generalities buried in the expert's calculations. That is, it brings to the fore the very problems, especially problematic assumptions, that have been overlooked by standard policy analysts. Second, participation in decision-making helps to build both credibility and acceptance of research findings (Dutton, 1984; Friedmann, 1987), the critical failure facing the contemporary approaches.

To the conventionally trained scientist, both physical and social, the idea of participatory research often sounds outrageously unscientific. In response to this concern, there are at least two replies. First, it is a methodology primarily designed for research problems characterized by a mix of technical and social problems. Scientists concerned with pure research in physics generally have little need to consult the ordinary citizen. Second, where the methodology is used, it is in most ways only the scientific method made more time consuming and perhaps more expensive, at least in the short run. In the next section we briefly examine an example of participatory research in hazardous waste policy.

Risk assessment as lay epidemiology

There is no better example of participatory research than that which took shape in Woburn, Massachusetts in the late 1970s and early 1980s. Although Woburn is scarcely the only experience along these lines, it represents one of the most highly developed illustrations of participatory research to date (Brown, 1990; Brown and Mikkelsen, 1990). In response to the discovery of the presence of toxic wastes, coupled with an inordinately high degree of childhood leukemia, community members in Woburn mobilized themselves to investigate the problem and to challenge state and local authorities with the data they were able to assemble.[3]

The residents of Woburn were shocked in 1979 to learn that construction workers had found more than 180 large barrels of waste materials in an abandoned lot alongside a local river. In reaction to citizens' concerns, the Woburn police department notified the State Department of Environmental Quality Engineering which, after investigation, discovered high levels of carcinogens in several local water wells and ordered them closed. Additional investigation, moreover, revealed that a few years earlier an engineer from the state had detected high concentrations in the same water supplies, although state officials failed to investigate the matter. Local residents further learnt that the city had received complaints about the water – e.g. a foul taste, dishwater discoloration and peculiar odours – and had commissioned a consulting firm to examine the matter, which in turn led to a state investigation. At the time, however, it was thought that the problem stemmed from the interaction of chlorine with other minerals in the water supply. City officials thus ordered a change in the town's chlorination system.

The community's own efforts to come to grips with the problem had, in fact, predated the closing of the wells. Anne Anderson, a local resident whose son had been diagnosed with leukemia, began 'gathering information about other cases by word of mouth and by chance meetings with victims at stores and at the hospital where her son was being treated' (Brown, 1990, p. 79). Given the surprising number of cases that surfaced in the inquiries, she began to speculate about the origins of the leukemia cases; perhaps they had resulted from something in the water supply. She registered her concern with the state agency, but was informed that the agency could not test the water on the basis of citizen requests.

Approximately six months later, the Woburn press reported that the state agency had itself discovered another toxic waste site in the area, but had again decided to withhold information. At this point, a local minister grew sceptical about the state's earlier reports, and suspicious of its lack of interest in further investigation. Together, he and Anderson placed an advertisement in the local paper; they asked fellow citizens with knowledge about other leukemia cases to contact them. Stunned by the feedback, they consulted a local physician and proceeded to plot a map that clustered the cases. Convinced of the significance of the clustering, the physician notified the Center for Disease Control (CDC) of the apparent danger. At the same time, 'the activists spread the word through the press and persuaded the city council . . . to ask the CDC to investigate' (Brown and Mikkelsen, 1990, p. 12). Furthermore, Anderson, Young and about 20 other citizens founded 'For a Clean Environment' (FACE) to mobilize community concern about their findings.

Shortly after the Woburn City Council made a formal request to the CDC, the Massachusetts Department of Public Health submitted a report that took sharp issue with the Anderson–Young leukemia map. According to the department, there was no reason to take the map seriously. Said to show no significant evidence of a cluster, it was dismissed as the work of amateurs. Despite this public setback, the community activists were bolstered by a growing national awareness of toxic hazards in the environment, as well as community efforts in other places. In fact, in the context of this growing climate of concern, Anderson and Young were invited by Senator Edward Kennedy to testify at congressional committee hearings pertaining to the toxic waste problem in the country as a whole.

Eventually, in response to the local physician and the city council, the CDC dispatched a scientific team, in affiliation with the Massachusetts Department of Public Health, to investigate the Woburn complaints. About six months later the researchers submitted a report attesting to the fact that leukemia and kidney cancer in the area were higher than normal. None the less, they concluded the data to be inconclusive. In particular, 'the case-control method failed to find characteristics that differentiated victims from nonvictims. Further, a lack of environmental data for earlier periods was an obstacle to linking disease with the water supply' (Brown, 1990, p. 79). But the families and friends of the victims once again were unwilling to accept the conclusions of the report and began to question the scientific study itself. As one journalist put it, a 'layperson's epidemiology' began to emerge (DiPerna, 1985, p. 106–8).

The first major step towards a more sophisticated lay investigation came when an interested Harvard professor invited Anderson and Young to discuss their findings in a seminar at the university's School of Public Health. Present was

Marvin Zehlen, a biostatistician who became intrigued with the case. In an effort to elicit more conclusive data, Zehlen and a colleague decided to undertake a more detailed investigation of the health problems in Woburn, in particular environmentally related reproductive disorders and birth defects. To do this, the Harvard biostatisticians and the FACE activists officially agreed to team up with one another in what was to become a major epidemiological study. FACE co-ordinated some 300 volunteers to administer a telephone survey designed to reach 70 per cent of the population; the Harvard scientists, in turn, supplied the volunteers with training on how to conduct the health survey, in particular how to avoid bias in asking questions and recording answers. In the view of Brown and Mikkelsen (1990), the project became a prototype for a popular epidemiological alliance between citizens and scientists.

Altogether, the scientists and citizens assembled research data that included detailed information on 20 cases of childhood leukemia, a careful examination of the Department of Environmental Quality Engineering's data on the regional distribution of water from the wells and the results of the community health survey. The biostatisticians, moreover, conducted a variety of analyses to detect bias in the data. At the end of the research process, the team concluded that leukemia was in fact significantly associated with exposure to the water from the well.

The public distribution of the Harvard/FACE report immediately encountered harsh criticisms from the Center for Disease Control, the Environmental Protection Agency and the American Cancer Society. Even the Harvard Department of Epidemiology took issue with the findings. Many of the criticisms, to be sure, were based on legitimate scientific concerns. For one thing, they pointed out that in such a study there would never be sufficient numbers of each of the numerous defects (Brown, 1990, p. 81). What is more, they showed that their groupings were appropriately based on the chemical literature concerning birth defects. Finally, they argued that if the groupings were in fact incorrect, they would not have uncovered positive statistical correlations.

The harshest criticisms were directed at the very idea of public participation in science. Because of its 'unorthodox methods', the study was said to be biased, and thus invalid. The main complaint was that it relied on a health survey conducted by non-scientific citizen volunteers, who in turn were motivated by community interests. Whereas science is said to be impartial, the research was founded on political goals. For present purposes, however, it is exactly this characteristic that made the case interesting. All things considered, the affected families had through their own efforts confirmed the existence of a leukemia cluster and demonstrated that it was traceable to industrial waste carcinogens that leached into the drinking-water supply. They were able to initiate a series of actions that resulted in a civil law suit against two major corporations, one of which the court judged to have negligently dumped its chemical waste products. The legal case then moved to a subsequent stage in which the plaintiffs were obliged to prove that the chemical wastes were in fact responsible for the leukemia cases. As this part of the process got underway, the judge determined that the jurors had not adequately comprehended the epidemiological and environmental data crucial to the case and ordered it to be retried. To avoid the possibility of an extremely punitive verdict, the corporation at this point agreed to an out-of-court settlement with the community plaintiffs. In short, the efforts of FACE paid off.

Not only had the case helped to demonstrate nationally that corporations are responsible for dumping toxic wastes and their resultant health effects but it also offered a valuable example of lay detection and communication of risk to scientific experts and government officials. The exercise has been described as a 'prototype' for 'low-cost' epidemiology (Raloff, 1984; Brown and Mikkelsen, 1990). For Brown (1990), such efforts are best referred to as 'popular epidemiology'.

Popular or lay epidemiology provides a sharp contrast to the standard approach. Epidemiology, the first step in an health-related risk assessment, is generally defined as the 'study of the distribution of a disease or a physiological condition in human populations and of the factors that influence their distribution' (Lillienfeld, 1980; Wartenburg, 1989). The data of such a study is typically used to explain the etiology of the condition and to provide preventive public health, and clinical practices to deal with the condition. By contrast, Brown (1990, p. 78) describes 'popular epidemiology' as 'a process in which lay persons gather statistics and other information and also direct and marshall the knowledge and resources of experts in order to understand the epidemiology of disease. It also includes attention to the basic structural features – social and communicative – of both the community and larger society of which it is a part. It is also explicitly political and activist in nature . . . [which] is also a form of risk communication by lay persons to professional audiences, and as such demonstrates that risk communication is indeed an exercise of political power'. In this respect, an increasing number of experiences shows that mobilized communities have succeeded in identifying and communicating hazards and risks in ways that have facilitated significant political, economic and cultural victories. It thus seems fair to conclude that the participatory methodology can play an important role in refocusing the ways that lay citizens, scientific experts and public officials deal with health hazards and risks.

Conclusion

The cases of Alberta and Woburn demonstrate participatory risk assessment to be more than a speculative concept. Alberta makes clear the advantages of participatory forums in policy formulation and programme implementation; Woburn illustrates the ability of a mobilized community to enter the research process itself. Both cases reveal the need for new kinds of relationships between citizens and scientists. The experiences of FACE, moveover, underscore the importance of bringing the 'local knowledge' of the community to the scientific establishment, as well as the need for the scientist to stand in the middle of such processes, rather than above them. Contrary to the conventional wisdom, the experiences also show that citizens are capable of acting intelligently in cases involving complex technological decisions (Di Chiro, 1992). Collaborative research relationships are thus more than academic issues; as the cases illustrate, they bear directly on the outcomes of the research process itself. Indeed, problem-solving in the case of a problem as intractable as Nimby may literally depend on such collaborative methodological innovation.

But how can participatory risk assessment be brought more directly into environmental policy-making? In so far as risk assessment has mainly developed as a tool for guiding and managing the corporate-bureaucratic state, its methods largely serve top-down policy decision-making processes. Risk policy analysis is thus in many ways built on political and methodological foundations antagonistic to authentic democratic participation. In fact, democratic theorists have commonly dismissed it as technocratic and élitist.

Here we have seen that the discipline's top-down methods are becoming increasingly problematic for a specific class of intractable or 'wicked' problems now confronting state decision-makers, and that this development offers new possibilities for the introduction of participatory methods. Indeed, the two cases show that participatory practices – mainly emerging outside traditional state practices – hold out potential for solving such problems.

Participatory research does not constitute a reconstruction of science *per se*. Rather, it seeks to build in a normative discourse about the social assumptions upon which scientific research rests, social scientific research in particular. Here, as we argued, the scientist has no privileged knowledge or legitimacy. Such assumptions pertain to the nature of society itself, including how we wish to organize it. Science can explore the implications of adopting particular assumptions but it has no privileged methods for choosing among them. In a democratic society these are questions for the citizenry.

In theoretical terms, participatory research can be understood as building in the human emancipatory component associated with participation. Here the perspective of critical social theory, the analytic task of participatory policy analysis can be approached as that of an 'interpretive mediator' between theoretical knowledge and competing practical arguments. Participatory policy analysis, in such a conceptualization, involves first an assessment of a given social problem and an evaluation of the alternative policy solutions in terms of emancipatory criteria, derived from an interaction between analytical frames of reference and the interests and needs of the relevant social actors (Habermas, 1973, p. 33). As a method, participatory policy analysis sets up confrontations between the analytical frameworks of social science and the proposed policy practices, mediated by the actors subject to the policy's manifestations. Such a dialectical exchange can be likened to a 'conversation in which the horizons of both participants [social scientists and citizens] are extended through confrontations with one another' (Dryzek, 1982). The task, in the language of postpositivist epistemology, is to develop a synthesis of social scientific theory and the 'local knowledge' of the community, normative as well as empirical. It is to reshape the interactions among the analysts, citizens and policy-makers as that of a conversation with many voices, adjudicated by the procedural ethics of discourse and deliberation. Seen this way, the social distance between the policy expert and the citizen would be radically reduced; the analyst might simply be described as a kind of 'specialized citizen' (Paris and Reynolds, 1993).[4]

In the age of high technology this is lofty-sounding language. But if we are to take democracy seriously we must confront directly the question of the relation of science to participation. Democracy without citizen participation and discussion is a meaningless concept. If a complex technological society renders such discussion impossible, we must then rethink our commitment either to democracy or technology. Participatory research, as the cases in Alberta and Woburn suggest, offers an innovative approach to this conflict, too often relegated to the realm of either/or. While the conventional argument suggests that citizens need science, the cases above show that science needs an active, informed citizenry.

Finally, for those who argue that decentralized decision-making and citizen participation are basic to a sustainable future, the possibility of participatory research is an important step forward. Basic to the technocratic arguments advanced by the administrators of the large-scale corporate-bureaucratic system is the contention that society is too complex technologically to return to simpler organization forms. While participatory research is no panacea, it surely shows that there is much more room here for exploration than the leaders of the technoindustrial system either recognize or are willing to concede.

Notes

1. Portney (1991, p. 11) gives the following example: 'Nearly everyone seems to agree that more prison space is needed if the criminal justice system is to be able to treat convicted criminals as harshly as the public mood warrants. Yet no one wants a prison in his or her city or town . . . Most people seem to agree that such facilities are a necessary and acceptable result of living in an industrial society.'

2. Participatory policy research is not as unique as it might sound. According to its own theorists, it is in many ways only a more progressive version of a method already well known in the managerial and policy sciences, namely 'action research' (Argyris *et al.*, 1985). Like action research developed after the second world war by the German émigré Kurt Lewin, participatory research is designed as a methodology for integrating social learning and goal-orientated decision-making. Where the former was co-opted by the managerial sciences to serve the rather narrowly defined needs of bureaucratic reform (typically identified as 'participatory management'), participatory research is an effort to carry through action research's earlier commitment to democratic participation (Fernandes and Tandon, 1981; Reason and Rowan, 1981; Kassan and Mustafa, 1982; Merrifield, 1989). Much of the effort to develop this methodology has taken place in the third world, especially among alternative social movements concerned with environmental issues and the use of appropriate technologies.

3. This account of the event in Woburn is drawn from the works of Brown and Mikkelson (1990).

4. The job of the participatory policy analysts, so understood, would be to help citizens obtain an authentic deep understanding of the historical forces that shape their situation. Borrowing from Bernstein (1976, p. 217), we can understand this to mean that 'such theory can only become efficacious – a material force – to the extent that it correctly interprets this situation and initiates self-reflection'. The theoretical task is 'intimately related to the formation of a political consensus among those engaged in strategic action, [but] it does not and cannot play the role of legitimating and justifying what is to be done'. The implication of this, as Habermas (1973, p. 33) explains, is that 'decisions for the political struggle cannot at the outset be justified theoretically and then carried out organizationally'. The only ones who can decide the course of action they are willing to undertake are those who know the risks and expected outcomes, i.e.

those who are conscious of their common interests and possess knowledge of both their circumstances and the predictable consequences – primary and secondary – of the proposed action.

References

Argyris, C. *et al.* (1985) *Action Science.* Harvard University Press, Cambridge, Mass.

Barber, B.R. (1984) *Strong Democracy.* University of Calfornia Press, Berkeley, Calif.

Beneveniste, G. (1987) 'Some functions and dysfunctions of using professional élites in public policy,' in S. Nagel (ed.) *Research in Public Policy Analysis and Management. Vol. 3.* JAI Press, Greenwich, Conn.

Bennett, D. (1986) 'Democracy and public policy analysis,' in S. Nagel (ed.) *Research in Public Policy Analysis and Management. Vol. 3.* JAI Press, Greenwich, Conn.

Bernstein, R.J. (1976) *The Restructuring of Social and Political Theory.* Harcourt Brace Jovanovich, New York.

Bernstein, R.J. (1983) *Beyond Objectivism and Relativism: Science, Hermeneutics, and Praxis.* University of Philadelphia Press, Philadelphia, PA.

Bookchin, M. (1982) *The Ecology of Freedom.* Chesire, Palo Alto, Calif.

Brown, P. (1990) 'Popular epidemiology: community response to toxic waste-induced disease,' in P. Conrad and R. Kern (eds) *The Sociology of Health and Illness in Critical Perspective.* St Martin's Press, New York.

Brown, P. and Mikkelson, E.J. (1990) *No Safe Place: Toxic Waste, Leukemia, and Community Action.* University of California Press, Berkeley, Calif.

Cancian, F. and Armstead, C. (1992) 'Participatory research, in E.F. Borgatta and M.L. Borgatta (eds) *Encyclopedia of Sociology.* Macmillan, New York.

Chess, C. and Sandman, P.M. (1989) 'Community use of quantitative risk assessment,' *Science for the People,* January–February, p. 20.

Churchman, C.W. (1971) *The Designing of Inquiring Systems.* Basic Books, New York.

Collette, W. (1987) *How to Deal with a Proposed Facility.* Citizen's Clearinghouse for Hazardous Wastes, Arlington, Va.

Davis, C.E. (1993) *The Politics of Hazardous Waste.* Prentice-Hall, Englewood Cliffs, NJ.

Dear, M. (1992) 'Understanding and overcoming the NIMBY syndrome,' *Journal of The American Planning Association,* Vol. 58, Summer, pp. 288–300.

deLeon, P. (1989) *Advice and Consent.* Russell Sage Foundation, New York.

deLeon, P. (1992) 'The democratization of the policy sciences,' *Public Administration Review,* Vol. 52, March–April, pp. 125–9.

Di Chiro, G. (1992) 'Defining environmental justice: women's voices and grassroots politics,' *Socialist Review,* no. 2, pp. 93–130.

DiPerna, P. (1985) *Cluster Mystery: Epidemic and the Children of Woburn.* Mosby, St Louis, Mo.

Dryzek, J.S. (1982) 'Policy analysis as a hermeneutic activity,' *Policy Sciences,* Vol. 14, pp. 309–29.

Dryzek, J.S. (1990) *Discursive Democracy.* Cambridge University Press.

Durning, D. (1993) 'Participatory policy analysis in a Georgia state agency,' *Journal of Policy Analysis and Management,* April, Vol. 12, no. 2, pp. 299–322.

Dutton, D. (1984) 'The impact of public participation in biomedical policy: evidence from four case studies,' in J.C. Peterson (ed.) *Citizen Participation in Science Policy.* University of Massachusetts Press, Amherst, Mass.

Edelstein, M.R. (1988) *Contaminated Communities.* Westview Press, Boulder, Colo.

Elliot, M.L.P. (1984) 'Improving community acceptance of hazardous waste facilities through alternative systems of mitigating and managing risk,' *Hazardous Waste,* Vol. 1, pp. 397–410.

Eulau, H. (1977) *Technology and Civility.* Hoover Institution, Stanford, Calif.

Fernandes, W. and Tandon, R. (eds) (1981) *Participatory Research and Evaluation: Experiments in Research as a Process in Asia.* Indian Social Institute, New Delhi.

Fischer, F. (1980) *Politics, Values, and Public Policy: The Problem of Methodology.* Westview Press, Boulder, Colo.

Fischer, F. (1990) *Technocracy and the Politics of Expertise.* Sage, Newbury Park, Calif.

Fischer, F. (1991) 'Risk assessment and environmental crisis: toward an integration of science and participation,' *Industrial Crisis Quarterly*, Vol. 5, pp. 113–32.

Fischer, F. (1992) 'Participatory expertise: toward the democratization of policy science,' in W. Dunn and R. Kelly (eds) *Advances in Policy Studies since 1950.* Transaction Press, New Brunswick, NJ.

Fischer, F. (1993) 'Citizen participation and the democratization of policy expertise: from theoretical inquiry to practical cases,' *Policy Sciences*, Vol. 26, no. 3, pp. 165–87.

Foucault, M. (1973) *The Order of Things.* Vintage Books, New York.

Friedmann, J. (1987) *Planning in the Public Domain.* Princeton University Press, Princeton, NJ.

Gaventa, J. (1980) *Power and Powerlessness: Quiescence and Rebellion in an Appalachian Valley.* University of Illinois Press, Urbana, Ill.

Gaventa, J. (1988) 'Participatory research in North America,' *Convergence*, Vol. 21, pp. 19–29.

Gibbs, L.M. (1982) *Love Canal: My Story.* University of New York Press, Albany, NY.

Gutin, J. (1991) 'At our peril: the false promise of risk assessment,' *Greenpeace*, Vol. 4, March/April, pp. 13–18.

Habermas, J. (1970) *Toward a Rational Society.* Beacon Press, Boston, Mass.

Habermas, J. (1973) *Legitimation Crisis.* Beacon Press, Boston, Mass.

Harmon, M.M. and Mayer, R. (1986) *Organization Theory for Public Administration.* Little, Brown & Co., Boston, Mass.

Hawkesworth, M.E. (1988) *Theoretical Issues in Policy Analysis.* State University of New York Press, Albany, NY.

Hirschhorn, L. (1979) 'Alternative service and the crisis of the professions,' in J. Case and R.C.R. Taylor (eds) *Co-ops, Communes, and Collectives: Experiments in Social Change in the 1960s and 1970s.* Pantheon, New York.

Hoppe, R. and Peterse, A. (1993) *Handling Frozen Fire.* Westview Press, Boulder, Colo.

Kann, M.E. (1986) 'Environmental democracy in the United States,' in S. Kamieniecki, R. O'Brien and M. Clarke (eds) *Controversies in Environmental Policy.* SUNY Press, Albany, NY.

Kassan, Y. and Mustafa, K. (eds) (1982) *Participatory Research: An Emerging Alternative in Social Science Research.* African Adult Education, Nairobi.

Kotz, N. (1981) 'Citizens as experts,' *Working Papers*, March–April, pp. 42–8.

Laird, F. (1993) 'Participatory analysis, democracy, and technological decision making,' *Science, Technology, and Human Values*, Vol. 18, no. 3, pp. 341–61.

Lasswell, H. (1951) 'The policy science orientation,' in D. Lerner and H. Lasswell (eds) *The Policy Sciences*, Stanford University Press, Palo Alto, Calif.

Levine, A. (1982) *Love Canal: Science, Politics, and People.* Lexington, Boston, Mass.

Lillienfeld, A. (1980) *Foundations of Epidemiology.* Oxford University Press, New York.

Mason, R. and Mitroff, I. (1981) *Challenging Strategic Planning Assumptions.* Wiley, New York.

Mazmanian, D. and Morell, D. (1992) *Beyond Superfailure: America's Toxics Policy for the 1990s.* Westview Press, Boulder, Colo.

Mazmanian, D. and Morell, D. (1993) 'The "NIMBY" syndrome: facility siting and the failure of democratic discourse,' in M. Kraft and N. Vig (eds) *Environmental Policy for the 1990s.* Congressional Quarterly Press, Washington, DC.

Merrifield, J. (1989) 'Putting the scientists in their place: participatory research in environmental and occupational health,' in P. Park *et al.* (eds) *Voice of Change.* OISE Press, Toronto.

Miller, P. and Rose, N. (1990) 'Governing economic life,' *Economy and Society*, Vol. 19, no. 1, pp. 1–31.

Paehlke, R. (1990) 'Democracy and environmentalism: opening the door to the administrative state,' in R. Paehlke and D. Torgerson (eds) *Managing Leviathan: Environmental Politics and the Administrative State*. Broadview Press, Peterborough, Ontario.

Paehlke, R. and Torgerson, D. (1991) 'Toxic waste as public business,' *Canadian Public Administration*, Vol. 35, Fall, pp. 339–62.

Paris, D.C. and Reynolds, J.F. (1983) *The Logic of Policy Inquiry*. Longman, New York.

Participatory Research Network (1982) *Patricipatory Research: An Introduction*. Society for Participatory Research in Asia, New Delhi.

Pateman, C. (1970) *Participation and Democratic Theory*. Cambridge University Press.

Piller, C. (1991) *The Fail-Safe Society: Community Defiance and the End of American Technological Optimism*. Basic Books, New York.

Plough, A. and Krimsky, S. (1987) 'The emergence of risk communications studies: social and political context,' *Science, Technology, and Human Values,* Vol. 12, no. 3–4, pp. 4–10.

Portney, K.E. (1991) *Siting Hazardous Waste Treatment Facilities: The Nimby Syndrome*. Auburn House, New York.

Rabe, B.G. (1991) 'Beyond the Nimby syndrome in hazardous waste facility siting: the Albertan breakthrough and the prospects for cooperation in Canada and the United States,' *Governance,* Vol. 4, April, pp. 184–206.

Rabe, B.G. (1992) 'When siting works, Canada-style,' *Journal of Health Politics, Policy and Law*, Vol. 17, pp. 119–42.

Raloff, J. (1984) 'Woburn survey becomes a model for low-cost epidemiology,' *Science News*, 18 February.

Reason, P. and Rowan, J. (eds) (1981) *Human Inquiry: A Sourcebook of New Paradigm Research*. Wiley, New York.

Rittel, H.W.J. and Webber, M. (1973) 'Dilemmas in a general theory of planning,' *Policy Sciences,* Vol. 4, June, p. 1.

Sandman, P.D. (1986) 'Getting to maybe: some communications aspects of hazardous waste facility siting,' *Seton Hall Legislative Journal*, Vol. 9, Spring, pp. 437–65.

Schon, D. (1983) *The Reflective Practitioner*. Basic Books, New York.

Scott, W.G. and Hart, D.K. (1973) 'Administrative crisis: the neglect of metaphysical speculation,' *Public Administration Review*, Vol. 33, September–October, pp. 415–22.

Stanley, M. (1978) *The Technocratic Consciousness: Survival and Dignity in an Age of Expertise*. University of Chicago Press, Chicago, Ill.

Stull, D.D. and Schensul, J.J. (eds) (1987) *Collaborative Research and Social Change*. Westview Press, Boulder, Colo.

Sullivan, W.M. (1983) 'Beyond policy science,' in N. Haan, P. Rabinov and W.M. Sullivan (eds) *Social Science as Moral Inquiry*. Columbia University Press, New York.

Susman, G.I. (1983) 'Action research: a sociotechnical systems perspective,' in G. Morgan (ed.) *Beyond Method*. Sage, Beverly Hills, Calif.

Thornton, J. (1991) 'Risking democracy,' *Greenpeace*, March/April, pp. 14–17.

Tribe, L. (1972) 'Policy science: analysis or ideology,' *Philosophy and Public Affairs*, Vol. 2, pp. 66–110.

Wartenburg, D. (1989) 'Quantitative risk assessment,' *Science for the People*, January/February, pp. 18–23.

Whyte, W.F. (1989) 'Advancing scientific knowledge through participatory action research,' *Sociological Form*, Vol. 4, pp. 367–86.

Wildavsky, A. (1988) *Searching for Safety*, Rutgers University Press, New Brunswick, N.J.

Winner, L. (1986) *The Whale and the Reactor: A Search for Limits in an Age of High Technology*. University of Chicago Press, Chicago, Ill.

Wynne, B. (1987) *Risk Management and Hazardous Waste: Implementation and the Dialectics of Credibility*. Springer-Verlag, Berlin.

11

Industrial and environmental crises: rethinking corporate social responsibility

PAUL SHRIVASTAVA

Bucknell University, USA

Introduction

Modern technological progress has come at a price – a price that we are starting to pay now, in terms of large-scale environmental damage; a price that many generations will continue to pay well into the future. It is this heavy price, the downside of technological progress, that is the focus of this chapter. More specifically, I focus on technological, industrial and environmental crises. These crises involve industrial technologies and they have devastating effects on human and natural environments.

Past research on industrial crises has focused on understanding their causes and consequences (Perrow, 1984; Mitroff and Pauchant, 1990; Shrivastava, 1992). Crises have been examined from the multiple perspectives of key stakeholders. These stakeholders include corporations, government agencies and communities (Bucholz, Marcus and Post, 1991).

Past studies of corporate social responsibility have articulated many different concepts of responsibility. They have described stages that companies go through as they mature into socially responsible firms (Carroll, 1979; Fredrick, 1986; Sethi and Steidelmeir, 1991; Wood, 1991).

It seems that the crisis literature and the corporate social-responsibility literature have grown in parallel and independence of each other. As a consequence there is no serious analysis of the social responsibility corporations bear for industrial/environmental (I/E) crises.

The purpose of this chapter is to articulate corporate social responsibility for I/E crises. It begins by clarifying what I mean by I/E crises. The next section identifies the weakness of the existing discourse on corporate social responsibility in dealing with these crises. This is followed by a conception of corporate responsibilities for I/E crises. These responsibilities are embedded in the concepts of ecocentric management, sustainable development and prevention and management of industrial crises. The final section uses data from the

Bhopal crisis to illustrate what happens to companies that do not fulfil these corporate responsibilities.

Industrial and environmental (I/E) crises

Industrial crises are events and processes in which the failure of technology causes *immense harm* to human life and the natural environment. They are occasions for *strategic decisions* and *force restructuring* of affected systems. They usually originate within corporate and government organizations, which own most technologies in operation today (Shrivastava, 1992).

Crises originate from sudden events such as industrial accidents, environmental pollution incidents or product injuries. They can also evolve slowly through the accumulation of environmental harm, environmental pollution and degradation, the emergence of new hazard information or the low-level health effects of technologies (Shrivastava *et al.*, 1988).

Examples of crises caused by sudden events include the Chernobyl nuclear-power plant accident, the *Exxon Valdez* oil spill and the Union Carbide pesticide plant accident in Bhopal. Slow emergent crises are exemplified by the Love Canal toxic waste crisis and the Minamata Mercury poisoning in Japan. This notion of I/E crises encompasses other chronic global environmental crises. These include ozone depletion caused by chlorofluorocarbons, global warming caused by industrial atmospheric pollution, acid rain, urban air pollution, toxic and nuclear wastes, the extinction of natural resource and a decline in biodiversity (Clark, 1989; Brown *et al.*, 1988; 1989; 1990; 1991; Pryde, 1992).

With the continuing increase in world population and the arrival of new, complex and hazardous technologies, the frequency and devastation caused by I/E crises has increased dramatically in the past two decades (Shrivastava, 1992). This has occurred within the context of two hundred years of ecologically unsustainable economic and industrial development. This industrial development strategy has brought great benefits to 25 per cent of the world – primarily the industrial west. But it has left 75 per cent of the world living in developing countries, in poverty, hunger and extreme deprivation.

We now realize that current patterns of industrial economic development are not environmentally sustainable into the future. The world population will double itself to 11 billion in the next 40 years. Providing basic amenities to this population will require increasing production and energy consumption by 5–30 times the current levels. Our current production has brought the environment to the present threshold of crisis. One can only imagine what quintupling this production would do (Commoner, 1990; MacNeil, Wisemius and Yakushiji, 1991; Starik and Carroll, 1991; Stead and Stead, 1991; Shrivastava and Hart, 1994).

It is not feasible for developing countries to model their economic growth on the pattern of the west. If India and China were to industrialize like the USA, this would cause catastrophic ecological damage. Although we now realize these limits, there is no moral basis for denying developing countries their growth aspirations. We also lack the political commitment, economic means and technological know-how to provide them with an alternative path to development (Meadows and Meadows, 1992).

The ecological limits that we face have severe implications for corporations, which are the main engines of economic development. Corporations need to rethink what their social and economic purposes are. They need to rethink their products, energy and resource usage, production systems, distribution systems, and waste and pollution management strategies. This is clearly a very large intellectual task. This chapter begins this task of reconceptualizing corporations by focusing on one key aspect – corporate social responsibilities for I/E crises (Throop, Starik and Ranks, 1993).

The corporate social responsibility (CSR) discourse and its limitations

Within this context of I/E crises and the unsustainability of our current industrial practices, what is the meaning of corporate social responsibility? Historically, the discourse on CSR has addressed ecology as one of the myriad other social issues that confront corporations, such as class, race and gender discrimination, business ethics and fraud, corporate philanthropy, minority concerns, community welfare, stakeholder demands, etc.

There are three popular positions on the broad issue of corporate social responsibility. Each position has different implications for corporate responsibility for I/E crises:

1. There are those who believe that the only responsibility of business is to make profits. They believe *free markets* are responsible for and can handle all environmental problems. Their basic assumptions are that the negative consequences of economic production are not very severe. They believe all ecological impacts can be reduced to economic measures of costs and benefits. Then they can be handled by creating economic incentives and disincentives to elicit appropriate behaviour from businesses (Friedman, 1962).

   One solution proffered by adherents to this position is creating 'pollution rights' that can be freely traded in the market-place. This is not an adequate solution for two reasons. First, we simply do not know all the natural resources that can have a market value. We have systematically studied and documented less than 2 per cent of all existing plant and animal species. Second, we do not have an adequate accounting system/calculus for accurately costing ecoresources (Cairncross, 1991; Costanza, 1992). These limitations make this solution more an ideology than a set of practical ideas.

2. There are those who acknowledge that corporations have significant environmental side-effects. These can be handled by *reforming corporations* and their production systems. Companies, governments and communities in partnership should be responsible for modifying products, production systems and waste management processes. They advocate a combination of regulations and voluntary corporate actions to achieve corporate reformation (World Commission on Environment and Development, 1987; Freeman and Gilbert, 1988; Daly and Cobb, 1989; Hoffman, Fredrick and Petry, 1990; MacNeil, Wisemius and Yakushiji, 1991).

3. Finally, there are those who believe that modern corporations are the root cause of environmental crises. They are designed to exploit the natural environment. It is their core purpose, their basic logic to convert environmental resources into market-valued commodities. They cannot be modified or reformed. It is the responsibility of the public to reject the environmentally destructive industrialization process we have pursued for the past 150 years. They call for *radical transformation* of the economy, the corporation and our life-styles (Naess, 1987; Nash, 1989; Brown *et al.*, 1991; Manes, 1991; Smith, 1992).

My own position lies between reform and radical environmentalism. I believe some part of the industrial system can be reformed, and should be reformed. Some reformation can occur from within companies. Some can be imposed through government regulations and public pressures.

However, there are other industrial products and processes that will not be environmentally sound and safe for humans, even with reformation. These should simply be eliminated. For example, the destruction of the protective stratospheric ozone shield is a problem that cannot be handled through incremental reforms. It could take five to ten years to eliminate the use of CFCs that destroy ozone. In addition, there is a 12-year inventory of CFCs already in the atmosphere that will eventually rise to the stratosphere. Even the most expeditious incremental reform strategy will continue to destroy the ozone shield for over 20 years. This can cause catastrophic damage to the earth's ecology.

Guided by these general orientations, business researchers have studied corporate social responsibility for environmental problems. There is now an extensive literature on the topics of business ethics, CSR and business and society relations which deals with environmental problems (Carrol, 1979; Preston, 1985; Hoffman, Fredrick and Petry, 1990; Post, 1990; Bucholz, Marcus and Post, 1991; Sethi and Steidelmeir, 1991).

The recent *Business and the Environment Resource Guide* (1992) lists about 400 publications in its business, government and society section, and an equal number in the management and strategic management sections. Most of these authors have provided enlightened and progressive views of corporate social responsibility.

However, this discourse suffers from three important limitations in assessing corporate responsibility for dealing with ecological crises and sustainability:

1. First, the very idea of corporate *social* responsibility is *anthropocentric*. The concept of social responsibility is orientated towards human societies, communities, institutions and agents, and not towards the natural world. Concerns about the natural world enter into the discourse only to the extent they affect human/social issues. Nature does not have any rights of its own. It exists for human welfare, subservient to human interests. Without acknowledging the rights of nature it is not possible to develop a deep concept of responsibility towards it (Devall and Sessions, 1985; Nash, 1989).

   A more ecocentric conception of corporate responsibility would see nature as having rights to exist regardless of its instrumental value to humans.

Corporations (and humans) would then be required to deal with all ecological resources and not only ones that currently have market and social value.

2. The CSR discourse is *northwestern centric*. It has occurred within the intellectual milieu of late western industrial capitalism. It has largely occurred among business practitioners, business school academics and economists. Consequently, it addresses concerns important to these participants. It has rarely included genuine voices of the developing south. It only peripherally addresses the responsibility of corporations for dealing with core problems of developing societies, viz.: population, food, poverty and environmental degradation.

The north–south conflict is examined within the paradigm of international capitalism. Accordingly, corporations are usually spared any meaningful responsibility for dealing with social problems in developing societies. The state or government is held responsible for social development. Even in situations where the state is far less powerful and capable than corporations, it has complete responsibility for social development.

3. CSR discourse is *located at the margins* of business practice. Business studies and decisions are centred on economic and financial concerns. Although ethics and corporate social responsibility are becoming increasingly important, they still play a marginal role in strategic business decisions. Financial, market, technological and regulatory considerations still remain the main guides to business decisions.

Because of these limitations the natural environment is not accorded the central importance the public gives it. It is treated as a peripheral issue, not as a survival issue. Recent Gallup polls in 22 countries show that the public considers environmental protection more important than economic growth. The public is willing to sacrifice some convenience, pay higher prices for environmentally friendly products and learn about being environmentally responsible (Gallup International, 1992). In June 1992, leaders from 178 nations gathered in Rio de Janiero for the World Conference on Environment and Development. They signed treaties to build ecologically sustainable economies. The CSR discourse does not reflect these public sentiments.

Corporate responsibility for I/E crises

The task of saving the natural environment from the ravages of industrialization is daunting. As a society we are better off making our strongest institutions the defenders of the environment. We need to place new responsibilities on them, test and monitor them, and challenge them. We need to establish checks and balances on them to ensure an acceptable level of environmental performance.

Ironically, our strongest institutions – modern corporations – are also our worst environmental polluters. Corporations are the basic vehicles of industrial development. They possess technological know-how, financial resources and organizational capacity for environmental protection. They are the primary users of environmental resources. It is in their long-term interest to protect the environment.

But appointing corporations as defenders or stewards of the natural environment is fraught with many intellectual and practical difficulties. Before we do so, we need clarification of exactly what their responsibilities should be, how they will fulfil them, what performance we can expect of them and how we can control them.

Corporate responsibility for I/E crises can be understood in terms of three concepts – ecocentric management, sustainable development, and crisis prevention and management. These three concepts broadly capture the spirit of a new and different sense of corporate responsibility. This view of CSR is based on the assumption that the long-term viability of the earth and consequently organizations depends on ecological sustainability. Corporations must be managed in an ecologically responsible manner. They must accept responsibility for sustainable development. Past industrial practices have created an inventory of hazards that hold crisis potential. Corporations must accept responsibility for preventing and managing crises in their ongoing operations.

Ecocentric management

Ecocentric management is the theoretical counterpoint to anthropocentric management that pervades corporations today. It rests on a holistic view of the human community as an integral part of nature. Humans belonged to this larger community and are related to it through complex interdependencies. Humans are not separate from and superior to nature. They are a part of it. They evolved from animals (Darwin, 1859). Darwin established the principle continuity of life forms. He argued that species changed form over time, and there was no basis for treating one (human) species as being superior to others. He gave animal and plant species a new and heightened status in the process of human evolution.

Ecocentrism rejects the idea that nature is simply a resource to be used for human welfare. The natural world is seen to have a moral standing in its own right, not simply as an accessory to human well-being. It defines human nature relationships through the idea of 'ecological egalitarianism'. This refers to the 'intrinsic' right of every form of life to function normally in the ecosystem, to blossom, live and flourish. It gives nature a status and rights similar to those that humans have arrogated to themselves. The protection and conservation of nature is seen as part of our individual and collective moral responsibility (Ehrenfeld, 1978; Devall and Sessions, 1985; Naess, 1987).

From this set of beliefs we can construct an alternative paradigm of ecocentric management. It is management that respects nature and uses it with care and responsibility. This is not remedial management aimed at repairing environmental damages even as companies continue to further damage the environment. It is proactive management that aims at eliminating environmental damage and living in harmony with nature.

Table 11.1 contrasts traditional anthropocentric management with ecocentric management. The two differ in fundamental ways in goals and values, in their concept of organizations, in their choice of products, strategies and production technologies, and in their view of organization–environment relationships.

Table 11.1   *Traditional versus ecocentric management*

Traditional industrial management	Ecocentric management
Goals	
Economic growth and profits	Sustainability and quality of life
Shareholder wealth	Stakeholder welfare
Values	
Anthropocentric	Ecocentric
Rationality and packaged knowledge	Intuition and understanding
Patriarchal values	Postpatriarchical feminist values
Products	
Designed for function, style and price	Designs for the environment
Wasteful packaging	Environmentally friendly
Production system	
Energy and resource intensive	Low energy and resource use
Technical efficiency	Environmental efficiency
Organization	
Hierarchical structure	Non-hierarchical structure
Top-down decision-making	Participative
Centralized authority	Decentralized
High income differentials	Low income differentials
Environment	
Domination over nature	Harmony with nature
Environment managed as a resource	Resources regarded as strictly finite
Pollution and waste are externalities	Pollution/waste elimination and management

Source: Based on Porritt (1984).

Ecocentric assumptions lead organizations to a different sense of environmental responsibility. Fulfilling this responsibility requires the redesign of products and packaging to be environmentally friendly, the use of cleaner technologies, energy and resource conservation, and the management of pollution and wastes. It requires corporations to give primacy to the health of workers, customers and the public. It requires developing internal systems, culture and structures that are responsive to environmental problems.

Leading corporations are beginning to move towards this paradigm of management. Companies such as The Body Shop, Merck, 3M and Proctor & Gamble have developed techniques of ecocentric management. These techniques include total quality environmental management, life-cycle analysis, conservation technologies, design and manufacturing for the environment, green organization design and industrial ecology networks, which have been described elsewhere (Ruckelshaus, 1989; Shrivastava, 1996; Shrivastava and Hart, 1994).

Sustainable development

My vision of corporate responsibility towards the environment is embedded in the concept of sustainable development. Sustainable development acknowledges that our past patterns of global economic growth are ecologically unsustainable. It allows us to move the corporate responsibility discourse from its current northern centric orientation towards a global orientation.

Sustainable development refers to economic growth that is mindful of the limited natural resources available on the earth. It is growth that moderates the pace and type of industrialization. It seeks to meet our needs without jeopardizing the needs of future generations. It is an economic development strategy that jointly addresses the key components of global ecological sustainability (i.e. population control, food security, ecosystem resources, energy consumption) and sustainable economies (World Commission on Environment and Development, 1987; Daly and Cobb, 1989).

Sustainable population control does not mean simply controlling population growth in developing countries. That clearly must be done. But sustainability also requires managing the environmental impacts of affluent life-styles in industrialized countries. Environmental impacts are a function of Population × Affluence × Technology (Ehrlich and Erhlich, 1990). The limited population of industrialized countries (about 1.4 billion) is responsible for most of the world's pollution and consumption of resources.

Sustainability involves ensuring food security for the world. Without food security it is not possible to maintain world social and political order. The world now produces enough food to feed its entire population. Yet millions of people die of starvation each year, and hundreds of millions remain malnourished. Sustainable development must find ways of equitably distributing food resources. It must encourage land reforms and agricultural practices that allow rural peasants to sustain themselves in their locations.

Sustainable use of ecosystem resources means limiting the use of natural resources to a pace where they can renew themselves through natural processes. It involves reducing the rate of resource usage to below the 'carrying capacity' of ecosystems. This minimizes the extinction of species and resources.

A key resource for development is energy. Per-capita energy consumption has experienced colossal growth in the past two centuries. Current patterns of energy consumption and growth are not sustainable (Clark, 1989). The sustainable use of energy requires conservation and reducing energy waste. In addition, we need to reduce the use of fossil fuels and increase the use of renewable energy sources (Brown *et al.*, 1990; MacNeil, Wisemius and Yakushiji, 1991).

Finally, sustainable development must be built around sustainable economies. Economic policies guiding industrialization, science and technology, energy, urbanization and international trade must be consistent with the objectives of sustainable development (Daly and Cobb, 1989; Commoner, 1990).

Sustainable development, as briefly sketched here, is not a perfect solution to all our ecological problems. There are many critiques of the inadequacy of these notions of sustainable development (Redclift, 1989; De la Court, 1991). However, sustainable development is a good starting point for dealing with many industrial and environmental crises. It can serve as an orientating concept for thinking about corporate environmental responsibility.

Corporate responsibilities for sustainability

Corporations are the main engines of development. For sustainable development to succeed, corporations must become ecologically sustainable. Corporate responsibilities for sustainable development are extensive. The Business
Council for Sustainable Development (ICC, 1990) describes these responsibilities in terms of 16 principles, which may be paraphrased as follows. Corporations should have environmentally responsive strategies, products, production
systems, policies and systems. They should promote resource and energy conservation and adopt cleaner production technologies. They should minimize
and manage waste streams, recycle and reuse materials and reduce pollution.
They should engage in customer, employee and public education on environmental issues. These actions will help them to reduce technological risks and
protect the environment and human health (Hunt and Auster, 1990; Buzzeli,
1991). In addition, corporations must extend themselves to fulfilling the
broader goals of sustainability with respect to patterns of consumption, global
food security and ecosystem resources.

Historically, corporations have thrived on and have encouraged the emergence of consumer societies. Uncontrolled consumption has been encouraged
through aggressive promotion and advertising. This has bred a consumerist,
even anti-conservationist ethic. More controlled and thoughtful patterns of
consumption in the future may mean a need for more differentiated products,
less use of mass production and a rethinking of promotion and advertising.

Corporations can play a pivotal role in ensuring global food security. They
control many parts of the food production and distribution chain. In industrialized countries, food production is organized along corporate lines, as any
other industry. Agricultural productivity is enhanced through industrial processes involving plant genetics, pesticides and fertilizers. There are fewer than a
dozen grain-trading companies that control trade, prices and movement of
food across national borders. With such power over food resources goes the
responsibility for ensuring food security.

Corporations are the main users of natural resources. Many industries, such
as agriculture, metals and mining, forest products, and oil and derivative
chemicals, are entirely dependent on the exploitation of natural resources.
Corporations in these industries have a special responsibility for protecting
ecoresources. They also possess the knowledge and financial resources necessary for environmental protection. They must accept an environmental stewardship role that stops irresponsible exploitation of natural resources.

These environmental sustainability responsibilities can ameliorate crisis preconditions in the long run. Over time they will make companies less crisis prone.
However, corporate responsibilities must also address the more immediate
threats of I/E crises. These responsibilities are discussed in the next section.

Crisis prevention and management responsibilities

If we were to harness corporations to the task of preventing and managing I/E
crises, what would we require them to do? Corporate responsibilities in this

regard are multifaceted, and stretch over the phases or stages of crises. It must be acknowledged that industrial crises threaten the survival of corporations. They are not a peripheral concern of business but rather a key problem in the 1990s. If companies are to survive and flourish, they must make attempts to prevent crises and systematically manage the ones they cannot prevent.

Past research shows that major crises occur in discernible stages (Turner, 1976; Shrivastava, Miller and Miglani, 1991):

- Crisis preconditions.
- Triggering events and emergency management.
- Postcrisis long-term recovery.

Crisis preconditions refer to the stage in which there is a build-up of hazards to the natural environment and human health. This occurs through an escalation in technological complexity, operating size and the use of hazardous and unstable materials. Simultaneously, there is a lack of development of safety infrastructure. There is a lack of safety regulations, physical services (sewage, water, electricity, housing, etc.) and social services (education, communication, health care, etc.). Environmental hazards may also build up because of overuse of environmental resources, unsafe disposal of wastes, pollution and a lack of attention to maintenance and safety.

During this period many small technological failures occur. They usually cause little damage and serve as warning signals. However, companies ignore these warnings because they lack technological solutions or because of high costs.

The *triggering event* is the event that sets off the crisis. It can be a sudden event like a fire, an industrial accident or a product injury. Alternatively, crises can be triggered through slow evolutionary processes. For example, the long-term accumulation of toxic wastes, new information about exposure to hazards or occupational diseases can trigger crises. Crises are caused by multiple simultaneous failures in technology, organizational policies, regulations, infrastructure and community preparedness.

Corporations react to these events by engaging in *rescue and emergency management*. They attempt to mitigate damages from the crisis. They rescue endangered people and environments and protect them from further harm (Kasperson and Kasperson, 1988). This is also the phase in which crises expand into economic, political and cultural domains. They engulf many individuals and organizations and bring about restructuring of systems.

The last and longest phase is the *postcrisis long-term recovery*. It takes months and sometimes years for crisis-affected communities and environments to recover from direct and indirect impacts. It is the period of economic, ecologic, social, political and cultural normalization.

In each of these phases, corporations have different responsibilities, as suggested below:

1. *Crisis preconditions:*

   - Product and process research
   - Early-warnings systems

- Prevention measures
- Crisis preparedness measures
- Environmental sustainability

2. *Triggering event:*

- Damage control
- Rescue
- Investigations
- Immediate relief
- Environmental clean-up
- Protecting at-risk public
- Medical response
- Communications

3. *Postcrisis long-term recovery:*

- Environmental restoration
- Conflict resolution
- Victims' recovery
- Business recovery
- Social/political normalization

In the above discussion I have attempted to articulate a different notion of corporate responsibility for environmental crises. This notion goes deep into the philosophy of management, attitudes towards nature and operational responsibilities for crises prevention.

To make corporations responsible in this deep sense is a challenging task. It is not a surface, cosmetic, rhetorical acceptance of responsibility. Instead, this type of CSR must be institutionalized within companies and within the broader society in which companies operate. It must guide the choice of products, production technologies, strategies, structures resource allocations, systems and procedures, and stakeholder communications. It must be inculcated as a deep cultural trait.

The consequences of not accepting this broad concept of responsibility can be severe. In the future, companies will simply not be able to survive without doing so. I would like to illustrate this by focusing on corporate responsibility reflected in Union Carbide's Bhopal crisis.

Union Carbide's responsibilities in Bhopal

On 3 December 1984, a major industrial accident occurred at the Union Carbide pesticide plant in Bhopal, India. Forty tons of methyl isocyanate leaked from an underground tank, and spread over the city. It immediately killed 2,200 people. Today the death toll from the disaster stands at nearly 4,000. It injured another 300,000 people, of which 100,000 were seriously and permanently impaired. Thousands of animals and birds died. There was immeasurable damage to the natural environment.

For the company the accident was devastating. Its stock price plummeted and stable investors abandoned it. Within three months of the accident, the company declared that it was caused by employee sabotage. It accepted 'moral responsibility' but rejected legal liability. It distanced itself from its Indian subsidiary company, blaming most of the failures on it. It unsuccessfully tried to help victims. It was thwarted in this attempt by an unco-operative government (of India) and a hostile ideological environment. For ten years it fought bitter court battles against the victims, public interest groups and the government. The battle still continues today.

In August 1985, the GAF Corporation attempted forcibly to take over Union Carbide. To remain independent the company had to restructure itself financially. It sold its most profitable consumer products business. By 1987 it emerged as a much smaller but profitable company. In 1989 it reached an out-of-court settlement with the government of India to pay $470 million in compensation for damages. This money could not be distributed to the victims because of the lack of medico-legal documentation of damages. In 1991, the Supreme Court of India ordered the government to set up special courts to distribute this money to victims. It also cancelled Union Carbide's immunity from criminal prosecution.

In March 1992, new criminal cases were filed against the company. A Bhopal district court judge requested extradition of the former CEO, Warren Anderson, to stand trial in one case. Legal wrangling is likely to continue for many more years. The victims still await full compensation for the disaster that struck them ten years ago.

How did Union Carbide see and fulfil its responsibilities in terms of ecocentric management, sustainable development, and crisis prevention and managaement? What have been the consequences of its actions following the Bhopal crisis? Some assessments of these questions are outlined below (Morehouse and Subramaniam, 1988; Shrivastava, 1992; Lepkowski, 1993).

Ecocentric management
Union Carbide pursued goals, values, products and strategies typical of traditional chemical companies. It exhibited little concern for the environment in its choice of product portfolio. It produced heavy chemicals, pesticides, batteries, carbon products, consumer products and plastics. The inherent hazardousness and environmental damage from these products did not dissuade the company from them.

UCC's environmental policies were aimed at regulatory compliance. Its risk management practices aimed at minimizing corporate financial liabilities. These policies and practices were driven primarily by legal and economic concerns, and not by ecocentric concerns of preserving and enhancing nature.

Despite its stated policy of uniform worldwide safety and environmental standards, the Bhopal plant lacked the level of safety and environmental protection present at the company's other similar plants.

Sustainable development
The Indian subsidiary of Union Carbide attempted to address the development concerns of its local environment. It was engaged in a partnership with the

government of India to promote family planning and population control. It provided well paid and stable jobs to over 30,000 workers. Its products were consistent with conventional economic development needs and local consumer demands. But they did not cater to the needs of ecologically sustainable development. Its agricultural pesticides ostensibly improved food production efficiency but, in the long run, degraded soil, crops and groundwater.

UCC did not have any explicit stance on environmental stewardship. It did not strive for sustainable use of natural resources. The main raw material used in many of its products (chemicals and plastics) was oil, which is non-renewable. The products themselves were environmentally harmful (pesticides, heavy chemicals) and difficult to dispose (plastics, batteries).

Crisis prevention and management

In preventing and managing the Bhopal crisis, Union Carbide was reactive and defensive. It reacted to the Indian government intiative of expanding pesticide production in the country. After making an initial commitment to establish a production facility, it did not back out even though it knew that the Bhopal plant could not be run profitably. To cut its losses, the plant was operated with minimum personnel and safety standards. The parent company did not provide strong oversight on safety issues. The plant personnel ignored early warning signals from an environmental/safety audit survey. The plant lacked emergency plans, and crisis prevention and readiness measures.

After the accident Union Carbide could not organize an effective emergency management plan. It was unable to play a significant role in rescuing victims and providing medical help. Its half-hearted attempts at providing relief were thwarted by the government and local activists. It did not participate in the long-term rehabilitation of victims. It did not do environmental impact assessment or clean-up after the accident. The Methyl Isocyanate (MIC) inventory in the plant was neutralized by a government of India taskforce.

The company claimed 'moral responsibility' but denied legal liability for damages. It quickly entered litigation over liability and fought aggressively to defend itself. Its defence lay in blaming the accident on 'sabotage' by a worker and mismanagement by local managers. This defence was based on evidence the company gathered through its own internal investigations, and never released to the public or the courts.

Much of the company's postcrisis management effort focused on business recovery and restructuring. It defended itself from a hostile takeover attempt by GAF Corporation by selling off its most profitable businesses. It reached a settlement with the government of India and paid $470 million in 1989 to settle all claims. After that it remained disengaged from social and political issues that shaped postcrisis conditions in Bhopal.

The end result of this half-hearted acceptance of responsibility was the continuous debilitation of the company over the ten years since the accident. The struggle to survive this crisis took a heavy toll on the company. Union Carbide today has a risky and uncompetitive business portfolio of mostly commodity chemicals. This is a cyclical business, highly dependent on petrochemical feed stocks. It is a minor player in an industry dominated by giants. It is unable to maintain a pace of investment in R&D and capital programmes that can match its rivals.

Its workforce witnessed continued decimation since the accident. Many bright and competent managers departed. Employees at plants were demoralized.

Its stock has been volatile and it has shown lack-lustre performance. A *The Wall Street Journal* article argued that, because of these reasons, UCC is not a financially viable company. It could again become a target for takeover (McMurray, 1992).

The lesson for corporations is that accepting corporate responsibility is not only an ethical matter but it is also a matter of long-term survival. It is in the self-interest of companies broadly to conceptualize their responsibilities on safety, health and environmental issues and to fulfil them vigorously. By doing so they are likely to act with more caution and more concern for the human and environmental impacts of their activities. This caution and concern can reduce their crisis chances.

This assessment does not imply a cause–effect relationship between meeting corporate responsibilities and survival (or decline). Corporate survival is a function of more than how companies meet their social responsibilities. It depends on corporate strategies, environmental conditions and chance, among other things. Here my point is that only envisaging corporate responsibility in the broader sense suggested above can facilitate survival. A broader conception of responsibility gives rise to a broader repertoire of actions for preventing and coping with environmental crises.

Acknowledgements

I thank Dan Gilbert, Bucknell University, and Ed Stead, University of Eastern Tennessee, for thoughtful comments on an earlier draft of this chapter, and Walter Nord and John Jermier, University of South Florida, for encouraging me to think through the issues presented here.

References

Brown, L. *et al.* (1988, 1989, 1990, 1991) *State of the World.* W.W. Norton, New York.
Bucholz, R., Marcus, A. and Post, J. (1991) *Cases in Environmental Management.* Prentice-Hall, Englewood Cliffs, NJ.
Buzzelli, D. (1991) 'Time to Structure an Environmental Policy Strategy,' *Journal of Business Strategy*, March–April, pp. 17–20.
Cairncross, F. (1991) *Costing the Earth.* Harvard Business School Press, Boston, Mass.
Carroll, A.B. (1979) 'A three dimensional conceptual model of corporate social performance.' *Academy of Management Review*, Vol. 4, pp. 497–505.
Clark, W. (1989) 'Managing planet earth,' *Scientific American*, September, pp. 47–59.
Commoner, B. (1990) *Making Peace with the Planet.* Pantheon, New York.
Costanza, R. (1992) *Ecological Economics.* Columbia University Press, New York.
Daly, H.E. and Cobb, J.C. (1989) *For the Common Good.* Beacon, Boston, Mass.
De la Court, T. (1991) *Beyond Sustainable Development.* Zed Books, London.
Devall, B. and Session, G. (1985) *Deep Ecology: Living as if Nature Mattered.* Peregrine Smith Books, Salt Lake City, Utah.

Ehrenfeld, D. (1978) *The Arrogance of Humanism*, Oxford University Press, New York.

Ehrlich, P. and Ehrlich, A. (1991) *The Population Explosion*, Touchstone, New York.

Frederick, W. (1986) 'Toward CSR3: why ethical analysis is indispensable and unavoidable in corporate affairs,' *Californai Management Review*, Winter, pp. 126–41.

Freeman, R.E. and Gilbert, D. (1988) *Corporate Strategy and the Search for Ethics*. Prentice-Hall, Englewood Cliffs, NJ.

Friedman, M. (1962) *Capitalism and Freedom*. University of Chicago Press, Chicago, Ill.

Gallup International (1992) *Survey of Environmental Attitudes*. Gallup International, Princeton, NJ.

Hoffman, W., Frederick, R. and Petry, E. (1990) *The Corporation Ethics and the Environment*. Quorum Books, New York.

Hunt, C. and Auster, E. (1990) 'Proactive Environmental Management: Avoiding the Toxic Trap,' *Sloan Management Review* Vol. 31, pp. 7–18.

ICC (International Chamber of Commerce) (1990) *Business Charter for Sustainable Development*, ICC, Geneva.

Kasperson, R.E. and Kasperson, J.X. (1988) 'Emergency planning for industrial crises: an overview,' *Industrial Crisis Quarterly*, Vol. 2, no. 2, pp. 81–8.

Lepkowski, W. (1993) The restructuring of Union Carbide since Bhopal,' in S. Jasanoff (ed.) *Lessons of the Bhopal Disaster*. University of Pennsylvania Press, Philadelphia, Pa.

MacNeil, J., Wisemius, P. and Yakushiji, T. (1991) *Beyond Interdependence*. Oxford University Press, New York.

Manes, C. (1991) *Green Rage: Radical Environmentalism and the Unmaking of Civilization*. Little, Brown & Co., Boston, Mass.

Mckibben, R. (1989) *The End of Nature*. Random House, New York.

McMurray, S. (1992) 'Union Carbide offers some sober lessons in crisis management,' *The Wall Street Journal*, 28 January.

Meadows, D.H., Meadows, D.L. and Randers, J. (1992) *Beyond the Limits: Confronting Global Collapse, Envisioning a Sustainable Future*, Chelsea Green, Post Mills, VT.

Mitroff, I. and Pauchant, T. (1990) *We are so Big and Powerful Nothing Bad can Happen to Us*. Carol Publishing, New York.

Morehouse, W. and Subramaniam, A. (1988) *The Bhopal Tragedy*. Council on International and Public Affairs, New York.

Naess, A. (1987) *Ecology, Community and Lifestyle: Ecosophy*. Cambridge University Press.

Nash, R. (1989) *The Rights of Nature*. University of Wisconsin Press, Madison, Wis.

Perrow, C. (1984) *Normal Accidents: Living with High Risk Technologies*. Basic Books, New York.

Porritt, J. (1984) *Seeing Green: The Politics of Ecology Explained*. Basil Blackwell, New York.

Post, J. and Altman, B. (1991) 'Corporate environmentalism: the challenge of organizational learning.' Paper presented at the Academy of Management, Miami Beach, 12 August.

Preston, L. (ed.) (1985) *Research in Corporate Social Performance*. JAI Press, Greenwich, Conn.

Pryde, R. (1992) *Environmental Management in the Soviet Union*. Cambridge University Press, New York.

Redclift, M. (1989) *Sustainable Development: Exploring the Contradictions*. Methuen, London.

Reich, M.R. (1991) *Toxic Politics: Responding to Chemical Disasters*. Cornell University Press, Ithaca, NY.

Ruckelshaus, W. (1989) 'Toward a sustainable world,' *Scientific American*, September, pp. 166–75.

Sethi, S.P. and Steidelmeir, P. (1991) *Up Against the Corporate Wall*. Prentice-Hall, Englewood Cliffs, NJ.

Shrivastava, P. (1992) *Bhopal: Anatomy of a Crisis* (revised edn). Paul Chapman Publishing, London.

Shrivastava, P. (1996) *Profiting the Corporation and the Environment*. Thompson Executive Press, Cincinnati, OH.

Shrivastava, P. and Hart, S. (1994), 'Greening organizations 2000,' *International Journal of Public Administration*, Vol. 17, nos. 3/4, pp. 607–35.

Shrivastava, P., Miller, D. and Miglani, A. (1991) 'The evolution of crises: crisis precursors,' *International Journal of Mass Emergencies and Disasters*, August, Vol. 9, no. 3, pp. 321–37.

Shrivastava, P., Mitroff, I.I., Miller, D. and Miglani, A. (1988) 'Understanding industrial crises,' *Journal of Management Studies*, Vol. 25, no. 4, pp. 285–304.

Smith, D. (1992) *Business and the Environment*. Paul Chapman Publishing, London.

Starik, M. and Carroll, A. (1991) 'Strategic environmental management: business as if the earth really mattered.' Paper presented at the International Association for Business and Society.

Stead, E. and Stead, J. (1991) *Management for a Small Planet*. Sage, Beverly Hills, Calif.

Throop, G.M., Starik, M. and Rands, G. (1993) 'Sustainable strategy in a greening world: integrating the natural environment into strategic management,' in P. Shrivastava, A. Huff and J. Dutton (eds) *Advances in Strategic Management, Vol. 9*. JAI Press, Greenwich, Conn.

Turner, B.A. (1976) 'The organizational and interorganizational development of disaster,' *Administrative Science Quarterly*, Vol. 21, no. 2, pp. 378–97.

Wood, D. (1991) 'Corporate social performance revisited,' *Academy of Management Review*, Vol. 16, no. 4, pp. 691–718.

World Commission on Environment and Development (1987) *Our Common Future*. Oxford University Press, New York.

12

Strategic management and business policy-making: bringing in environmental values

JO McCLOSKEY and DENIS SMITH

Liverpool Business School and University of Durham, UK

Introduction

Accepted economic thinking in postwar industrial countries tended to promulgate ideologies which stated that the way forward for sustainable future development was through growth via increasing consumption of resources. Mass production resulted in what appeared to be limitless products and services, and industry developed a range of new technologies that enabled faster production and distribution of those products. The free enterprise system that prevailed in these economies ensured rapid economic growth and high productivity and encouraged mass consumption and freedom of choice by consumers. However, by the middle of the 1970s, changes in the physical environment were beginning to manifest themselves and this combined with the findings of research studies which revealed a correlation between environmental damage and industrial practices that had arisen from industrial activities. The publication of Rachael Carson's *Silent Spring* and the Club of Rome's work on the limits to economic growth combined with media coverage of environmental issues to heighten public awareness and concerns about the range and extent of environmental problems. These issues included the need stringently to treat water in order to make it safe for consumption, the extensive damage to landscapes by intensive farming and forests, the risks from nuclear power production, the effects of pesticides and the eutrophication of lakes. By the early part of the 1990s, the extent of these issues had widened considerably to include global problems of environmental impact, such as the erosion of the ozone layer, acid precipitation, global warming and hazardous waste disposal. The biosphere, which had always been regarded as a free good that could be almost endlessly exploited, was under serious threat (McIntosh, 1991). Increased awareness of global environmental damage, combined with the downturn in productivity and consumption and mounting trade deficits, highlighted the need for societies to adjust their economic ideologies from those which had concentrated on short-termism to more sustainable strategies for development. This chapter seeks to explore the interface between business activities and environmental quality in the light of post-industrial economic decline.

Developing environmental values

The free enterprise system is characterized by the enormous amount of decisions which are reached independently by producers and consumers in order to promote a certain quality of life while preserving individual autonomy. However, rapid developments in information technology, consumer education and sophistication and numerous product and process scares have resulted in changes in individual purchasing behaviour. These changes, coupled with collective consumer pressure on producers, mean that it is no longer enough for manufacturers to supply products that simply fulfil narrowly based consumer requirements for product performance. Public groups are increasingly demanding environmentally friendly products that are produced by using materials and processes which do not threaten the environment or society. These social and political pressures are forcing manufacturers to consider the complete life-cycle of the product and this includes disposal and/or recycling of the product at the end of its useful life. This cradle-to-grave approach raises fundamental questions about the moral responsibilities of both producers and consumers alike and brings into sharp focus the global inequalities that exist between nation-states. Such a swing in consumer behaviour requires industry to redesign mass production, distribution and consumption mechanisms so that the lowest feasible level of resources can be used to provide society with optimal standards of living and commensurate quality of life. Such a shift to conservation requires that pollution be reduced through rigorous efforts to eliminate waste, inefficiency and mismanagement (Gunn, 1991).

While most organizations acknowledge that virtually all company operations today have some form of environmental implications, one of the major problems facing industry is the confusion as to what exactly constitutes 'environmentally friendly' initiatives or practices. Companies who proclaim to be environmentally aware and corporately responsible have formulated environmental policies into their mission statements and strategic plans. However, these initiatives rarely give specific practical guidance as to how and where environmental efforts should be applied within the range of activities undertaken by the organization (Hooper and Rocca, 1991). Without principles to guide such decisions, it is impossible to communicate how environmental affairs can fit into the broad strategies of the company. It is imperative that such principles should reflect the perspectives of operations, environmental affairs, legal, financial and other relevant functions and should be constructed to parallel critical decision-making processes and major company activities.

Business strategy and the environment

The strategic management process seeks to ensure that the organization achieves a fit with its environment and optimizes its resources to achieve

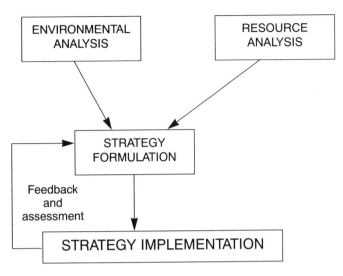

Environmental scanning
Value-chain assessments: Environmental auditing
Competitor analysis: sector-wide greening
Ecological aspects of corporate environment
Regulatory assessment

ENVIRONMENTAL ANALYSIS

RESOURCE ANALYSIS

STRATEGY FORMULATION

Feedback and assessment

STRATEGY IMPLEMENTATION

Intergenerational effects
Distribution and extent of costs and benefits
Continual environmental auditing

Figure 12.1 *A green perspective on the strategic management process (Source:* Smith, 1992)

competitive advantage. The means by which competitive advantage can be achieved are many and varied and there has been considerable debate within the literature concerning the role of technical expertise in achieving such an advantage. Indeed, a school of criticism has developed around the work of Mintzberg (1994) which is opposed to the rational planning school of thought. Critics of business planning, as epitomized by the rational planning school, have pointed to the difficulties faced by planners when attempting to plan beyond anything but the short term. In more recent years, some authors have suggested that the inherent chaos and uncertainty within the broad business environment necessitates that organizations revise their decision-making to incorporate such uncertainty and to recognize the limitations of technical expertise in the process (see, for example, Stacey, 1991).

In theory the incorporation of 'green' issues within discussions of strategic management should be relatively simple to accomplish. (In the context of our discussions, 'green issues' is used as a label in order to differentiate these problems from those more general issues which are grouped under the label of the 'business environment'. Although the term 'environment' is often used within the business literature, it is narrowly defined and often restricted to a discussion of environmentally based issues.) If the strategic management process is broken down into its constituent parts (Figure 12.1) then it is possible to identify a number of critical areas where attention could be focused across a range of 'green issues'. The strategic management process is essentially concerned with the interaction of business and its competitive environment. Consequently, the process should seek to help managers develop strategies that allow organizations to achieve a best 'fit' with the environment in which they operate. The use of the term 'environment', however, has usually been seen in terms of barriers to entry, the economic buying power of buyers and suppliers and the economic exploitation of the resource base in order to gain competitive advantage (Porter, 1985). There is now, however, a need to broaden this economic interpretation of the environment to encompass those factors in the micro and macroenvironment which present opportunities for, and/or threats to, environmentally benign business practices (see Shrivastava, 1993; Smith, 1992; 1993; McCloskey and Maddock, 1994). Some organizations, particularly those with a high environmental profile, have already incorporated both environmental audits and environmental impact assessments into their environmental and resource analysis procedure, and already apply an ecological perspective to their existing economic considerations. Those organizations that carry out both ecological and economic environmental scans and audits will benefit from improved statutory compliance, along with a more accurate identification and management of environmental risk. Such a process should also lead to enhanced environmental awareness and corporate responsibility throughout the organization (Smith, 1991). Ultimately, this will lead to better financial and insurance planning and will provide the organization with ever-increasing opportunities for gaining competitive advantage and increasing profits (North, 1992). Put simply, incorporating environmental (ecological) values into corporate decision-making will ultimately result in greater organizational sustainability.

Environmental values and the strategy process

The strategic management process places considerable weight on the values held by senior staff within the organization. Indeed, there are those who have suggested that, ultimately, 'Almost all questions of corporate strategy are questions of ethics . . . [and] . . . the very best corporations can and should be managed in a way that is consistent with a strategy built on a foundation of ethics' (Freeman and Gilbert, 1988, pp. 7–8). If we accept this relationship between values and strategy, then it should be a relatively simple matter to incorporate more radical ecologically based values into the main strategy theories. However, the transformation of business strategy in this regard has proved to be problematic and business schools have shown some considerable reluctance to take such an ecologically and ethically based transformation on board (see Smith, Hart and McCloskey, 1994). Events such as Bhopal, Chernobyl, Love Canal and the pollution problems in the former communist-bloc countries will eventually force through change in organizations as social concerns transform political pressures into tighter regulatory frameworks. It is our contention here that organizations can gain a long-term competitive advantage by anticipating such changes and improving their environmental performance now before they are forced to make expensive changes by the governments.

Analysing the environment and measuring environmental impact therein is crucial to the implementation of any environmental strategy. However, the pollution process recognizes no political or economic boundaries and any systematic attempt at analysing the global effects of specific businesses and industry sectors on the biosphere is at present virtually impossible. None the less, it is now widely recognized that business has a major role to play in providing the answers to many of our pollution problems through resource reduction and better managerial processes. Within a resource analysis it is desirable to assess the effective utilization of resources and their subsequent influence on environmental impact. Porter's (1985) value chain provides a useful framework within which to consider such issues. The value chain attempts to profile those activities that will add value through its business strategy. The value chain includes both direct *value creating* activities – inbound logistics, operations, outbound logistics, marketing and services – as well as *support activities* such as procurement, technological development, human resource management and management systems. For example, an organization pursuing a low-cost strategy will attempt to focus its attention on operations and logistics and less on marketing and sales. In capital-intensive industries (which have been accused of being among the major polluters) such as the automobile, chemical, steel and heavy electrical industries, significant value is usually added in logistics and operations. These industries typically opt for global standardization as customized or country-specific products would be prohibitively costly. However, if the value-chain analysis was to be linked with the process of environmental auditing, it would be possible to highlight those aspects of the organization's activities which contribute significantly to its 'portfolio of degradation' and take necessary corrective action. Alternatively, more value could be added through the various marketing and services activities by formulating or marketing new environmentally benign products and processes, thereby creating opportunities to gain a competitive edge.

If we move away from viewing the environment as a common 'good' towards an ecologically driven model, then the value of the organization's products and services needs to take into account the environmental impact associated with its production (Smith, 1992). If polluters were unable to see pollution as an externality on the production process but had to incorporate the costs of such pollution, then we would see a move towards waste minimization strategies being incorporated into the strategic decision-making process. The costs of pollution, if calculated to account for the spatial and temporal dynamics of that pollution process, would force many organizations to reassess their modes of production and sectoral activities. This would also provoke changes in consumer behaviour as the costs of greater pollution control would be passed on to the consumers who would revise their preferences accordingly.

Table 12.1 *Greening Porter's value chain*

	Inbound logistics	Operations	Outbound logistics	Marketing and sales	Service
Procurement	Transportation impacts Storage modes	'Green consumables' Clean technologies Recyclable packaging	Storage modes Transportation modes	Raw materials sourcing and supply	Receipt and environmental disposal of used product or product components
Technology development	Waste minimization through source reduction Alternative raw material sources	Clean technologies Pollution minimization and control	Finished product recyclability	Packaging minimization and disposal innovatory 'Green' products and processes	Dissembly and reconstruction
Human resource management	Staff selection Supplier selection	Corporate culture training programmes Corporate environmental awareness	Subcontractual arrangements	Internal and external communications and community liaison	Incentives Rewards for environmental ideas and practices
Management systems	Inventory reduction Recyclability	'Just-in-time' processes	'Cradle-to-grave' responsibility for products Recycling and recovery infrastructure	Green new-product development committees Research & development	Quality circles and environmental standards assurance

Table 12.1 illustrates some of the elements that are likely to prove of importance in securing an ecologically based competitive advantage. The value chain can serve as a useful framework for assessing the impact that an organization and its activities have on environmental quality; and the potential for organizations to take a more fundamental approach to greening their activities is considerable, given the range of activities listed. After completing the processes of environmental and resource analysis, the strategy process moves into the formulation and implementation stages. Here it is possible to identify a number of important areas which have an impact on the greening process. These include the limits of technical expertise in decision-making; the process of short-termism; and the nature of competitor activity.

The use of technical expertise

There is a large and varied literature that examines the process of human reasoning and the role of bias therein (Evans, 1989). A considerable element of this research has sought to explore the role of technical expertise within decision-making and the often debilitating effects that technocracy can have with regard to environmental performance and, more specifically, technological risk (see, Collingridge and Reeve, 1986; Fischer, 1990; 1991; 1993; Smith, 1990; 1991; 1994).

Environmental affairs have long been a technical or scientific function performed by specialists, with little emphasis placed on developing a broad management perspective among environmental personnel. Such specialism allows a technocratic approach to environmentalism to prevail and this can create the illusion of infallibility of science and technology (see Collingridge and Reeve, 1986). These specialists, whether external or internal, are aware of, or may even be part of, the company culture. They are, or will be made aware, of the corporate image that the company wishes to portray to the outside world and the need to preserve the status quo. They are often under pressure, real or imagined, to produce reports that side-step the issue by referring to the historical record of the business practice (or process) without acknowledging an adequate enough time lag between the polluting activity and the pollution damage. For example, the causal relationship between asbestos pollution and lung cancer proved difficult to verify because of the latency period needed for cancer to develop, by which time blame can be levelled at other forms of exposure. Similar comments can be made over the relationship between smoking and lung cancer and with the disposal of hazardous chemical wastes, which also display a longevity and toxicity that creates major intergenerational problems for those concerned with environmental policy. Alternatively, specialist reports can be couched in such scientific and technical language that it is difficult either to prove or disprove their findings, or to assess the thoroughness of the investigations. The high degree of uncertainty that accompanies new technological and scientific developments, and the imbalance in the distribution of expertise, highlights the need for a more open, democratic approach to the strategic process (see Fischer, 1990). Participative management, involving a range of specialist personnel covering the whole spectrum of the organization's activities, could provide a foundation for reciprocal accountability and would produce a more egalitarian communication and control system than the current specialist, hierarchical management structures found in most organizations. Such a move, while essential to achieving sustainability, will require fundamental changes in the dominant forms of decision-making used by industry and government alike (see Sheldon and Smith, 1992).

The process of short-termism

As has already been mentioned, economic growth through mass production, distribution and consumption has been the tenet for sustainable development in free market economies since the 1940s. This philosophy rests on the growth of wealth and assets and is loosely measured in material living standards and gross national product (GNP). However, living standards are measured in material terms only and GNP simply records total output regardless of what resources have been used. The fast accumulation of wealth brought about by quick turnover led to increased capital expenditure on plant and machinery and investment in more efficient manufacturing and distribution processes. The upwards spiral of production, growth and profits justified the free market ideology until the 1980s when evidence of environmental degradation and decline in production and consumption became apparent. The focus on 'growth of assets' has started to lose ground to a philosophy of 'productivity of assets'. Organizations have begun to operate strategies that maximize the value that their activities add to the economy and, while profit maximization will always be fundamental to any business organization, there is now another fundamental objective that must be addressed if businesses are to be sustainable in the longer term – that objective is the minimization of environmental mismanagement. Unfortunately, the environmental perspective has hitherto been pitted against, or imposed on, manufacturing initiatives by legislation and regulation rather than being integrated with a more proactive operations management. This conflict has developed from the erroneous belief that environmental activities rarely contribute to profit generation and can even hinder such efforts. However, the business community has now begun to realize that there is a need to improve their environmental performance if organizations are to remain competitive. This realization is due to the growing concerns currently being expressed by a variety of stakeholders, some of which can be listed as follows:

1. Consumers are not only demanding environmentally friendly products but are now also starting to question the materials and processes used in production.
2. Forthcoming EC legislation could decree that banks and other lending institutions would be at least partially liable for the environmental damage caused by companies with whom they do business. Future legislation could mean that banks who hold a mortgage over contaminated land may be sued for any resulting pollution damage associated with that investment.

3. Environmental damage claims accounted for over 50 per cent of the £509 million losses reported by Lloyds of London in June 1991. Latest policies now include specific time limits and are much more specific as to the damage claims which will be covered. It is conceivable that insurance companies will not insure against environmental damage unless businesses adhere to strict environmental policies and processes (Greenpeace Business, 1991).

As major stakeholders become increasingly wary about investing in companies that are engaged in unsound environmental processes, more organizations are realizing that unless they comprehensively clean up their activities they will not be sustainable in the market-place.

The nature of competitive activity
The notion of competition remains one of the most fundamental and pervasive conditions of business practice. Business rivals capitalize on their strengths and efficiencies to gain competitive advantage and the ultimate objective is to force their rivals out of the market and thereby to achieve total dominance. The total cost of such competition must include loss of productivity and expenses incurred in bankruptcies and liquidations (Gunn, 1991). These costs have to be absorbed in the cost of operating the economy, which, in turn, lowers the standards of living and the quality of life – the foundation on which free enterprise is based! The purpose of competition should be to increase the chances of survival by achieving maximum productivity, while simultaneously conserving resources and minimizing waste and costs. Some companies (notably The Body Shop and Loblaws Industries) have shown that it is possible to achieve competitive advantage through conforming to high environmental standards, irrespective of the actions of their competitors.

As the criterion for success in organizations changes from 'growth of assets' to environmentally sound productive efficiency, competition will become a cost-effective form of rivalry whereby organizations compete against their own past performance. Self-competition will dominate and accentuate the use of co-operation, collaboration and teamwork to achieve optimal output using environmentally benign materials and processes.

Conclusions

It is evident that consumers are becoming increasingly concerned about environmental issues and industry has begun to think more carefully about the effects their products and processes may have on the environment. Given the more stringent demands of key stakeholders such as banks, lending institutions, insurance companies and the media, organizations have realized that they must incorporate ecological issues into their business practices and processes if they are to survive in the market-place in anything other than the short term.

Managing environmental affairs is no longer an incidental or secondary function of company operations. Product design, manufacturing, transportation, customer use and the ultimate disposal of a product should not merely reflect environmental considerations but must be driven by them. While many models and techniques for greening business have been developed, one of the major difficulties remaining for organizations is that of implementing a green strategy and integrating environmental management systems and policies with the strategic management process. The main areas of controversy centre around the interaction of technical and scientific expertise, the continuing ethos of short-term profit rather than long-term sustainability and the nature of competition which currently favours 'survival of the fittest' rather than 'survival of the species'. In addition, the conflict of interest between the competitive and ecological environments on the one hand, and between societal concerns and political manoeuvring on the other, provide for a complex setting within which the strategic management process is framed.

Organizations must realize that to be effective they need to articulate practical principles to guide the organization's environmental efforts; integrate environmental affairs within company operations; and develop environmental professionals to meet mounting environmental requirements (Hooper and Rocca, 1991). However, while a small number of industries lead the way in new technology, the majority of organizations are still trying to keep abreast of the ever-increasing developments in new technology. It is important that industry realizes the significance of the changes that are brought about by such developments and recognizes the need to communicate the implications for business and the impact on the environment clearly to the public, if conflict and controversy are to be avoided.

References

Chakravarthy, B.S. and Lorange, P. (1991) *Managing the Strategy Process*. Prentice-Hall, N.J.

Collingridge, D. and Reeve, C. (1986) *Science Speaks to Power*. Francis Pinter, London.

Evans, J. St B. (1989) *Bias in Human Reasoning: Causes and Consequences*. Lawrence Erlbaum Associates, Hove.

Fischer, F. (1990) *Technocracy and the Politics of Expertise*. Sage, Newbury Park, Calif.

Fischer, F. (1991) 'Risk assessment and environmental crisis: towards an integration of science and participation,' *Industrial Crisis Quarterly*, Vol. 5, no. 2, pp. 113–32.

Freeman, R.E. and Gilbert, D.R. (1988) *Corporate Strategy and the Search for Ethics*. Prentice-Hall, Englewood Cliffs, NJ.

Gunn, B. (1991) 'Competruism: strategic implications,' *Management Decision*, Vol. 25, no. 5, pp. 16–27.

Hooper, T.L. and Rocca, B.T. (1991) 'Environmental affairs: now on the strategic agenda,' *Journal of Business Strategy*, May/June, pp. 26–30.

McCloskey, J. and Maddock, S. (1994) 'Environmental management: its role in corporate strategy,' *Management Decision*, Vol. 32, no. 1, pp. 27–32.

McIntosh, A. (1991) 'The impact of environmental issues on marketing and politics in the 1990s,' *Journal of the Market Research Society*, Vol. 33, no. 3, pp. 205–7.

Mintzberg, H. (1994) *The Rise and Fall of Strategic Planning*. Prentice-Hall, London.

North, K. (1992) *Environmental Business Management: An Introduction*. International Labour Office, Geneva.

Porter, M. (1985) *Competitive Advantage: Techniques for Analyzing Industries and Competitors*. Free Press, New York.

Sheldon, T.A. and Smith, D. (1992) 'Assessing the health effects of waste disposal sites: issues in risk analysis and some Bayesian conclusions,' in M. Clark, D. Smith and A. Blowers (eds) *Waste Location: Spatial Aspects of Waste Management, Hazards and Disposal.* Routledge, London.

Shrivastava, P. (1993) *Bhopal: Anatomy of a Crisis.* Paul Chapman Publishing, London.

Smith, D. (1990) 'Corporate power and the politics of uncertainty: risk management at the Canvey Island complex,' *Industrial Crisis Quarterly*, Vol. 4, no. 1, pp. 1–26.

Smith, D. (1991) 'The Kraken wakes – the political dynamics of the hazardous waste issue,' *Industrial Crisis Quarterly*, Vol. 5, no. 3, pp. 189-207.

Smith, D. (1992) 'Business strategy and the environment: what lies beyond the rhetoric of greening?', *Business Strategy and the Environment,* Vol. 1, no. 1, pp. 1–9.

Smith, D. (1993) 'The Frankenstein factor – corporate responsibility and the environment,' in D. Smith (ed.) *Business and the Environment: Implications of the New Environmentalism.* Paul Chapman Publishing, London.

Smith, D. (1994) *Bhopal as a Crisis of Ethics: Corporate Responsibility and Risk Management. Crisis Management Working Paper* 3. The Home Office Emergency Planning College/Liverpool Business School.

Smith, D., Hart, D. and McCloskey, J. (1994) 'Greening the business school: environmental education and the business curriculum,' *Management Learning*, Vol. 25, no. 3, pp. 485–98.

Stacey, R. (1991) *The Chaos Frontier: Creative Strategic Control for Business.* Butterworth-Heinemann, Oxford.

Appendix

Global warming and the greenhouse effect: implications for international environmental policy

RODNEY WHITE

University of Toronto

New limits, new changes

Human beings are a rapidly expanding species and, like other species that have suddenly become more populous in relation to the resources provided by their niche in the biosphere, they make surprising discoveries about the nature of that niche. The press of their numbers forces them continually to evaluate the resources available for continued expansion and to anticipate the shortages they might face. This process of discovery is full of stops and starts – moments of panic and retreat, followed by longer periods of expansion and consolidation.

The European 'discovery' of North America (called the 'new world' by the newcomers, and which they rushed in to exploit) was followed up by the circumnavigation of the globe. Magellan's voyage (like that of the Apollo spacecraft), demonstrated that the globe was one single system, accessible to anyone determined enough to make the effort. Eventually, the European colonizers spread their culture and their people to almost every patch of the globe.

The pictures of the earth, taken from the Apollo 12 spacecraft in 1969, are widely credited with the acceptance of the idea that the world is one, finite system, the communal home of the human species. Interestingly this physical demonstration of what now appears to be obvious has been favourably reported and the pictures have been reproduced countless times. However, the computational exercise that provided the basis for *Limits to Growth* – a numerical examination of the implications of the earth's finitude – provoked some angry reactions (Meadows *et al.*, 1972). It is interesting to note that a re-examination of the model 20 years later has confirmed its accuracy over that intervening period (Meadows, Meadows and Randers, 1992).

Global warming – the enhancement of the natural greenhouse effect by human activities – contains elements of these major changes in the way we view the world and live in it. The basic science of the greenhouse effect is relatively simple, but the implications of changing it by human agency are highly complex and remain very contentious. Some commentators see the probable result as the end of the world as we know it. These include individuals such as Adrian Atkinson (1991, p. 72): 'We have arrived very suddenly at the edge of the abyss, beyond which lies a very brutal ecological dénouement'; and institutions: 'It is now widely accepted that the planet Earth is in danger of becoming uninhabitable and that urgent measures, at every level, are essential to protect the global environment' (Metropolitan Toronto Government, 1991, p. 16). What then is the greenhouse effect and how have we destabilized it? Having begun the destabilization process, what remedial policy options are open to us at the urban, national and global scales?

The enhanced greenhouse effect: its evolution and its probable impact

Life on earth depends on incoming radiation from the sun which warms the earth's surface. Some of this warmth is absorbed at the surface and another portion is radiated back through the atmosphere. A portion of this reradiated energy is absorbed by water vapour and trace gases in the atmosphere. Natural trace gases (sometimes known as greenhouse gases) include carbon dioxide, methane, nitrous oxide and ozone, to which human beings have added some synthetic compounds – the chlorofluorocarbons (CFCs). The natural greenhouse effect – which has remained quite stable throughout the human tenancy of the planet – keeps the temperature at the earth's surface an average of 32°C warmer than it would otherwise be. Without this blanket of trace gases the earth's surface would be as cold as Mars and human life would not be possible.

The principal greenhouse gas is carbon dioxide. Carbon occurs on the surface of the earth as an important component of soils, litter and biomass, especially trees. Carbon is released to the atmosphere when vegetation decomposes or burns. It combines with oxygen to form carbon dioxide where it stays in the atmosphere for about 100 years before being absorbed by plant material on the earth's surface, or by the ocean itself or by carbonaceous marine organisms. This carbon cycle – like the phosphorous cycle, the nitrogen cycle and all the other biogeochemical cycles on which life on earth depends – is made up of many processes operating at different speeds, the geological portion being relatively slow, and the vegetal portion being relatively rapid, but the cycle as a whole has maintained its stability over very long periods, much longer than the human timescale.

Human beings began to affect this cycle first by removing the tree cover, beginning in Neolithic time some 10,000 years ago. Extensive deforestation occurred in the temperate zone, especially in the zone of broad-leaved forests (oak, ash, chestnut, etc.) where the soils proved to be most suitable for agriculture. The evergreen forests (fir, spruce, pine, etc.) remained relatively intact until the nineteenth century when the demand for timber and wood pulp moved into the industrial phase; the turn of the great tropical forests awaited this century. The human burning and cutting of the forests affects the carbon cycle by accelerating the release of carbon to the atmosphere and by reducing the vegetal 'sink' which absorbs atmospheric carbon.

These assaults on the world's forests have had major impacts on soil erosion in many regions and in other regions are believed to have negative effects on rainfall; the global climatic role of the tropical forests is now a matter of serious concern. The impact of deforestation on the global carbon cycle is, however, small compared with the impact of the human combustion of fossil fuels – coal, oil and natural gas. Reforestation would have numerous beneficial effects for the biosphere, including reducing the build-up of carbon dioxide in the atmosphere, but that *alone* could not compensate for the overloading of the cycle by industrial activities fed by fossil fuels.

Evidence from cores of ice at the poles containing bubbles of air (trapped as snow fell and became compressed into the ice sheets) gives us a detailed and reliable measurement of the composition of the atmosphere over several hundred years. Until 1750 carbon dioxide remained at about 280 parts per million (ppm). Since then it has risen steadily, so that it now stands at 350 ppm and is still rising (Firor, 1990, p. 50). Since 1957 detailed measurements have been taken directly from air, monitoring our continuing impact on a regular basis. The trend is irrefutable: it falls in summertime as vegetal growth absorbs carbon dioxide, and then rises again in winter. *But each summer it starts at a higher concentration.*

No one disputes the data. Emissions of carbon dioxide and the other greenhouse gases are increasing and they are overloading the atmospheric 'sink', and hence building up in the atmosphere. Scientific opinion is almost unanimous in declaring that this build-up will lead to a warming up of the climate, expected to reach an average increase (over the surface of the globe) of between 1.5° and 4.5°C by the time the carbon dioxide concentration in the atmosphere has doubled. On present trends, this doubling is expected before the middle of the next century. The science of the greenhouse effect, and the build-up of greenhouse gases due to human agency, has been checked, and rechecked, by individuals and by international panels of scientists. It is a fact of modern life.

The implications of the build-up are more difficult to predict; indeed some sceptics think it may not necessarily be disastrous at all. First, let me briefly summarize the various positions of the sceptics, or optimists. Some think that an initial increase in temperature will increase humidity and hence cloud formation, and that the additional cloud cover will reflect away at least enough incoming solar radiation to compensate for any temperature increase at the surface. Others concede a temperature increase but think increased humidity will produce more precipitation, in the form of snowfall, over the mountains and poles. Such a change would counteract any tendency to sea-level rise – which is seen by most scientists as a likely consequence of global warming due to the thermal expansion of the oceans. Another optimistic viewpoint concedes all the expected biospheric changes but assumes that these will be small enough, and will occur slowly enough, to allow the ever-adaptable human species to survive by managing its resources more efficiently.

There is a great deal of uncertainty both in understanding the likely impacts of human beings on the biosphere and in estimating human responsiveness to those impacts that do occur. However, these uncertainties are not sufficient to delay mitigative action, now, to slow the rate of global warming which most scientists believe we can now expect. In broad terms, warming is expected to occur, and to result in a sea-level rise which threatens the world's populous (and food-producing) lowlands and coastal cities. Drier conditions in the continental interiors are expected to reduce further the world's grain harvest. Warmer conditions are conducive to increased storm activity, especially in the tropics. These climatic and coastal conditions are expected to occur rapidly enough to preclude large-scale human adjustment through peaceful migration and the introduction of more suitable crops.

Some possible implications of global warming

Whereas there is still some resistance to the idea that we must act immediately to lessen the impacts of global warming, many institutions and individuals have moved swiftly to take, or at least to recommend, precautionary measures (see, for example, Mintzer, 1992; White, 1992a; 1993a; 1994a; 1994b). The implications may be divided into the technological and the political although, at their root, they are both interlocked. Although methane and nitrous oxide have a partly agricultural source, the basic difficulty is that our modern societies which emerged from the industrial, transportation and information revolutions of the last 200 years are heavily dependent on fossil fuels. Other important sources of power – such as hydroelectric power and nuclear power – have their own environmental problems and could not be expanded, in the current circumstances, to replace entirely the fossil fuels. The logical alternatives are to use less power (through demand restraint and greater efficiency of use) and to make wider use of renewable energy sources such as wind and water power, solar power and biomass. Initially these power sources may be more expensive and less convenient for our society as it presently functions, especially with regard to the automobile and its dependence on fossil fuels. The internal combustion engine has provided the greatest advance in personal mobility since the saddle and the stirrup, and it will not be easy to learn to live without it.

However, the political adjustment is going to be more fundamental than learning to live without cheap energy and without a personal automobile. First, we must change the time horizon over which we make decisions. The *minimum* timeframe for thinking about adjustments to global warming is 50 years – almost the lifetime of children and teenagers alive today. Second, we must enlarge the scope of our thinking to include *all* the world's people, not just the people belonging to our neighbourhood or even our nation (White, 1992b; 1993b). This is implied in the 'Gaia hypothesis' which states that the earth behaves as a single organism, to regulate its temperature, the composition of the atmosphere and other physical attributes. The concept was developed by James Lovelock (1991, p. 186), whose expectations for human beings as stewards of the earth are not high:

> I would sooner expect a goat to succeed as a gardener than expect humans to become responsible stewards of the Earth . . . We must learn to live with the

Earth in partnership. Otherwise the rest of creation will, as part of Gaia, unconsciously move the Earth into a new state, one where humans may no longer be welcome.

Purely technological responses to the environmental challenge will fail, because the problem is not just one of technology. A battery-powered, or even a solar-powered, automobile will not make much difference, because the fuel savings per vehicle will be negated by the increasing number of vehicles, the population of which is growing much faster than the human population, for which the growth rate is already exponential. We have to look at rates of change at the global scale – humans, automobiles, carbon dioxide – and see where we fit in the global biogeochemical cycles and what we must do to live in harmony with them.

Because carbon dioxide stays in the atmosphere for about 100 years (as do ozone layer-destroying CFCs), we need a long timeframe to understand how the warming phase we have initiated might be brought under control. Thus the reason for the longer timeframe is set by the nature of the process we have unleashed. But why do we have to think of *all* the world's people? (If you think that this may be difficult, note that Lovelock points out that we have to think in terms of the world's *species*, not just the people.) The answer to this question also lies in the long duration of carbon dioxide in the atmosphere; because, while it is up there, constant turbulence ensures that it becomes well mixed. You cannot distinguish the origin of the gas, either by country or by type of activity. Everyone's carbon dioxide is mixed together and contributes to the enhanced greenhouse effect. The gas we exhale from our lungs, the gas from our factories and automobiles, the forests burning in Amazonia, the gas flared from the oilfields in Nigeria, the firewood burned in Nepal, the huge quantities of coal burned in India and China, all release their carbon dioxide to the atmosphere where it is well mixed and stays for decades.

Thus North America, Japan and the European Community could do an exemplary job of reducing their carbon dioxide emissions but that alone would not avert the implications of global warming scenario *in the slightest way*. India and China *alone*, on the present trajectory (even with China's strenuous efforts to reduce population growth), could negate the entire efforts of the older industrial nations, unless they are counted in as prime players in the efforts to reduce the human-enhanced greenhouse effect. And this means dealing with the root causes of their current situation. In today's world, rapid population growth is a function of poverty and high mortality rates. As the richer countries of the world look at energy demand management they must also look at the reasons for continued poverty in the poorer nations of the world. If development and underdevelopment are two sides of the same coin, then we must address those problems vigorously, even if that means changing some of the hallowed precepts of the market economy, such as the survival of the fittest.

This is what Lovelock and other ecologically minded people are trying to tell us. One species cannot exist without the complex ecosystems maintained by a host of other species. In other words, the stock exchange is one kind of reality, but the atmosphere is another.

References

Atkinson, A. (1991) *Principles of Political Ecology.* Belhaven Press, London.

Firor, J. (1990) *The Changing Atmosphere.* Yale University Press, New Haven, Conn.

Lovelock, J. (1991) *Gaia. The Practical Science of Planetary Medicine.* Gaia Books, London.

Meadows, D., Meadows, D., Randers, J. and Behrens, W. (1972) *The Limits to Growth.* Potomac Associates, Washington, DC.

Meadows, D., Meadows, D. and Randers, J. (1992) *Beyond the Limits. Global Collapse or a Sustainable Future.* Earthscan, London.

Metropolitan Toronto Government (1991) *Strategic Plan, May 1991.* Metropolitan Toronto Government, Toronto.

Mintzer, I.M. (ed.) (1992) *Confronting Climate Change. Risks, Implications and Responses.* Cambridge University Press.

White, R.R. (1992a) 'The international transfer of urban technology. Does the north have anything to offer for the global environmental crisis?', *Environment and Urbanization*, Vol. 4, no. 2, pp. 109–20.

White, R.R. (1992b) 'The road to Rio – or the global environmental crisis and the emergence of different agendas for rich and poor countries,' *International Journal of Environmental Studies*, Vol. 41, no. 3/4, pp. 187–202.

White, R.R. (1993a) 'Convergent trends in architecture and urban environmental planning, a commentary', *Society and Space, Environment and Planning D*, Vol. 11, pp. 3–6.

White, R.R. (1993b) *North, South, and the Environmental Crisis.* University of Toronto Press, Toronto.

White, R.R. (1994a) 'Strategic decisions for sustainable urban development in the third world,' *The Third World Planning Review* (special issue on sustainable urban development), vol. 16, no. 2, pp. 103–16.

White, R.R. (1994b) *Urban Environmental Management: Environmental Change and Urban Design.* Wiley, Chichester.

Index